CALLUS
ON MY SOUL

CALLUS ON MY SOUL

A MEMOIR

DICK GREGORY with Shelia P. Moses

KENSINGTON PUBLISHING CORP.
http://www.kensingtonbooks.com

DAFINA BOOKS are published by

Kensington Publishing Corp.
850 Third Avenue
New York, NY 10022

Originally published in hardcover by Longstreet Press
Book design by Megan Wilson

ISBN 0-7582-0202-4

First Kensington Trade Paperback Printing: February 2003
10 9 8 7 6 5 4 3 2 1

Printed in the United States of America

Dedication

This book is dedicated to the unsung heroes and sheroes all over the world whose names most people don't ever stop to ask: the porters, the taxi drivers, the dishwashers, and the bell captains at the hotel; the valet at the airport, the waiters and waitresses, the cooks, the teachers, the bus drivers, the garbage collectors, and the maids. I don't know your names, but God knows who you are and He/She knows your names one by one. So I'm placing this blank scroll here for you and your families. Put your name here and every day at noon, for the rest of our lives, we will pray or meditate together. Let us say a special prayer for the struggling single parents, the handicapped, and those who are disabled. Remember the struggling farmers and the forgotten human rights workers. We will not forget those who leave home before the sun rises and who never make it back before it sets.

God bless you all,
Dick Gregory

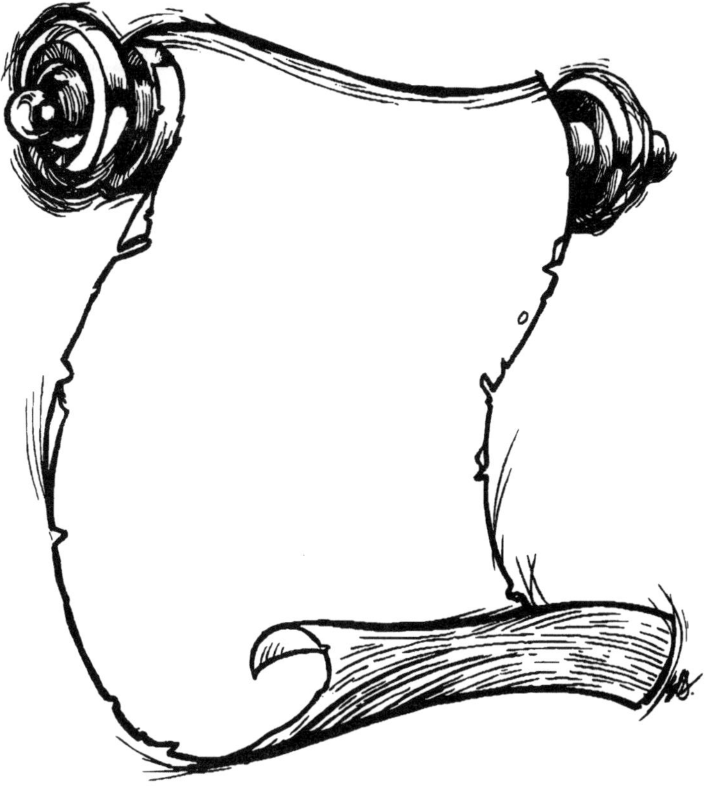

Acknowledgments from Dick Gregory

How do you say thanks to millions of people? How do you tell people you have never met that you love them? I really do, and I hope that this book is a reflection of that love. I have gone from welfare child to track star to being labeled "a comedy star." But the real show started in 1961 while my coauthor was still in her mother's womb. The Movement called and I answered. Twenty years later I was fighting hunger and fasting as I developed the Formula Four X. All the time, I was protesting and going to jail for Black folks and oppressed people all over the world. So many people helped me along the way, and I acknowledge my appreciation to you all. Let me start by saying thanks to the Black mothers and fathers who prayed for me and patted me on the back in airports and said, "I'm proud of you, son." I know that they really meant it.

I want to acknowledge the soldiers we lost while writing this book — Albert Turner, Dr. Alvenia Fulton, Stokely Carmichael, Jim Farmer — as well as those we lost so long ago: Dr. Martin Luther King Jr., Medgar Evers, Viola Liuzzo, Chaney, Goodman and Schwerner, Roy Wilkins, Dr. Benjamin Mays, Robert and John F. Kennedy, Malcolm X, Tom Skinner, Bob Johnson, Ralph Abernathy, Betty Shabazz, Jim Sanders, Reverend John Nettles, and those four beautiful little girls from Birmingham. I would also like to say thanks to the good, honest, decent White folks who walked in the shadow of the valley of death with us during the Movement and today.

I would like to acknowledge my friends from the entertainment world such as Richard Pryor, Harry Belafonte, Ossie Davis and Ruby Dee, Bill Cosby, Miles Davis, Sidney Poitier, and Paul Mooney, who all understand the creative journey as I do. There are just so many people who have been there every step of the way: John Fairman, Bertram Lee, Jim Kelly, Adam Bourgeois, and Reverend Randel Osburn. Not to forget Steve Jaffe, who has been such a good friend that I forget he is also my publicist. Mark Lane and I will always share a special bond through our mutual struggle to place the facts about the assassinations of President Kennedy, Dr. King and others before the people because of our loyalty to the truth.

Then there's John and Eunice Johnson, who dared put Emmett Till's picture on the cover of *Jet* magazine over thirty-five years ago. And their daughter, Linda Johnson, who has become a shining light in the publishing world. One day, when the real historians tell the truth about the Civil Rights Movement, they will turn to *Jet* and *Ebony* for their research, and say thanks to the Johnsons.

To my agent, Bob Silverstein, who fought for this book: *Thanks, man.* A special thanks to Longstreet Press for the literary freedom you gave us to tell the truth. I would be remiss not to thank my coauthor, Shelia P. Moses, who did research and writing for this book for three years and never wavered. She worked tirelessly to find the facts, to tell the truth, and to maintain the essence of what my life has been.

A special thanks to my ten children: Michele, Lynne, Pamela, Paula, Stephanie (aka Xenobia), Gregory, Christian, Miss, Ayanna, and Yohance. They understood that I could not be at home and a part of the Movement simultaneously, and I appreciate their loyalty to me and to the Black folks who needed me more than they did. They are ten blessed children, because God gave them Lil Gregory as their mother.

I was equally blessed because God gave me Lil, my wife, my partner, and my best friend for forty-two years. She mothered eleven children, buried one, and never missed a beat. She went to jail pregnant, with babies at home, for righteousness. She has one of the brightest minds in this country. No one on this planet has had the effect on me that Lil has and will always have. For her, for my children, I thank you, God.

Acknowledgments from Shelia P. Moses

All of my life I've wanted to write. To paint pictures with words, real pictures. The opportunity to write Dick Gregory's memoir has allowed me to go even farther than my childhood dreams. With that came a price that I willingly paid, including being away from my family and friends and living out of a suitcase for almost three years in order to tell the story of one remarkable man.

I am so grateful to my Momma, Maless Moses, who never questioned my ability to finish this book, and to my nine sisters and brothers, Barbara, Daniel, Johnny, Scarlett, Ben, Leon, Loraine, Gayle, and Jackie, who have loved me on the brightest and darkest days of my entire life.

My dear friends Marie Showers, Debra Rogers, April Russell, Wanda Linden, Kim Abnatha, and Melanie Crenshaw have truly understood what I'm trying to accomplish as a writer and most of all as a woman.

Also my friend Steven Mckinney, who died too young, too soon, and left us broken-hearted. "We miss you, Stevie."

I am forever indebted to the people who mentored me through this book: Sonia Sanchez, Paul Benjamin, Bill Duke, Barbara Austin, Dr. Patricia Johnson, Shelia Frazier, Karen Tangora, and Xernona Clayton.

On behalf of Dick and myself, we are so grateful to Longstreet Press, who wasted no time in picking up the publishing rights to this book and who provided us with two wonderful editors, Sherry Wade and Tysie Whitman. To Bob Silverstein, my agent and friend, thank you for believing in me. Not to forget Blanche Richardson, who is a mentor to writers all over the country. The most difficult part of this book was the research, and I had little angels from coast to coast helping me put the pieces together: Tim Hunter, George O'Hare, Ferdy Banks, Steve Jaffe, Dolores Gregory Hill, Reggie Toran, Ronald Gregory, Herb Jubirt, and Patrick Mckinney. They did everything from gathering news articles and pictures to picking me up at the airport.

Thank you to Dick Gregory's friends and family who were never too busy to talk with me. There are no words in the dictionary to express my gratitude to Lillian Gregory. She has been a silent force in my life and in the success of this book. I am grateful to her and to the Gregory children for sharing Momma and Daddy stories with me.

Finally, I thank my coauthor and friend, Dick Gregory. We have truly gone the distance. Thank you for sharing your story with me and the world. I really can't imagine this universe without you, nor do I want to. We are all indebted to you, my friend. You have carried the torch so long, a torch others dared touch. You ran the race for us and let the world know that even a little Black welfare boy from St. Louis, Missouri, could plant a seed. That seed, Dick Gregory, gave us hope.

TABLE OF CONTENTS

TABLE OF CONTENTS (continued)

CALLUS
ON MY SOUL

She had a third-grade education. *Momma, everything I've done, I've done for you. I've done it for my wife and for your grandchildren. I've done it for all the little children in the world. You know what I was thinking the other day, Momma? I was thinking about Vanessa Williams and how beautiful she is. You know, she was the first Black woman to be crowned Miss America. Well, not really. You were; at least you were to me. Now that I am a man, I look back on all those years you suffered and went without the things that my Miss America should have had. That Vanessa Williams is so strong. She fought back and won. Just like you, Momma. It cost you your life, but, like so many other Black women, never did you sell your soul — not even for us.*

1 Momma

It was the summer of 1942 in St. Louis, Missouri, the "Show Me" state. I was ten years old and all I wanted to do was to go outside and play like the other children. But I guess, in many ways, we were never like the other children. There were six of us. Presley was the oldest, then me, then Dolores. The youngest were Garland, Ronald, and the baby, Pauline. I was the leader, when it came to getting into trouble.

We were so poor and our clothes were so raggedy that the other children in the neighborhood laughed at us. The neighborhood was probably full of poor children, but when you are one of them, you can only feel your own pain. Like the pain I felt when Momma told us we had to stay in the house all summer while she was out working for White folks because she didn't want us to be laughed at. But it wasn't just because of our raggedy clothes — she was afraid for us. Back then little children were getting hit by cars and having accidents every day. Every time the phone rang at the White folks' house, poor Momma thought they were calling to tell her we were hurt or worse. She was so desperate to keep us safe she actually hid our clothes under the bed mattress, thinking we would stay inside until she got home from work. But we did not care; we were dying to get outside. So Presley and I decided to break the rules.

Momma had all these nice, fancy dresses that the White folks had given her. She had them all put away to wear to funerals or some special occasion. Presley and I decided they would be perfect summer attire. We wasted no time putting the dresses on and going outside to play. The neighborhood children laughed at us so hard that first day, it was almost unbearable. But it still wasn't as bad as sitting in the house for the entire summer. The next day we did the same thing, and the children continued to laugh. By the third day, word had gotten out, and children and adults from other neighborhoods would come by just to see the Gregory boys in Momma's White folks' dresses. For a while they would come around pointing at us and laughing, but eventually we were just part of a normal, hot summer day. That summer, as a little Black boy in St. Louis, I learned the pure joy of doing what I had to do, even when others didn't understand.

Well, it was bound to happen. One of the neighbors told Momma what we were doing and all hell broke loose. We didn't need those dresses anymore because Momma put us on punishment for the rest of the summer. By the time we needed clothes again, it was time to go back to school.

I was in the fifth grade. School provided a whole new set of kids to laugh at us because we didn't have nice clothes. But Helene Tucker never laughed. She treated me really nice and every day I looked forward to class just to be near her. Helene Tucker was my first love. Puppy love, but love all the same. It was because of Helene Tucker that I first experienced the mean spirit of poverty.

It was Friday, the day when our teacher would call on each member of the class to stand up and tell how much money his parents were going to give to the Community Chest. The Community Chest was a program for people on relief. The parents would donate money, and the money would go to relief kids like me and my brothers and sisters. This Friday was going to be different. I was going to buy me a daddy and impress Helene Tucker. All I had to do, I figured, was to top whatever donation Helene Tucker's daddy made. My teacher went all around that classroom, calling everyone's name except Richard

Gregory. Helene Tucker donated five dollars. *Five dollars,* I thought, *I have to top that.* I raised my hand, but the teacher raised her animosity towards little children like me higher than I could reach. She ignored my hand, so I stood up.

"What is it, Richard?" my teacher asked, very annoyed.

"My daddy wants to make a ten-dollar donation," I said proudly.

It was the first time I'd seen that look on someone's face, but it was a look I've seen a thousand times since that day. It was a look I prayed other children would not ever have to see, though I know they have.

"Richard," she said, setting the stage for one of the worst moments in my childhood, "sit down. This money is for your kind. If your daddy had money, you wouldn't be on relief."

Through the tears in my eyes I could see some of the other children laughing, and I could see this strange look in Helene Tucker's eyes. I ran out of that classroom and all the way home. I never told Momma what that teacher said, and she died not knowing the hurt I felt that day. I ducked school for a long time after that. I didn't want to face the teacher who had caused me so much pain.

It would be years before I understood why it was so easy to hurt a child the way that teacher hurt me. It hurt worse than any physical pain I had ever felt. My pain had always been a temporary thing. I'd been laughed at before, but it was always because of the clothes on my back or my little greasy lunch bag. And I was teased by children, not adults. But this pain, this laughter, was because of my condition of pure poverty. This was something I couldn't change.

It hurt worse than the time I was shining shoes at the tavern downtown. Even with the "No Colored Folks Allowed" sign on the front door, the owner allowed me to shine shoes inside. One day, a White woman asked me to shine her shoes. I was glad to do it because women always gave better tips. As I was shining her shoes, I touched the back of her leg to get a better grip on her shoe. This White man across the room saw me touch her lily-White skin and went crazy! He came over and hit me in the mouth so hard, it knocked out my front teeth. The owner made me leave and told me I couldn't come back anymore. Now ain't that a bitch!

At ten years old, racism and poverty had already cost me my girlfriend, my job, and my two front teeth.

I still couldn't tell Momma. She had her own problems, like paying the rent. So I lied and told her I fell down the stairway. It would have been nice to have told my daddy. His name was Presley Sr. We called him "Big Prez." Big Prez's visits were as rare as a child being born in our house. I could count the times he came home by our ages. I think Big Prez's absence in my life was the reason I started praying at such an early age for things I wanted and needed. If I prayed to God, I didn't have to worry Momma with so much. She was drowning in her own pain and problems.

One day she came home from work to find us children and everything we owned sitting on the sidewalk at the corner of North Taylor Street. My brothers and sisters and I stood among our belongings with our heads down in front of that big old red building. I don't know if the building was really so big or if it just looked that way because I was feeling so small. Little did I know the stone steps that led to our front door would later serve as the stage for the telling of my first joke, leading to my career as a comedian. But that day, as a little Black boy evicted with no place to go, I wanted to hide under that old building. We just stood there and waited for Momma to rescue us from the neighbors who whispered as they passed by. Some people just peeped out of their windows, hoping that they would not be next.

Momma finally showed up, thank God. She was tired from cleaning houses all day and from getting no sleep the night before. She was in constant pain from diabetes and she came home to find us evicted. She didn't cry; she rarely did. She just put on her "mercy face" and went to beg the absentee landlord to let us back in, just until payday. Of course he did; he always let us back in. I think he got a kick out of watching my Momma beg. I often wonder how that man positioned his face when my Momma was begging for a place for her babies to sleep, how he positioned his hands to pick up those orange crates we used for chairs and set them outside on the street.

The rent was only eighteen dollars a month and it couldn't have made that much difference to his eating or sleeping. But that didn't matter. He evicted us so many times that it wore Momma's spirit down. I always thought that if he would just come by early enough to see Momma wrap her old shoes in plastic so that her feet wouldn't get wet when she walked to work, or if he could see her standing on the corner selling sandwiches to the streetcar drivers, he would know that my momma was a queen. But he never did, or at least he never acknowledged it.

No matter how badly that landlord treated Momma, she never had any hatred in her heart for him, or anyone else. I can still hear her voice when she talked to White folks, calling them Mister So-and-So and Miss So-and-So. Of course, they called her just plain Lucille. Never in her forty-eight years on this earth did I hear a White person address my momma as Mrs. Gregory or even Miss Lucille. Even their children called her Lucille. It was almost as if she were two different people. In our neighborhood, the children loved Momma and they addressed her the same as we addressed their parents, Mr. or Mrs. The minute she walked in the door at those White folks' houses, with their disrespectful children, she was Lucille. But Momma never complained; she was just so kind and loving to everyone.

I thought about Momma when I saw Mother Teresa receive the Nobel Peace Prize. Something she said in her speech just touched my soul. When asked why she had helped so many people, she responded, "You have to love them first." Somehow that's what Momma did. She loved people who were unkind to her and to us. "You have to love them first." Yes, that's what Momma did, she loved them first. I wish I could have done more for her.

Momma died before I was able to give her the love and respect she deserved from me as her son. As a child, I didn't understand how or why we had to live on relief and other families didn't; I was just too young. I was ashamed of Momma's clothes and her lack of education, but it never diminished my love for her. I just felt ashamed. I wanted her to have something. And I wanted her to have something to give to us. I wanted Momma to be loved like a queen, and I wanted her to stop waiting.

She was always waiting for something — waiting to get a check, waiting for relief food. But most of all she waited for Big Prez to come home. I hated watching her wait for him. She didn't wait for days or weeks. She waited months and even years for him. Sometimes he wouldn't come home for two or three years, but Momma just kept waiting. And every time he came home, she got pregnant. He hardly knew his children, and I didn't want to know him. He didn't even come home for holidays, except for one year when Momma said he was definitely coming for Christmas. She was so excited as she dressed up in those White folks' clothes. Then the waiting began.

Christmas Eve night, after my siblings had gone to bed, Momma called me to her. "Richard, this is for you. Now don't tell the other children I gave it to you. It's our special little secret."

I looked inside the old box she handed me. It was a really nice wallet. I wondered how Momma had found a way to buy me an extra gift. I laughed to myself because I knew she had given all the other kids something special, too. She always got each of us a "special gift," and told us not to tell the others. Later, of course, my sisters and brothers would get into fights about who Momma loved the most and everyone would pull out their special gift that the others were not supposed to know about. That's how wonderful Momma was. She wanted each of us to feel special, even when she did not.

"Thanks, Momma. I'm going to carry it with me every day." And I gave her a big hug.

"Oh, I'm so glad you like it, Richard. Now go on to bed, it's getting late."

"No, Momma. I want to wait up with you. I want to wait for Big Prez."

I didn't really think he was going to show up, but I didn't want Momma to sit there in those White folks' clothes all alone.

It was very late when there was a knock at the door. Momma ran to the door, but it wasn't Big Prez. It was a neighbor who told us that Big Prez was down the street at her house drinking and crying. She said he didn't want to come home because he got off work late and all the stores were closed. Big deal, I thought, that means no gifts for us this year, just like all the other Christmases. Poor Momma put on her White folks' coat and went to get him. When they came back, all the children jumped up out of bed and ran to say hello. They were so happy, especially my little sister, Pauline. She had no idea that she would be a teenager when she saw her daddy again.

I ran to the bedroom. Momma followed me and Big Prez followed her. I looked up and there he was, a man I barely knew. He was all dressed up and I wondered where he got all his fine clothes. I bet he didn't get them from White folks.

"Richard, what is wrong with you? Give your daddy a hug," Momma said. I hid my head deeper in the bedsheets.

"Hi, Richard," Big Prez said, "How are you?" I couldn't believe it. He acted like it was a normal day and he had just walked in from work. I gave him a hug to make Momma happy and listened to him make excuses for not having any gifts for us. Then he pulled out a big roll of money and gave each of us a handful. My sisters and brothers were so happy, but I was thinking about how we barely had any food in the house, except for what the White folks had given us.

Christmas flew by with Big Prez sitting around telling stories and everyone else sitting around listening to him. Then things started getting back to normal. It began when I saw him in the kitchen, kissing Momma. I went berserk. I walked up to him like a man and told him to get his goddamn hands off my momma. He grabbed me before I could run. He took off his belt, and while Momma held me down, Big Prez beat me real bad. The licks didn't hurt as bad as Momma holding me down so that stranger, who wouldn't help her feed me, could beat me. I felt so betrayed. Then they made me go to bed.

It wasn't long before I could hear Big Prez yelling about how out of control I was and how Momma thought she was better than he was. He called her every name he could think of and started beating her from one end of the kitchen to the other. Every time he knocked her down, I could hear her get back up. She was crying and my brothers and sisters were screaming for him to stop. I knew how bad he had beaten me and I wasn't going to let him do Momma that way. But when I rushed into the kitchen to save Momma, Big Prez was kissing her and telling her how much he loved her. She started kissing him back and didn't notice that I had picked up a knife and was swinging it towards Big Prez's head. When she realized what was happening, she grabbed my hand to keep me from cutting him.

Big Prez didn't get mad. He didn't yell at me or at Momma. He just stood there with this look of surprise on his face. Then he looked at Momma and said the words I knew would come sooner or later.

"It's all right, Cille. I'm leaving."

I knew it. I just knew it! I thought to myself.

Big Prez walked out that door and broke Momma's heart one more time, like he had been doing for the past fifteen years. But I wasn't going to let him off the hook that easy. Not this time. I followed him. He walked with his head down until he reached the tavern down the street and went inside. I sneaked in and hid behind the bar, just inside the door. And there she was: the real reason he had beaten Momma. She was all smiles, fussing and hugging on him all at the same time.

"Where have you been, Presley?" she asked him.

"Had to beat Cille before I left. I beat her for nothing and I beat Richard for running his mouth at me. . . ." Before he could finish his sentence, she cut him off.

"I don't want to hear nothin' 'bout Cille, and I sure don't want to hear nothin' 'bout your little bastards. 'Sides, you don't even know if they yours."

I couldn't believe what happened next. Big Prez got mad at her for talking about Momma and me. Before I knew it, he was beating her worse than he'd beat Momma. Two men sitting at the bar got up and tried to help her, but Big Prez pulled a razor out of his pocket and threatened to kill them all. I was still hiding behind the bar when Big Prez just up and walked out, leaving that woman beaten on the barroom floor. He never looked back to see if anyone followed him. He didn't seem afraid at all. When I think back on that incident, I realize I probably inherited the ability to be fearless from Big Prez. Years later, I ran into some people in San Francisco who knew Big Prez. They told me he didn't take no stuff from anyone and that he made things a lot easier for Black folks who worked at the hotel where he was head chef. It was hard for me to imagine that, because Big Prez had never made Momma's life any easier.

I didn't follow him after he left the tavern. I knew he was going to the train station or the bus stop. I ran home to check on Momma. The other kids were asleep already, and Momma was back at that window with the same look on her face that she always had when Big Prez was away. For six months, she would go to work, come home and cook, then sit at that window. Big Prez never returned. He had wanted a reason not to come back and my pulling a knife on him gave him an out. I never felt guilty about it because I would rather have seen Momma sit alone at that window for the rest of her life than have Big Prez beat her for being human. I had watched her suffer so much for so long, but I always believed it was the waiting that eventually killed Momma. The landlord humiliated her, the White folks disrespected her, and the diabetes kept her in pain. But the waiting killed her spirit.

After Big Prez left, we were back to normal: no food, no clothes, and no love from a daddy. But we still had Momma. And eventually, she got up from that window and put a smile back on her beautiful face. She tried to be the best mother to us she could be. She was my best friend and I didn't even know it. Today, when people ask me who is my best friend, I always answer, "My wife, Lil, of course." But before Lil, there was Momma. And there was Charles Simmons.

We called Charles "Boo." Boo really liked me and I liked him. I guess you could say we loved each other as much as two little Black boys from St. Louis could love each other. Boo was an interesting cat. Boo had a daddy. A real daddy. On top of that, Boo's daddy had a real job; he worked as a chauffeur. Most of all, he was always nice to my brothers and me.

Boo, Presley, and I used to work paper routes, shine shoes, and shovel snow together. Sometimes Presley and I would work from sunrise to sunset together, but Boo didn't have to work as hard as we did. Boo had a daddy to pay the rent. I was so happy for him, happy that he had warm water to bathe in, glad that he had lunch money and full meals at home.

Most of all, I was happy that he had a man in the house. I think Boo felt sorry for me because he was always protecting me. I wasn't sixty pounds dripping wet, but Boo was a big dude who could hold his own. He was just a good fighter and a good all-around athlete. When children teased me really bad, Boo would beat them up. When he wasn't around, I would just run home and cry. One day, when Boo wasn't around, a strange thing happened. I stood up for myself. Not with my fists, but with words. Momma always told me that "there is freedom in laughter," and that advice finally kicked in one day when the bad boys of the neighborhood had me cornered.

"Hey, Richard! Where's your daddy?" one of them teased. They all laughed.

"Oh, he's at your house with your Momma!" I shot back.

Now the joke was on him and everyone was laughing at him instead of me. I had figured out what Momma was talking about and it felt real good. There really was freedom in laughter. After that, every time someone would laugh at me, I would hit them with a joke so tough, they'd stop teasing me and run home to try and think of something to top what I had said to them. It was there on the corner of North Taylor Street that I learned to make other people laugh. I got so good at it that people would come by just to hear what I would say to the next cat. Boo and I would just sit around waiting for the next kid to knock down with my jokes.

2 Relief

It didn't take long for me to override the pain of people on the street teasing me about my daddy, but nothing changed at home. The lights were still out most of the time because Momma couldn't pay the bills, and we didn't have any more food or better clothes to wear. Once a year, the relief clothes would arrive. I hated those orange pants and matching shirts more than the teasing they caused. In the winter, we got these sweaters with a reindeer on them. We would go to the movies and all the relief children would have on the same sweater. If trouble broke out, the other children would say the guy in the reindeer sweater did it. Hell, we would all get kicked out! It was an awful feeling to walk down the street dressed like the many other children who didn't have a daddy. I wonder if it ever occurred to the people running the welfare system how painful it was for us to wear clothes that separated us from the other children. When a person commits a crime, he is sent to prison and given a uniform to separate him from society. Those relief uniforms did the same thing to us. Those ugly orange shirts and pants made us feel like prisoners in our own community.

Probably one of the worst whippings I ever got was when Momma found my relief clothes in the trash can. She beat me and then put me on punishment. In my young mind, neither the beating nor the punishment was as bad as walking down the street wearing clothes that screamed, "I'm a poor little Black boy on relief with no daddy!" Little did I know, help was on the way.

God knew I didn't have a daddy. He started sending me daddies, like Mr. Coleman, the principal of Cote Brilliant Grammar School. He gave me a job as a patrol boy. Mr. Coleman said he was happy with my performance, except for one thing. I had been talked to so bad for so long, by so many people, that I thought that was the way to get someone's attention. As a patrol boy, I was always fussing and yelling at the kids. Man, I would stand out there and yell, "Get your ass across the street before that car run over you, boy!" Mr. Coleman did not agree with my tactics. I guess I had cussed one time too many and he summoned me into his office. He talked about my unacceptable behavior and it made me feel bad because I could see the disappointment in his eyes. He told me he would not allow me to be a patrol boy anymore if I continued to talk to people in that manner.

God, I didn't want to lose my patrol job. For the first time in my life, I was a part of something. I was always left out of everything at school. No one picked me to be on their team for any sport. But my patrol job changed all of that. I wasn't getting paid any money, but I was getting something I had never had before, except from Momma: respect. Being a patrol boy also gave me a sense of power that was new to me. Simply putting on that belt gave me a sense of power, and with power comes a sense of responsibility. What a feeling! So that day, when it was time for school to be dismissed, I changed my attitude and went out there and behaved like the Richard Gregory that Momma was so proud of. Thanks to Momma and men like Mr. Coleman, I had, at age fourteen, gained the power of respect for myself and for other people. Though I didn't know it at the time, my jokes on the corner of North Taylor Street and a job as simple as patrol boy were changing my life.

Mr. Ben was another daddy to me. He was a White man who owned the corner grocery store. I think there must be a Mr. Ben in every neighborhood; at least I hope there is. He was a good man with a big heart and a soft spot for Momma. Most of the people on relief had credit at his store, but he extended Momma's credit much further than he did the others'. Sometimes, I doubt that we would have eaten at all if it were not for Mr. Ben.

At fourteen, I started high school at Sumner High. I wasn't a patrol boy anymore. I started feeling a little down and not so important. But I did have new clothes for the very first time. The summer before, Boo, Presley, and I got jobs with the Red Cross. We spent the summer working on the river for the federal flood program. We had lied about our ages, so we were treated like men and were expected to work like men. At the end of the summer, the Red Cross discovered that we had lied about our age and said they were not going to pay us. It's amazing how good Christian Black women change when you mess with their children. Momma went down there and raised hell until they gave us our five-hundred-dollar checks. Five hundred dollars each was like a million dollars to us. We were so excited, we couldn't wait to go shopping for new clothes.

Unfortunately, my first shopping experience ended up reminding me of the time that teacher had hurt my feelings in front of Helene Tucker and the whole class. Not one store in all of St. Louis would let us try on clothes. We had to buy the clothes and pray they would fit. We were not allowed to return anything, even if the tags were still on the clothes and we had the receipts. As children, we were confined to areas that were segregated; we went to segregated schools, movies, and playgrounds. When we did come in contact with White folks it was to shine their shoes or wash their cars. But to be a young man and to finally earn a paycheck — five hundred dollars in real money — only to find, when you go out to buy new clothes, that you are treated like an animal instead of a teenage boy. It is almost like you stole something. It hits you in the face that these White folks aren't going to let you try on a shoe, a coat, a hat, nothing. They looked down on Negroes like we were dogs. So we learned a horrible lesson that day as Momma watched sadly. Then we took our nonreturnable clothes home.

We had new clothes, but we still didn't have hot water most of the time to bathe or do laundry. Momma's health wasn't getting any better, and I was finding it hard to focus on my schoolwork. To make matters worse, Helene Tucker was at Sumner. I just couldn't let her see me with clean clothes and dirty ears.

One day I was hanging around after school and noticed all the track team members taking showers after practice. So I asked the coach if I could be on the track team. I didn't want to run; I simply wanted access to the showers. Coach Smith wouldn't let me join the team, but he told me I could use the track as long as I stayed out of the team's way. I started running with them every day for one hour; then I'd take a shower and go home. One afternoon after the team had gone home and I was alone on the track, two girls passed by and I heard them talking about me.

"What is he doing?" one asked the other.

"He must be training for the big meet," the other one answered.

Hot damn! They noticed me! I was so excited, I kept running for hours. For the first time in my life I was noticed for something good. Those girls were not talking about my raggedy clothes, nor the fact that I didn't have a daddy at home. They didn't say "You are on relief"; they noticed my ability to run. I couldn't wait for the next day so I could get out there and run again. It was important for a Black boy on relief to be noticed. The people in the neighborhood around the school started to notice me, too. Sometimes they would stand beside the track or outside their homes, if I was running in the neighborhood, and watch me run. They didn't know that when I got behind the buildings where they couldn't see me, I'd stop and rest. I wasn't cheating; I was just plain tired. White people would stand on their porches and say, "Look at him running like Jesse Owens." Owens had come to St. Louis shortly after winning four gold medals in the 1936 Olympics. Can you believe he came there to race a horse? With all his talents and four gold medals, that was what White folks brought him to St. Louis to do: race a damn horse. But Jesse Owens outran that horse and Black folks went crazy. And even though White folks invited him there to race a horse, they knew he was an American hero. So when they saw me running, I had a name other than "nigger," because Jesse had already paved the way. It is ironic that thirty years later we became good friends and I actually delivered the eulogy at his funeral.

Running was only one of the things I did to survive. Boo, Presley, and I were still hustling every day, but I kept running and preparing for the "big meet" like those girls said I was. My ship finally came in when we returned to school after Christmas break. Coach Smith asked me to join the team, after he, too, noticed my ability to run for long periods of time. I was so proud. The coming fall semester, I would be on the track team. I would have my own locker and my own uniform. But I had to get through the summer first.

I was so tired of watching Momma work like a dog that I went out and got a full-time job working at the ammunitions plant. It was during the Korean War, and they would have hired anyone. They gave me a job loading forty-five-pound boxes of unfinished shells. It didn't matter what they asked me to do, I did it. I was making almost two hundred dollars each week — more money than Momma made all month. The money I was making gave her a chance to stay home and rest her aching feet for the first time in years.

It was obvious by then that Big Prez was not coming back and even if he did, he wouldn't help us. But with me working full-time, we had food, clothes, and things we never had before. Nothing made me happier than the look on Momma's face when I gave her that money each week. She even had extra money to buy fabric to make herself a nice dress, a dress of her own, not a hand-me-down. That was a funny thing about Momma. She would save pennies all year to have enough money to buy fabric to make a dress to wear when she had her picture taken. All the pictures we have of her show her wearing either White folks' clothes or something she made with her own special fabric. She was so beautiful when she dressed up, especially when it was something she had worked for and saved her own money to buy. Even her smile was different. There was just something about Momma's smile that made everything all right. It outweighed every inch of pain the racist system and Big Prez tried to put on Momma and us. When I think about Momma, even today, I remember her smile more than anything. We don't have one picture of her in those clothes she worked in all day. As a matter of fact, she didn't even wear them to work; she carried them. Even as maids, Momma and her friends never wore their work clothes on the street. Just before leaving work, they'd change back into the nicest clothes they owned and walk home like the queens that they were. Momma and her friends had so much pride. So when you looked up and saw Momma coming home, if you didn't look down at her run-down shoes, you would have thought she was a secretary at a law firm. She was always dressed. Always. That was enough to inspire the poorest Black boy in St. Louis: me! So I kept on working the night shift after school started in the fall. But trying to work, run track, and do my schoolwork was getting harder and harder. One night, while I lay in bed barely able to move my aching body, Momma came in and sat down beside me. "Richard, you look so tired. Why don't you stop all that running?"

She didn't understand that, as far as I was concerned, it was far more important to keep running than it was to go to work. She wasn't telling me this because she wanted the money. It was just all she knew. Black people were just programmed to think that way, programmed to believe that working for White folks was the only way out. But not this Black boy. Even though my job was helping the family, I knew it was a one-way street to nowhere. I felt sorry for Momma as a Black mother trying to raise her children, but that track field was my way out. I was going to have to risk breaking Momma's heart in order to move on for us all.

"Momma, do you remember telling me about the woman who saw the star on my forehead when I was born?" As a small child, Momma often told me the story of her encounter with an old psychic woman named Mother Poole, who took one look at me and told her that she saw a star on my forehead and that I was going to be somebody really special someday.

"Yes, Richard. Why?"

"Well, I think she may have been right. My coach said I'm really good. He said I could be a great runner one day. I have to quit that job, Momma. I want to concentrate on my running."

Momma held my head in her lap and rocked back and forth. She didn't say much. She didn't have to. I knew it was all right with her to leave a job that was never going to get us off North Taylor Street. I lay there and thought about what a good woman Momma was and how unkind life had been to her. I felt so bad — not because I was going to quit that job, but because even I had been unkind to her. I was always proud of Momma, but sometimes I had been ashamed of her, too. Like the time she came to see me play in the school band.

A couple of weeks earlier, one of the band's drummers hadn't shown up for practice. Since I had been playing around with the drums all school year, the band director asked me to stand in. The moment I touched those drums, I knew they belonged to me. That drummer never got his sticks back; I played with the band for the rest of the year. But the one and only time Momma came to see me play, I was embarrassed because she had on a shabby coat. Then I saw an usher direct Momma to the top of the bleachers and, God help me, I was glad. I didn't want anyone to see her.

I am more ashamed of myself now for feeling that way than I was embarrassed at her appearance all those years ago. I wonder now how my Momma felt that day. The night I told her I was going to keep running, I knew she only wanted the best for me. The next day, I quit the job at the ammunitions plant and, with Momma's blessing, made track my life for the next few years.

3 Her Last Mile

I slowly became something of a local star. Except for Momma and my brothers and sisters, the people around me began to change right before my eyes. Momma never came to track meets and she still expected me to do my chores and behave the same at home. But let me tell you, once I walked outside that house, everything was different. When I walked into Mr. Ben's grocery store, he would stop waiting on everyone else — including the White folks — and come over to help me. Not that he had ever ignored me; Mr. Ben was always a nice man. But things were different now. He wanted everyone to know that we were friends. I gladly talked to him and answered all his questions about my running. It was a way of saying thanks for not letting my family starve over the years.

The fall of 1951 was a turning point in my life. The previous spring I had become one of the fastest one-milers in the country. I was especially looking forward to the new Scholastic Track and Field book that was coming out. I knew it would have my name and picture in it. At the same time, the PTA of Sumner High and the NAACP were planning a march to the Board of Education to protest the overcrowded Black schools. I hadn't given any thought at all to joining the march until the Scholastic book came out and Richard Gregory's name and picture were not included. I couldn't believe it! My old coach, Lamar

Smith, had been replaced by a new one, Warren St. James. I ran to Coach St. James's office and told him a big mistake had been made; they had accidentally left me out of the book. Coach informed me that it was no accident. He told me that you have to run with the White boys to get your name in the book. I had won the Missouri state mile championship for Negroes. The book was — guess what? — "White only." I was so angry that I joined the march to protest my name not being in the book.

I guess my reputation as a patrol boy had spread because the march organizers asked me to keep the demonstrators in line. The press ran a story that stated that I was the leader of the march, and they even said my name on TV. They called me a communist and rumors started to fly. I didn't know what a communist was, but whatever it was, it upset Momma. But I was happy. Not only did I have a chance to tell all of St. Louis that there were eighty students in my classroom that was designed for thirty, I also told them about how my name had been left out of the Scholastic book after giving one of the best performances in the country.

That year I became an activist for change, though it would be fifteen more years before I would march again. Because of my first march, however, the high school cross-country program was integrated the next week — and not just in St. Louis, but in other cities throughout the state. The White schools started to demand some of the Black athletes run on their team. They didn't want us; they needed us. To this day, St. Louis takes pride in the fact they integrated their school system before the Supreme Court ruling *Brown vs. Board of Education* that would come two years later. That same year, I competed against the White boys at Wood River High. I won almost every race and my picture was on the front page of the *Argus*, St. Louis' first Black paper, and the White newspapers, the *St. Louis Star*, the *St. Louis Globe Democrat*, and the *St. Louis Post Dispatch.* I had gained a reputation as a leader and I was elected president of my senior class. But I have to admit that it was not a fair election because my friends threatened to beat up anyone who didn't vote for me.

Things got even brighter when Coach St. James told me he would help me enroll in his alma mater, Southern Illinois University in Carbondale, Illinois. In addition to attending Southern as an undergrad, Coach St. James had not one, but two Ph.D.'s. Like many Negroes with Ph.D.'s, because of segregation he couldn't find a job at the university level, so he had to teach at a high school. Coach St. James's help getting me into Southern was God sending me another daddy.

And thank God for Coach, because otherwise my grades were too low to be accepted at any of the one hundred colleges around the country that were trying to recruit me to run track. I kept running track at Sumner, but all I could think about was going to college in the fall. I would be the first Gregory to go to college! Everything else — high school, Momma, my friends, even track — took a back seat to college. I stopped training and started partying. In fact, I partied so hard that I came in seventeenth at my final meet. The press had a field day pronouncing "Dick Gregory Places Seventeenth" in all the papers. They didn't even talk about the winners, just "Dick Gregory Places Seventeenth."

In addition to my poor performance at the track meet, I failed to write the graduation speech that was part of my duty as president of my class. One of my teachers wrote the speech for me, and I delivered it like I was the president of the United States addressing the nation. Momma was so proud. I will never forget the look of pride on her face that day or the day she rode the city bus with me to the Greyhound bus station. I was going to Carbondale, Illinois, to enroll in college. God bless her, she fixed me a bag lunch of bologna and bread that I didn't want and left on the bus.

College was strange and wonderful, and God immediately sent me another daddy. Coach Leland Lingle was the head coach of the track team, and he began grooming me for stardom. He was not just interested in me as his star athlete. He had a genuine concern for me as a human being. We just talked about life and the problems that one might be confronted with as an adult. He talked to me about courage and character that one must have to overcome obstacles that will come your way. Coach Lingle told me why it was important not to waste my life being just an athlete. Now that I look back on my relationship with Coach Lingle and all the controversy that goes on with coaches and students today, I can honestly say that he never ripped me off. If anything, he made me a better man, and I wish that every college campus in America had a Coach Lingle to whisper life's little lessons in the students' ears. He even told me to take foreign languages and speech classes. He was the first White person other than Mr. Ben back in St. Louis to show any interest in me. But not everyone was as kind to me as Coach Lingle.

I learned that it was all right for me to run track with the White boys, but after a meet, I couldn't eat with them off campus. Revenge is sweet; I became captain of the track team and brought the half-mile record down to 1 minute 54.1 seconds. But God had a bigger plan for me; he sent me to the movie theater. All of my life I had been going to the movies and sitting in the balcony because we thought it was cool. But that was back in St. Louis in an all-Black movie theater where it didn't matter where you sat. The theaters were segregated back in St. Louis so seating was not an option. In college, I was so ignorant about racism that the first time I went to the movies, my date and I sat in the theater where all my White teammates were sitting. The manager came and asked me to go sit in the balcony. I refused. He called the police and I was asked to leave the theater. My date and I left, and she was in tears. But I didn't cry. Instead, I returned the next night and the night after that and refused to sit in the balcony. They continued to kick me out and I continued to return with more Black students until finally we were allowed to sit wherever we wanted. That was the first time in the history of Carbondale that the theaters were integrated.

But I still loved the balcony. It reminded me of the days when Boo and I would run all the way to the "Muni" to see an opera. The Municipal Opera House/Theater was an outdoor theater in St. Louis that had been built with one stipulation: Of the ten thousand seats at the Muni, one thousand must always be reserved for the "less fortunate." We were definitely less fortunate, so we went to the Muni almost every night we could to see plays and listen to opera. The trick to the one thousand free seats was that even if a Black millionaire wanted to buy a seat outside the "reserved for the less fortunate" section, he couldn't, because all the other seats were segregated. Even though I had fought for the right to sit anywhere I wanted in the Carbondale movie theater, I preferred the balcony. And that was where I was the night Coach Lingle came looking for me. He knew exactly where to find me when I wasn't on campus. He had this strange look on his face.

"Is it Momma?" I asked, knowing the answer.

"Just call home, Dick."

"Is she dead?"

"Just call home, Dick."

"Doc," I said, demanding an answer.

"I'm very sorry, Dick."

Momma was dead at forty-eight.

The next morning, I took the longest ride of my life back to St. Louis. It was so hard to walk into that run-down old house and not see Momma sitting there with a smile on her face. I just wanted to hug her one more time, smell her perfume one more time. I just wanted to tell her how much I loved her and how proud of her I was. The day of the funeral seemed to last an eternity. All of the White folks she had worked for over the years attended. Big Prez didn't. The neighborhood women helped with the funeral arrangements. Of course, Dolores had dressed Momma in those fine clothes the White folks had given her, and finally, she didn't have to worry about shoes. Momma had walked her last mile.

When the graveside service was over, they covered Momma's casket with dirt. The sound of the dirt hitting the top of the casket sounded to me like thunder. Can you imagine dirt in Momma's face? She wasn't dead in my heart; she was in heaven where angels belonged. But the workers putting dirt in Momma's face made it so final. God, that hurt. Afterwards I visited all of Momma's friends. I went from house to house just to listen to them talk about what a fine woman she was and how much they would miss her. As I walked those lonely streets, I saw Momma's face on every corner. Her footprints were embedded in those sidewalks she had walked to feed her babies.

The next day I packed my bag and got on the bus and headed back to college, leaving behind my sisters and brothers to return to the only home I now had. I thought about Momma and wished for that greasy lunch bag that she used to pack for me. I wished for her and for that old run-down house. I knew that I would never go back to North Taylor Street again — there was no need. The one sure thing I had in this world was gone, but so was her suffering. No more walking until her feet bled, no more begging the White man not to put us out on the street, no more waiting for Big Prez to come home. My sweet Momma, my queen, was gone.

4 On My Way

I went back to Southern Illinois University and continued to star on the track team of a college that dared me to eat with my White teammates off campus. I couldn't understand how the university could consider me a star athlete, then treat me so inhumanely when the press was not around. Back in St. Louis, I believed that poverty was the worst disease on earth. At Southern, I soon realized that racism was the true number-one killer. I'm not just talking about a White man hitting me in a bar because I accidentally touched a White woman's leg while shining her shoes; this was bigger, more insidious. Racism permeated every fiber of the university's social, political, and economic fabric. As far as the school system was concerned, I only existed on the track field. Off the field, I was just another nigger.

I remember one incident in particular. I was walking down the street in Carbondale when a White man stopped me outside a restaurant.

"Are you Dick Gregory?" he asked.

"Yes, sir, I am."

"Well, that's my son there in the car. Would you give him an autograph?"

I looked in the car and saw a little White boy in the passenger seat and a wheelchair in the back.

"Sure," I said, "You got a pen?"

He didn't have a pen, so I asked him if he would get one from the restaurant. He turned red as hell and took what must have been the longest walk of his life into the restaurant. Clearly he didn't appreciate being told what to do by a Black person, even if I was a track star. When he returned with the pen, I gave his son my autograph and walked away. I could feel his anger from behind, and wondered if he could sense my hurt. I wanted to turn around and tell him the reason I didn't get the pen: it was a "Whites Only" restaurant, and I wasn't permitted to go inside. But I just kept walking. It really didn't matter at that point — I was walking around in a daze anyway. Racism was wearing me down, and I was still grieving for Momma. I thought about her all the time. (I still do.) Life was so painful then, and I stopped caring about everything. That's when good old Uncle Sam called me to help keep the world safe from communism.

In 1954, the same racist system that told me where I could and could not eat drafted me into the United States Army. I was first stationed in Arkansas, but they quickly transferred me to Fort Lee outside of Petersburg, Virginia. The only thing I remember about that place is its famous street, Halifax Street, which is the longest street without an intersection in the country. When I got there, I did as little as possible. I spent my time joking around with the other draftees and getting into trouble. I would stay up all night telling jokes and horsing around. I overslept almost every day until finally I was summoned to the colonel's office.

The colonel must have lectured me for hours on my unacceptable behavior. He went on and on about my potential, my duty to my country, and the army's expectations. Then he said that since I thought I was so funny, he was ordering me to enter the Camp Talent Show. The joke was on him. I not only won that talent show, I won the next one, too. Eventually, I was transferred to Fort Hood, Texas, and there I qualified to enter the All-Army Talent Show at Fort Dix in New Jersey. The grand prize was a spot on *The Ed Sullivan Show*. Ed Sullivan had the number-one variety show in America at the time. His show was so big that when the Beatles came to the United States, they performed on Ed's show before anywhere else. But God knew I wasn't ready for the big time. I lost the talent show. I'm sure my act was too political to win anyway.

Two years in the army was more than enough for me. The only thing I got out of the whole experience was learning to handle myself onstage and meeting Jim Ellis. He was a lieutenant and an All-Army halfback, who was also an All-American at Michigan State. Jim became one of my best friends.

I was discharged in 1956 with no place to go. I decided to return to Southern, where a lot had changed in two short years. Doc Lingle was no longer head coach. Football was now the main sport, and the school was pushing him out. Coach Lingle left Southern shortly after I returned, and I decided to do the same.

I was determined to leave the university in style this time. In other words, I lied. Let's say it was a premature truth. What I did was send myself a telegram that read: "Come to Baltimore. Immediately. Guaranteed $25,000 per year. (Signed) Frank D'Alesandro." D'Alesandro was the mayor of Baltimore. I didn't know anyone in Baltimore and I didn't know Mayor D'Alesandro. I chose Baltimore because I had met the mayor's son when I was in the army. I showed the telegram to everyone on campus, including the president. I got comments like "Congratulations, Gregory. Go out there and make us proud!" and "Good luck, Greg. We love you." The power of stardom was serious! Not one person noticed that the telegram was sent from Carbondale. To this day, I am amazed at how important it makes some people feel to know a celebrity. I guess it gives them a ray of hope.

So I packed my bag, took my fake telegram, and headed for the bus station. A few of my friends who saw me off noticed that I was getting on the Chicago bus, not the bus to Baltimore. I told them I was stopping off in Chicago to see a woman, but I was really going to find my brother, Presley. He was working as a doorman, but I wasn't sure at which hotel.

I was so scared. I was going off on my own to a strange city, leaving behind a racist but at least familiar situation. I was so scared, in fact, that I got off the bus after a few miles and ran all the way back to the campus. When people asked me what I was doing back, I lied again.

"Hey man, I'm a star. I can't be riding on the bus. I'm catching the train!"

When you lie, and people believe the lie, you have to make it come true. So, sure enough, a few days later I was on the train headed for the Windy City. Let me tell you, there is no place in America as cold as Chicago in the winter. I weighed only 120 pounds, and that was mostly muscle. That wind coming off the lakefront cut through my clothes like a razor attack. I got even colder when I couldn't find my big brother. Presley had moved and left no forwarding address, but the people he had been renting from at the boarding house let me stay awhile.

I found a job at the post office that I somehow managed to hold onto for two months. I made so many mistakes on that job that I hate to think how many little children didn't get their Christmas presents that year. I had also been intentionally putting all the mail addressed to Mississippi in the foreign mail pouch. I knew it was wrong, but that, plus doing a pretty good unflattering imitation of my supervisor, helped me make it through the workday. I finally realized that I was not going to survive the post office. And the post office realized that it wasn't going to survive me. They fired me. But I can't ever stop thanking God for that job. I was assigned to sit beside a man who has been my friend for forty-four years, Herbert Jubirt. He is also a comedian and a good one at that. I have met a lot of people over the years and I have made some good friends after I became Dick Gregory, the comedian. But Herb, my wife Lillian, and my siblings loved me first simply as Richard Gregory. I had no fame, no money; I didn't even have a car. But they loved me. They still do.

I still hadn't found Presley, so I packed the few things I had, left the boarding house, and walked to the train station. I was standing on the platform in the cold, feeling lonely. I had my head down, wondering what I was going to do. When I looked up, I found myself standing right in front of one of my old high school classmates. We talked about old times and what each of us had been doing since graduation. I told him about my unfortunate army days and mentioned my friend, Jim Ellis.

"You mean 'Tank' Ellis?" he said.

I couldn't believe it! He knew Jim! He told me where Jim lived in Chicago and I must have outrun every car on the street getting to Jim's house. Man, it was great to see him. He showed me the same love and care he had shown me in the army. Jim helped me get a job at Ford Aircraft, and the sun began to shine again. Jim was trying out for professional football, and eventually he left Chicago. Before he left, he looked out for me, like he always did; he introduced me to a wonderful couple named Ozell and William Underwood, who let me rent their basement apartment. They were really nice people, about my age, and were more like family than landlords. Both of them are deceased now. William passed some years ago, and Ozell died while this book was being written. These good people made a big difference in my life, and I thank God for sending them to me.

With a steady job and a place to call home, I had some stability in my life. I wanted to check on my brothers and sisters to see how they were doing and tell them that I was fine. I knew to call Dolores first. Dolores is a blessing in all our lives. She always knows where each of us is and how we're doing. Dolores is the type of good woman who does all the mothering for the family, like visiting if someone is in the hospital. I felt so sorry for her when Momma died, because she was trying to work and raise her family, but she went to that hospital every day to visit Momma. The one day that she was late, waiting on our cousin to go with her, Momma died. Dolores took that really hard. It took her a long time to realize that she had done all she could for Momma. Pauline was only thirteen when Momma died, so she and Ronald went to live with Dolores. Dolores was like a mother to them; she was really like a mother to all of us. She still is. No matter where I am in the world, it's always been a comfort to know that Dolores can reach everyone in the family at any time.

Dolores gave me Presley's address and she told me how everyone was doing. Pauline was still living with Dolores and Garland had married a wonderful woman named Emma (who died a few years ago). They have five wonderful children. One of their daughters, Diana, would in later years spend a lot of time at the farm we lived on when she was a student at Boston University. She is a brilliant young woman who is now a senior key account sales manager at Anheuser Busch, where she has been employed for twenty-two years. All of my nieces and nephews are grown-up now, but I spent more time with Diana and Dolores's son Ferdy than I did the others. Ferdy lived with us for a few years and worked as a distributor with Corrections Connections. But his mother has always been like a walking yellow pages. Dolores also told me that my baby brother, Ronald, was now a track star at Notre Dame in South Bend. I was so proud of Ronald; it made me think how proud Momma would have been of her youngest son. I wished I could wake her from the dead and tell her that, unlike my experience, they even called Ronald by his real name. The minute I started running track and making a name for myself, the White press started referring to me as "Dick" Gregory. I didn't think it mattered until Momma came home one day and told me something that still brings tears to my eyes whenever I think about it.

"Richard," she said, "I did a terrible thing today."

I was shocked. Momma didn't do "terrible things."

"What did you do, Momma?"

"Well, I was listening to the radio while I cleaned my boss's house today, and they were talking all about some track star named Dick Gregory." She paused for a second and I realized that she didn't know they were talking about me.

"Is that White boy as good as they say he is, Richard?"

"Yes, Momma. He's really good."

"You know, son, I listened to that radio and I pretended that White boy was you. I mean, he had the same last name, but I know it's a terrible thing to steal another mother's son — even if it's just for a minute."

I'm sorry now that I didn't tell Momma they were talking about me, her son, Richard. I guess I was too young and too immature to appreciate her and her lack of understanding at the time. I just listened in silence while she bragged about a child that she thought was White. I wish she could have lived to see Ronald go to the University of Notre Dame. I wish she could have seen his name in the headlines. His real name. Ronald eventually made it to the U.S. Olympics finals. He met his wife, Joanna, in South Bend, and they moved back to St.

Louis, where they still live. In fact, all my sisters and brothers live in St. Louis now.

Dolores gave me Presley's new address and I found him the same day. We hung out together as much as we could, but most of the time we were both working and trying to keep our heads above water. When I wasn't working or hanging out with Presley, I would go to parties at my friend Thelma Isbell's house. We called them quarter or rent parties. If one of our friends was having financial problems, all the people in our little circle would get together and have a party to raise money for that person. One Saturday night she was having the party of the year, but I was in such a bad mood I decided not to go. I had no idea that not going to a party on a cold night in Chicago would change my life forever.

Instead I went to a nightclub called Club Delisa. A comedian named Alan Drew was serving as master of ceremonies. I listened to him for a while and decided I could do better. I paid him five bucks to let me onstage. I thought about Momma, and her words of wisdom kicked in once more: There is freedom in laughter. I joked about the cold weather in Chicago and about how broke I was. I guess almost everyone in the audience was broke too, because I got enough laughs that night to get up the courage to try it again. The next night I went to the Esquire Lounge. Jimmy White, Ted Scott and Luther Billingslea were the owners, and Flash Evans was the MC. I tried it again; I offered Flash five dollars to introduce me and bring me onstage. Flash gave me a shot and the audience went crazy!

That night, the owner of the Esquire offered me a job as MC for ten dollars a night, three nights per week, Friday, Saturday, and Sunday. I was to start in two weeks. I couldn't believe it! I knew then that I had found "my thrill." So I started doing what I would continue to do for the next forty years. I ran to the newsstand and purchased every newspaper I could afford. I read each and every one of them for material for my act. Today, in a normal week, I spend an average of three hundred dollars on magazines and about twenty daily newspapers. I spend five to seven hours a day reading. I purchase everything from *Jet*, the *Afro American, Black Enterprise, Upscale, Emerge,* and the *New York Times* to the *National Enquirer*. I read everything I can get my hands on to get a comprehensive understanding of what's going on in the world and use it in my lectures. While it's nice to collaborate with writers on your material, I haven't had a writer in years. All the material I ever needed for my act was in the newspapers.

I had two weeks to prepare for my first gig. I read everything I could buy, borrow, or find in the Underwoods' house. Thank God for family and friends. They were my practice audience and two weeks probably felt like an eternity to them, too. When the big night finally rolled around, the Esquire was packed because everyone was there to see the famous Guitar Red.

Now Guitar Red was, and still is, one of the best guitar players that ever lived in Chicago. I went on first, thank God, because no one wants to follow Guitar Red. I was willing to perform all night if I had to, but my jokes were weak compared to the way Guitar Red was playing that guitar. Red could, and did, play guitar with his toes better than most cats using their fingers. I watched him, studied him, because I wanted to be the best I could be. Guitar Red was a master guitar player, and Chicago loves him to this day. Not only did I want to be good like him, but I knew that as long as Guitar Red was in the house, I had a built-in audience, an audience that could relate to me, and I kept them laughing all night. There were two old-timers in the band, Paul Basken and Billy Martin, who pulled my coat to what show business was really like. I quickly learned that if you want to be good in the entertainment business, you have to work hard like the old cats. They worked night and day to master their craft. Guys like Billy Martin and Paul Basken weren't just successful because they were good; they were successful because they put in the time needed to be great.

5 Lily of the Valley

It took me a while, but eventually I had my own loyal fans. And with the local stardom came the women. I was never good with the ladies. I don't know why. Maybe I was still heartsick for Helene Tucker. But once I became well known at the Esquire, I started meeting all the fine women of Chicago. I met a woman named Martha Smith there one Friday night, and she told me she would come back the next night and bring her friends. That Saturday, she brought a whole tableful of pretty women. She called me over to her table and introduced me to her friends and to her sister, Lillian Smith, whom I have been married to for forty-two years.

"Hi," Lillian said shyly. She was pure as the driven snow.

"Hi," I answered. "I'm Dick Gregory. It's really nice to meet you."

She barely looked at me, but she seemed so familiar. It took me a while to realize that it wasn't her face I recognized; it was her soul. She was just like Momma from within. I quickly realized by talking to her a few minutes that she was very bright and was employed at the University of Chicago in the Business Department. I was a member of the University of Chicago's track club and I was over there every day, yet I had no idea my future wife was inside one of those buildings. We were two ships passing in the night, until that evening at the Esquire Night Club.

I cannot express in words how grateful I am to God for sending

Lillian to me. I didn't see it at first because I was so busy trying to find my next gig. But then I came down with yellow jaundice and was flat on my back in the hospital for six weeks. Everyone came by to visit, but Lil was there every day, nursing me back to good health. She brought me food, cigarettes, and even money. Lil always had money, while I was still making only ten dollars a night. When I got back on my feet, I went back to work at the nightclub right away. I approached Jimmy White and asked him for a ten-dollar-a-night raise. He refused and I quit. I knew enough owners by then to get gigs at a number of different clubs, but I was constantly looking for steady work.

One night, a customer told me about a nightclub called the Apex that was for rent out in nearby Robbins, Illinois. I convinced a track friend of mine, Ira Murchison, to drive me out there to see the owner. Not only was Ira the fastest living human being on the planet at that time, but he was also a nice guy. It was good for me to be around him and watch the amount of work he put into his athletic abilities. He was constantly on the track field, and I used to watch him for hours. I knew I had to be just as disciplined in order to be a good comic.

The Apex was so old and dirty, it almost seemed haunted. Stranger still was the club's owner, Sally Wells, who could tell fortunes better than anyone I have ever met. She told Ira he had been overseas and that he would go again soon. She was absolutely correct. Ira had just returned from a track meet in Moscow and was on his way back. When Ms. Wells finished with Ira she turned to me. I told her that I didn't want her to tell me anything about my future, because she was literally holding my fortune in her hands: the keys to the Apex.

She rented me the club for $168 a week. I gave her the money for the first week and would have to figure out a way to get the next week's rent later. Before I signed the lease, she told me my fortune anyway. She said that I would be a big star one day. She said she saw me traveling all around the world, carrying a brown briefcase. I was loving this old lady until she added that I would soon be married. I told her that I would have to be in love first, but she didn't respond. I wasn't going to debate the point; I wanted the keys to my nightclub. The keys to my future.

Once I had the keys, the first thing I did was to borrow eight hundred dollars from Lil. The second thing I did was to persuade a liquor-store owner to advance me a thousand dollars' worth of liquor. I promised him I would make it big and we would all profit one day. People just seemed to believe in me. I was in business!

Opening night was the hardest. I got to the club early and realized that I didn't have change to give customers who ordered drinks. I drove back into the city to find change. Ozelle must have really believed in me because she borrowed one hundred dollars in change from her boss at the drugstore where she worked. When the doors opened, I had four customers, but by the middle of the night, the place was half full. I was thrilled.

That night, for the first time in my life, I understood entrepreneurship. I understood the power and glory of not working for someone else. I understood why a farmer who owns his crops is willing to till his soil all day, unlike a sharecropper. But most of all, I understood Momma and the sandwiches that she had stood on the corner and sold. For all the indignity that she suffered while working for White folks who never called her Mrs. Gregory, her sandwich business was reparations. Now I understood the thrill Momma had when she stood on that corner waiting for the streetcar driver to buy his lunch from her. It felt good to her beautiful hands when he dropped in that dime for his sandwich. It felt different from the dimes that White folks were paying her. She had been an entrepreneur, the first one I had known personally. I hadn't known it then, but I did now.

The Apex worked me harder than the days when I loaded ammunition back at the plant in St. Louis. Everything that could go wrong, did. I was everything from the comic to the bartender. When the liquor ran out, I couldn't go back to the guy who had already given me merchandise because I hadn't paid him yet, so I would run back and forth from the club to the corner liquor store almost every thirty minutes and buy one half pint of liquor at a time to fill my orders. I also began to realize that this was just the beginning of a long, hard road. After weeks of struggling and not making a profit, I went to Lil to borrow more money.

She gave me three hundred dollars and told me that was all she had. She also told me that she was moving to Cleveland, Ohio, to live with one of her sisters. I couldn't believe my ears.

"Why, Lil, would you leave your job and your friends?"

She looked at me just like Momma used to look at Big Prez when she didn't want to give him bad news.

"I'm pregnant."

I was mad as hell, but I wasn't going to let my new queen know it. She deserved better, and I was going to do right by her. So Sally Wells was right! On February 2, 1959, I married Lillian Smith at her brother Christopher's house in Hyde Park. I married a girl I barely knew, but it was the best thing I ever did and I hope it was the best for her. I have probably made every mistake humanly possible in my life, but I have always tried to do right by Lil. I really have.

Now I had a new wife and a baby on the way, but no place for us to live. I was still living with the Underwoods and trying to make it in show business. My sister Dolores had never met Lil, but she agreed to let Lil stay with her until I could get on my feet. My new wife, my brother Ron, and I got on a bus and headed to St. Louis. Dolores has a heart of gold and I knew that she would take good care of my wife, but I hated leaving Lil there pregnant and afraid. It felt like leaving Momma when I went off to college. It was like quitting that job instead of quitting the track team. But in my heart, I felt that my actions would eventually make things better for us.

I returned to Chicago and the Apex Club, and struggled like no person should ever have to struggle. I was determined that nothing and no one would stop me from making it, not even the snow that was keeping my customers away. Things got pretty bad. I owed money to all of my friends. The Underwoods' phone had been disconnected because I hadn't paid the bill. When it was finally reconnected, I called St. Louis to check on Lil.

Dolores told me the baby was due in a week and that Lil would have to go to the city hospital, Homer G. Philips. That hospital was a place where I had been treated badly as a child. We are all products of our childhood experiences, and I still carry that city hospital in St. Louis with me. It left a bad taste in my mouth and a sick feeling in my heart. It reminds me of that teacher who hurt me because I was on relief; it reminds me of that White man who knocked my teeth out for touching a White woman's leg while shining her shoes. And it wasn't just the receptionists, the aides, or the nurses; some Black doctors had a way of making Black folks feel bad. One time a doctor was rude to Momma because I was dirty when she brought me in for an earache. He made me so mad, I bit the thermometer and it made my mouth bleed. The doctor slapped me, then made Momma and me go back to the waiting room. He wouldn't treat me until he'd seen all the other patients. Maybe I deserved to be punished, but that had nothing to do with the way he treated Momma.

I couldn't stand the thought of Lil's giving birth to our child at the city hospital. I was so disturbed by the call that I borrowed bus fare and went to St. Louis. Now that I look back on it, I guess people laughed at some of the things I did to survive. I went to the doctor in St. Louis who had operated on Ronald's hernias when he was at Notre Dame. I told him the situation and asked him to help Lil. The doctor never asked a single question; he just got on the phone and arranged for her to be admitted to a private hospital. I took Lil to the hospital and went back to Chicago feeling a lot better about the whole situation.

Little did I know the baby wouldn't come in the few days Lil stayed at the private hospital. The hospital sent her back home, and when I called in a week to check on Lil, Dolores was the maddest Black woman in St. Louis.

"Richard, you're going to be paying for this for the rest of your life!" Dolores was irate.

"Paying for what?" I said. "What are you talking about?"

"It's Lilly. She just had the baby on the floor!" My family always called her Lilly. It's an appropriate name for the woman who has stood by me for more than forty-two years, given us ten beautiful children, and never once raised her voice — not even, according to Dolores, when she was in labor for the first time.

My sister was talking a mile a minute. Apparently, one of the doctors at the private hospital sent Lil home because they thought it would be a few more days before the baby would come. I'm sure the real reason they sent her back home was because they didn't want a Black woman hanging around in the hospital. The baby came the very next day and my new wife had the baby on the floor of her room at Dolores's, all alone. Well, she wasn't really alone. Dolores had gone to work and my brother Presley was visiting when Lil went into labor. But, Dolores told me, Presley was too scared to go into the room. When Dolores returned home the baby had just been born.

"I'm telling you, Richard," Dolores yelled, "Presley said she didn't even holler! If he hadn't gone into her room, he would never have known she was having a baby." When the ambulance came, they couldn't get the stretcher on the elevator because it was too small, so they had to stand my Lilly up, strapped to the stretcher, to get her on the elevator.

"So where is she now, Dolores?" I interrupted.

"She's at Homer G. Philips Hospital." The city hospital! I didn't hear a word Dolores said after that. I froze. Lil was at the city hospital. She was still talking when I hung up the phone and ran to the bus station. I took the next bus to St. Louis, then ran from the bus station all the way to the hospital.

I couldn't believe it; nothing had changed at that hospital in all those years. All the women were lined up in beds just like they used to line us up in the hallway to get shots when I was a little kid. You really couldn't blame the hospital for being overcrowded; it was the only hospital that admitted Black folks. Even if you had money, most of the hospitals were still segregated in St. Louis and many parts of the country. So my new wife and new baby were at Homer G. Philips, where I had been slapped as a child.

However, what I failed to appreciate at the time was that Homer G. Philips had some of the best doctors in the country, and definitely the best internship program. Because of segregation, if you were a Black medical student at Yale University, chances are you couldn't intern at Yale's hospital or other White hospitals in America when you finished their academic program. Because of pure segregation, Homer G. Philips had a twelve-year waiting list. But the students on that waiting list were coming from Yale,

Howard, and other top medical schools across the country.

In fact, the very hospital I didn't want my child born in had saved Dr. Martin Luther King's life three years before. On September 20, 1958, while attending an autograph signing in Harlem for his book, *Stride Toward Freedom*, King was stabbed by a deranged Black woman. The doctor who performed surgery on Dr. King was a former intern from Homer G. Philips. And no doctors had more experience dealing with major cuts than those at Homer G. Philips, due to the meatpacking house in St. Louis. The employees did not necessarily get cut at work, they often were just violent from the psychological effects of cutting meat all day at the packing house. Most of the employees were Black, and when they got cut they were sent to Homer G. Philips. The media reported that, because of his wounds, if Dr. King had sneezed, he would have died. Everyone said, thank God, he didn't sneeze. I say, thank God the doctor was a product of Homer G. Philips. But it took me many years to understand what that hospital really stood for, just the way it took me all those years to understand Momma selling her sandwiches on the corner.

If I had understood then the way I do now, I would have walked into Homer G. Philips with pride to see my new family that was packed into a room filled with other women who had just given birth. Instead, I felt at that moment that I would rather have my child born on the floor at the home of people who love her than in that hospital. At least when Lil had stood up to go get in the ambulance, she had still had her dignity.

But Lil just smiled when I came into the hospital room. She didn't complain at all. We talked and she introduced me to all the women in the ward with her. She had told them all about the nightclub and how I was going to make it big. When I tried to apologize for having left her and to tell her how sorry I was that she had to have the baby on the floor at home, she wouldn't even listen to me. She acted as though she had just given birth at a palace and I was the king. We named our firstborn Michelle, and she was beautiful. I stayed in St. Louis as long as I could and then rushed back to Chicago to open the club on time. I hated having to leave my family, but it was Friday and I had to get back to the Apex to open up. Lil still didn't complain.

That night, I announced to the audience that I had just become a new daddy. I kind of hinted that they had better bring gifts and they did. The next night I had so many gifts for Lil and Michelle that I could hardly get them all on the bus back to St. Louis. The following Tuesday, Lil and Michelle were home from the hospital and I stayed with them at Dolores's house for three days. Those days are so beautiful to me now. I remember Lil lying in bed like Momma used to when she was resting from work. I wrapped my arms around her and Michelle and the three of us slept together for the first time. I tried again to say how sorry I was for not being there for her, how sorry I was that she had the baby at Dolores's home and not at the private hospital as we planned. Lil wouldn't hear it.

"Greg, you know when I was lying on that floor? Well, I just thought this child is going to say 'Dick Gregory's my daddy.' Our baby is never going to say 'I was born on the floor.' She's just going to say, 'Dick Gregory's my daddy.' You can do anything you want to do, Greg. You know that and I know that. Don't let anything stop you."

I listened to this woman who had just given birth to our child on the floor of her bedroom tell me that I could do anything. I wondered what in the world I had done to be so blessed. How could Lil have such faith in me, in our love, and in our family? Right then and there, I promised Lil and I promised God that our child would never be without a father. I kept that promise to Michelle and her nine sisters and brothers who followed.

That Friday, I returned to Chicago. God stepped in and brought the sun out of hiding. The club was sold out for the next few weekends. But the winter had been so rough that the sunshine couldn't repair the damage or erase the mountain of debt I'd incurred. I lost the nightclub and went back to work at the Esquire. I was grateful for the job, but I knew I was meant to make it big — bigger than the Esquire.

Herman Roberts owned the Roberts Show Club, the biggest and newest nightclub for Negroes in America. His nightclub was huge in more ways than one. He had some of the biggest stars in the country coming to perform there, Miles Davis, Duke Ellington, Sarah Vaughan, Count Basie, Sammy Davis Jr., and Nina Simone. Yes, these Black performers were playing downtown at the White clubs, but Herman was in the Black neighborhood and you didn't come to Chicago without stopping by his place. Herman also owned the Herman Roberts Motel. That's right, in the second largest city in the United States in the sixties, he had a motel. I was trying to get Herman Roberts to hire me, but I had to get him to see my act first. He was so busy with his nightclub that he just didn't have the time. So when I found out that the Pan-American Games were coming to town, I threw a party with borrowed money at his nightclub and invited him to come. Herman showed up and boy, did I perform! It worked and he offered me a job.

"How much do you want a week to be my new MC?" he asked.

"One hundred and twenty-five dollars!" I demanded.

"Is that all?" He looked surprised. I wanted to shoot myself. I should have said two hundred dollars. Well, at least I had the job.

The very first thing I did was to send for Lil and Michelle. We rented a little furnished place for twenty-five dollars per week and we became a real family for the first time. It was then that I came to understand what it had been like for Momma all those years, trying to keep a roof over our heads. It also made me think more about Big Prez. I wondered how he could have left Momma alone with not one, but six children to take care of. But I didn't have time to think too much about Big Prez; I was on a roll. Or at least I thought I was.

6 To Cast a Stone

Herman Roberts forgot to mention the fact that he only kept MCs for one month. So there I was, unemployed again. Lil and Michelle really went through a lot in those lean days, but thank God, Michelle was too young to remember and Lil was so supportive. She even got her old job back at the University of Chicago. I did what I had to do, picking up gigs here and there, until eventually Herman Roberts offered me my job back.

We were barely making ends meet. I was keeping Michelle during the day while Lil worked at the University. Every day, I would wrap Michelle in a blanket and we would make our rounds. We did everything from running errands for Lil to looking for new nightclubs for me to perform in. I'm surprised that poor child didn't fall through the floorboard of the raggedy old car we had at the time. In the afternoon, I would take her home to Lil and go to my next gig. I eventually left Herman's club and went out on my own again.

Night after night, I worked the clubs all over Chicago. Then the summer of 1960 came and so did the Republican Convention. By then, I was playing at some of the White clubs, too. The delegates to the Convention who were hitting the clubs talked about me to John Daly at American Public Broadcasting. He got the word that there was a Negro in town bold enough to stand up and talk about racism. I got a call that

John Daly wanted me to appear on a TV show called *Cast the First Stone*. I wasn't an activist back then and didn't care about the show; I just wanted the world to see the star on my forehead that old Mother Poole had told Momma about.

At the expense of everyone we could borrow from, Lil and I had eighty thousand fliers printed up advertising my appearance on the show. We worked night and day passing out the fliers. John Daly took two full minutes to introduce my act. When the moment came for me to do my thing, it lasted exactly twenty seconds. Twenty seconds! They had taped me for two hours, and then they edited it down to twenty seconds. My anticipated stardom, my dreams, all went up in smoke. I cried and so did Lil.

The next day, Lil and I didn't even mention it. She went back to work at the University and I went looking for my next gig. To our surprise thousands of letters came in from those twenty seconds. People were writing to congratulate me and to tell me how much they enjoyed my twenty seconds. Eventually, I managed to find yet another one-month gig at a coffeehouse on Rush Street. The Fickle Pickle was the type of place where people met and networked, like they do today at Starbucks. They were paying me $125 per week and I met some nice people who really wanted to help me. Joe Musse was one of those people, and he became my manager. Joe introduced me to Freddie Williamson, who worked out of the Chicago office of the Associated Booking Agency. Freddie was a good agent, but I could never get him to come to my show. So one day I took my show to his office and performed until he, too, believed in me. Ultimately, he got me a gig that was one of the turning points in my career and in my life.

Freddie booked me at a place called Eddie's Supper Club in Akron, Ohio. I took the job and went to Ohio to live with rats and roaches in a place where you had to share one bathroom with other men and women. At night, I had to pile clothes on top of myself to keep warm like we did when we were children. I was a grown man, a married man, but I cried myself to sleep every night. But when I was performing, I forgot all about that little room because things were changing for me. Eddie's was the largest all-White club I had ever seen. And after a month with those White boys, believe me, I was prepared for the big time. I could make them laugh all night, but when the laughing stopped, I couldn't sleep in their hotels. I didn't know what was next for me, but I sure knew I was ready to get back to Chicago. I made it home in time for Christmas.

That year, Lil and I bought each other gifts on credit the way Momma used to do. We even got a big TV on credit to go in our almost-bare living room. But Lil did some extra typing jobs at the University so she could afford to get me something special. Can you believe it? Lil was just like Momma, and I was thinking about Momma as I unwrapped the new brown leather briefcase. It reminded me of Momma giving me that wallet so long ago. I wished I still had that wallet to put in my new briefcase. Sally Wells was right again: I now had the brown briefcase that she had seen me carrying around the world. How lucky could one man be? No matter how poor I was, I had Lil and Michelle. Oh, how I wish Momma could have lived long enough to see her grandchildren. I was so grateful for my family and grateful for that brown briefcase.

Lil giving me that briefcase was just one more person, one very important person telling me that she saw that star in my forehead. By now I think a lot of people were seeing it, including one of the greatest musicians who ever lived, the amazing Miles Davis. I was still performing all over Chicago when I got a gig at the Regal Theater and Miles was there. Miles was so cool and I liked him right away. But one thing about Miles was he never talked to anyone unless he had to. So I was really surprised when he came over one night after I performed and just started talking.

"Dick Gregory, you are one funny motherfucker and you are going to be really big one day."

"Oh really, how do you know that?"

"Man, my sister don't like nothing. She will come up from East St. Louis every now and then to see me, but other than that she don't do nothing and don't like nothing. But she has been up here three times to see you. I'm telling you man, you going to be big." I guess the king of jazz was right because just when I thought the holidays were over, my agent called with the news that would take Lil, Michelle, and me out of that twenty-five-dollar-a-week hole-in-the-wall we'd been living in.

Irwin Corey was booked at the Playboy for the week but he didn't want to play for seven nights straight so they called wanting me, Dick Gregory, to fill in! I was going to play the Playboy Club! It was all a result of Hugh Hefner going to Herman's club a few weeks earlier. Sammy Davis Jr. was in town and no matter the location, everyone who could get in came to see Sammy. He was just a bundle of talent that came without the scuffle. It was there that Hugh Hefner saw me, as I served as MC for Nipsey Russell and Sammy Davis Jr. But Hugh almost didn't see me because earlier that week Herman had told me I could not work that night. I told him that they had better keep Nipsey because I was not coming back. When I said that, he told me I could come to work and MC, as long as I wasn't funny. That meant I had to restrain myself from being funnier than one of the main attractions. I was so upset. But I will never forget what happened when I went backstage. This old Black dude who worked the lights and sound equipment asked me what was wrong.

"Man, this could be the biggest night of my life and Herman told me not to be funny."

That old cat was so beautiful. He said, "Look son, as long as you are the MC, you have thirty seconds to bring on each act and in between that, you just say your funnies and keep moving. You have to be as funny in thirty seconds as you would be in an hour and a half."

I did what the old man told me, with Hugh Hefner sitting in the front row. If I had not kept a positive attitude, Hugh Hefner never would have seen me that night. That's how close I came to not making it.

And as for Sammy Davis Jr., he and I would later become friends. He was definitely a friend to the Movement. In addition to marching together, we put together a couple of fundraisers for various civil rights organizations over the years.

So there I was at the Playboy a few weeks later, for what was supposed to be one Sunday night. For the three days leading up to that engagement, I was so happy. That night when it was time for me to go to the club, I only had twenty-five cents in my pocket. I didn't care, because I was going to make fifty dollars that night. I wasn't familiar with Chicago and wouldn't you know, I got on the wrong bus and got off in a blizzard nine blocks away from the Playboy. It was now 7:30 and I was due on at 8:00. I just starting running and praying. I was about six blocks away from the club when I saw the Playboy sign shining through the snow. I soon realized that my being late was a gift from God.

When I got to the door, Hugh Hefner's right-hand man Victor Lounge met me and tried to change my mind. It seemed the house that night was packed with White Southerners in town for a frozen-food convention and they had bought out the entire club for the evening. But I was excited from being late, and I was determined — so determined that I ignored Victor. I thought about my new briefcase and Sally Wells's prediction. I thought about Momma and the wallet and the star that even I could now see on my forehead. Well, I just walked right past that White boy and into my future. I wasn't going to let Lil endure what Big Prez had put Momma through. I was certain that this was it. I looked into that audience and I didn't see Southern Whites; I saw Lil and my future. I went for it.

"Good evening, ladies and gentlemen," I began. "I understand there are a good many Southerners in the room tonight. I know the South very well. I spent twenty years there one night. . . . It's dangerous for me to go back South. You see, when I drink, I think I'm Polish. One night I got so drunk, I moved out of my own neighborhood. . . . Last time I was down South, I walked into this restaurant. This White waitress came up to me and said, 'We don't serve colored people here.' I said, 'That's all right, I don't eat colored people, no way! Bring me a whole fried chicken.' About that time, these three cousins came in. You know the ones I mean — Ku, Klux, and Klan. They said, 'Boy, we're givin' you fair warnin'. Anything you do to that chicken, we're gonna do to you.' About then, the waitress brought me my whole chicken and the cousins said, 'Remember, boy, anything you do to that chicken, we're gonna do to you.' So I put down my knife and fork, picked up that chicken, and kissed it!"

During my routine, I kept thinking back to North Taylor Street. Every time the audience cracked on me, I'd hit them with the kind of jokes I used on the bullies back in St. Louis. I guess I'd been onstage about three hours when my big moment came. Hugh Hefner himself came to the club and caught my act. Victor Lounge called him and told him to come and see the unbelievable. It was unbelievable, because these White Southerners were laughing, not trying to hang me. At the end of the night, Hefner offered me a six-week gig at $250 per week.

Everything changed that night, and my life has never been the same. About a week after I started at the Playboy Club, I got "the big call." Jack Paar read a review about me in *Time* and wanted me to come to New York to appear on his show. That review was due to the hard work of my publicist, Tim Boxer, and a lucky accident. I kept telling Tim to get me a review in *Time* so he went to visit their Chicago office in person. They told him no and that they didn't have anyone to come over to catch my act. As Tim was leaving, one of their science reporters from Cape Kennedy came in, telling the guys that he wanted to go to the Playboy. It was very difficult to get into the Playboy back then, almost impossible. So Tim was walking out the door as this writer was complaining about not being able to get into the club. They started yelling for Tim to stop and then they told him that this science writer would do the review, only because he wanted to get into the Playboy. That is when I really knew God was guiding my life. Remember, this guy was a science writer, not an entertainment writer. But Jack Paar read that review and it was my ticket to New York. The whole trip was out of this world, what an evening! In one day, I flew on a jet plane for the first time, stayed at the Mayflower Hotel, appeared on *The Jack Paar Show* and ran into Nat King Cole in the lobby. All in one night. At the end of the show, while I was still in New York, I did what I continue to do forty-two years later: I called Lil.

When I am away from home, I call her an average of ten times a day. Sometimes I don't want anything in particular; we will talk about the weather or the children. I just want to hear her voice. The night I called her after *The Jack Paar Show,* she was so excited I could see her face light up right through the telephone. Lil gave me my messages and, following the last message from a well-wisher, she said one of the funniest things she'd ever said:

"Oh, Greg. They repossessed our television today."

It was music to my ears. Lil must have thought I was crazy, I laughed so hard. I knew that it was only a matter of time before I could buy Lil ten TVs. And she wasn't upset about the television being taken away. That's one of the great things about her, she is always calm. Calm and beautiful. It has sustained me all these years — from my first television appearance to this very moment.

I told Lil about Joe Glasier, the president and CEO of Associated Booking, coming by my green room before I went on the show. He gave me an envelope that I put in the drawer until afterwards because I was so excited. Later that night I opened the envelope and found it had one thousand one-hundred-dollar bills in it. I went to find Joe and asked him what the money was for.

"Oh, it's for you and your family. Buy your wife a new house."

I thanked Joe and I gave him his money back. It's not that I didn't need it or that I wasn't appreciative — I just didn't want to be indebted to him or anyone else. That is why so many artists and athletes stay with the same managers and agents for life. Mainly the Black ones, because Black folks have that loyalty thing going and they are not about to betray the person who got them started. Even when they want to leave, they don't. It's almost like sharecropping: you get so indebted to old master that you owe them too much to leave. Then you buy a million-dollar house that you can't afford and your manager makes arrangements with the bank until the next season. Kind of like the sharecropper boss, making arrangements with the local grocery store to pay the bill until harvest time. It's a cycle that only benefits old master. You have kids in high school accepting houses for their mothers as they are taken off to college to star on a team. But I never did that, and I didn't have to remain loyal to people outside of my family when it came down to making business decisions. If I had taken that money, how could I have gone down South when the Movement called, if my managers and agent didn't want me to go? I didn't want to be held hostage and I didn't want anyone holding my talent hostage. If I am indebted to anyone it is Lil, my immediate family, and friends.

After I appeared on *The Jack Paar Show*, managers, agents, lawyers — you name it — started calling and the money rolled in. I was blessed to be surrounded by a team of people who didn't work for me, they worked with me. And we were a team that kept all bases loaded. I had good writers, like Jim Sanders and Ed Wineberger. Jim died years ago. Ed Wineberger went on to create *The Cosby Show* and my third writer, Bob Orben, was to comedy writing what Einstein was to physics. Ed and Bob were White, and Jim was Black. Ed and Jim traveled with me in the early days. When I became a part of the Movement, they were right there, running from the Klan with me. I'm sure when Ed was creating *The Cosby Show*, he understood the Black family because he had experienced our lives firsthand. In addition to having great writers, I had Bernard Klamen and Dick Shelton as my attorneys, and it didn't hurt at all to have Marv Joseph and Ralph Mann for agents. They took care of everything, and all I had to do was go on that stage and be funny. More important than working with good people, I have been surrounded by good friends all of my life, from Boo to Jim Ellis to Herbert Jubirt, and my best friend for life, Lil. I was like a kid in a candy store.

Lil was even more beautiful to me when I got back from New York. She was pregnant with our second daughter, Lynn, who was born on July 30, 1961.

My family was growing and so was my circle of friends. People I hadn't heard from in years started to contact me, including Big Prez. After twenty-nine years of not having a daddy, I got a call from Big Prez. He invited me to come to his house the next time I was in San Francisco. I knew he had remarried and become a head chef at one of the major hotels there. The last time I'd seen him, I'd wanted to kill him. But I agreed to see him in San Francisco, where I also met his wife and their children, my sisters and brothers. I don't know why we had always called him "Big Prez," because he didn't seem very big at all when I saw him. "Daddy" seemed to have settled down and I resented him for that. Momma was such a fine woman and she deserved all the nice things he was doing for his new wife. Also, to my surprise, he was nice and kind, the type of person all children want for a daddy. I was so hostile to him in a way I pray my children will never be towards me. But something Michelle said to me after she met Big Prez helped to ease my bitterness towards him.

"Daddy, you don't like Granddaddy, do you?" she asked.

"Not really."

"Well, I do," she said with a smile on her little innocent face. Then she asked, "Can I go by there sometimes without you?" That's a hell of a thing for a child to say to you! I said yes and we left San Francisco. Michelle had softened me about Big Prez, but the way I saw it, I wasn't his son at all. I was "Dick Gregory, the famous comedian," allowing him to play Daddy for the moment. I was glad to leave San Francisco and get back home to my real family where I belonged.

Weeks later, I would become guilty of doing to my family what Big Prez had done to us for all those years — but for a different reason. The Civil Rights and Human Rights Movements came calling, and suddenly I was never at home. Forty years later, I am still away from home about ten months out of the year. The difference between Big Prez and I was that I always came back, and if my family ever wanted for anything, it was me.

While all sorts of old friends and wannabe friends were showing up in my life, I couldn't imagine having fame without Lil. She always made it worthwhile. The two most exciting things that happened to me in 1961 were Lynn's birth and being able to give Lil all that I thought she was supposed to have. I bought her a brand-new Thunderbird. Lil didn't even have a license (and she still doesn't), but I wanted her to have that car.

I have the kind of respect for Lil that a country has for its president. If it has been in my power, Lil has never had to do anything she didn't want to do. Oh, how I enjoyed that Thunderbird sitting in our driveway just for Lil. I drove her wherever she wanted to go. When the kids got older, they would drive her. After all Lil had endured with me, after all she'd sacrificed for me, she deserved the best.

My life and that of my family was changing as my fame grew. But fame demands a price, and I was about to pay. The price I would pay would completely change the direction of our lives. It was the sixties, I was considered a famous and outspoken Black man, and civil rights leaders started to call on me to help with various causes. I willingly spoke at rallies, prisons, and schools. But I was in no way ready when Medgar Evers called.

7 BLINDED BY THE LIGHT

A fear came over me when Medgar called to ask me to come to Mississippi. It's one thing to be bold in New York or in Chicago — it's a whole other matter to be bold in Mississippi. You have to understand how I felt about Mississippi. Back in St. Louis, Mississippi was always the butt of all the jokes. When you talked about a "bad White boy," you weren't talking about Hitler; you were talking about a redneck Mississippi cracker. You didn't think there was anything more vicious than a blond, six-foot, blue-eyed Mississippi sheriff. When Mississippi wasn't a joke, it was the subject of some true horror story that some old person was telling: "Let me tell you about those White men cutting that Black boy's nuts out last year." Later, I would make my own jokes about the place that had put so much fear in my heart as a child.

"A White moderate in Mississippi is a cat who wants to lynch you from a low tree."

Bob Johnson, editor of *Ebony* and *Jet* magazines, had confirmed my childhood fear of Mississippi in 1955 when he dared to print a picture of fourteen-year-old Emmett Till, who had been mutilated and murdered by grown White men in Mississippi. The picture was published on the cover of *Jet* and sent around the world. Some White folks couldn't understand that picture, but the Whites of Mississippi understood it well. And Black folks around the globe understood it in the marrow of their bones. It was the price you paid for "reckless eyeballing." In Mississippi, you could go to jail just for looking at a White woman — or you could wind up like little Emmett Till. That picture confirmed my fear and fortified my desire never in this life to go to Mississippi.

But Medgar, one of the finest men I've ever known, had no fear. He didn't just talk the talk, he walked the walk. I still miss him and I miss knowing that there is a Black man in Mississippi who would rather die and leave behind his beautiful wife and children than be somebody's nigger. His spirit was so fearless that I couldn't say no when he called.

I was on my way to Mississippi.

Before I left to join Medgar and his fight for justice, I had a long talk with Lil. We made a promise to ourselves and to God that Black folks would always come first, even before our own children. It was a promise we've kept for more than forty-two years. The Movement was a battlefield. You had to make that kind of commitment because every time you stepped onto the battlefield, it could very well be your last step. It was like the war movies Boo and I watched as kids, where you have all those soldiers willing to die for their country.

Medgar's call and my decision to go to Mississippi forced me to evaluate my life, my politics, my responsibilities, and my priorities. First of all, I would never go back into the army. I didn't understand a Black man fighting for a country that didn't allow him to eat in the restaurant with White folks. I had my own battle to fight right here at home. The fight was for things that we deserved as human beings: the right to eat in a restaurant, to go to a movie, or to drink from a water fountain. I had no interest in being a soldier for a racist system that didn't consider me human.

The call from Medgar made me realize that the heroes in the movies were just a fantasy. I idolized men like Clark Gable. When Momma would tell me to do my chores, I'd stand in the mirror and say, "Frankly, my dear, I don't give a damn." And man, John Wayne was my hero. I was programmed to idolize those cats like you'd program a computer. Going to Mississippi to help Medgar changed my programmed mind. When I stepped off that plane, it was not about cowboys and Indians. This was real, and I knew the difference. I was so scared that I had to remember Momma's smile and think of Lil and the children.

Lil was pregnant again, and we were hoping for a boy, our first son. I had to think about my unborn son's being able to go to Mississippi one day without the fear I was experiencing, and not leaving in a box like fourteen-year-old Emmett Till from Chicago. Till's mother, Mamie Bradley, had sent him down to spend the summer with his uncle, Mose Wright, a sharecropper who lived outside of Money, Mississippi. After being accused of saying "Hey, baby" and whistling at Carolyn Bryant, the wife of a White grocery-store owner, young Till was taken from his uncle's house in the middle of the night by Carolyn's husband, Roy, and Roy's half-brother, J. W. Milam.

Till was beaten and shot in the head, then barbed wire was put around his body and he was tied to a seventy-five-pound cotton-gin fan. But that wasn't enough to satisfy the evil that lived in Mississippi. With a bullet in his head, they threw his body into the Tallahatchie River. On August 31, 1955, a fisherman found Till's body floating in the river. The local authorities tried to do a quick burial, but Till's mother insisted that his body be brought back to Chicago. It was there that she laid out the body of her son in a church and allowed the world to see what Mississippi was made of.

The trial of Till's murderers was almost as sad as what had been done to Mamie Bradley's son. There was not one Black person on the jury. To serve on a jury, you had to be a registered voter and there was not one Black person in the entire county who was registered to vote. Even if any Blacks had been registered, they probably would not have been selected for that jury. There were only three White attorneys in Sumner County and they all offered their services free of charge to the defendants. Did you hear me? Free to the defendants, not Emmett's mother.

The defendants were allowed to bring their children to court and the children played with — of all things — guns, while they ate ice cream with their fathers. Emmett's mother sat through the entire trial and listened while they made her son's life seem worthless. The White woman that Till had allegedly whistled at was referred to in court as "Mrs. Bryant"; like Momma, Emmett's mother was addressed as "Mamie." But the high point in the trial, as far as Black folks were concerned, was when Till's Uncle Mose stood up in the courtroom and said "tere he!" (there he is) and pointed his finger right at the accused men. Uncle Mose was old, illiterate, and poor, but he stood up for his nephew and he stood up for me. Surely I could do the same for my own unborn son.

Those murderers must have beaten Emmett Till for hours. Some people believe that he was beaten all night, but it took the jury only one hour and seven minutes to return a verdict of not guilty.

As if they had not insulted Black people enough, the following year *Look* magazine featured an article about Emmett Till's fatal night. Because Till's murderers had been acquitted, they could not be tried again for the same crime. They were able to sell their horrible story to *Look* for four thousand dollars. I had to go to Mississippi.

When I arrived, I was amazed to see a Mississippi that no one told Black folks in St. Louis about: the Black teacher, the Black preacher — just success story after success story. No one had told me about the Black schools, Acorn University, Jackson State University or the Black church; I had only heard the negative things. When that plane landed, Medgar was standing there waiting for me, not with fear on his face, but a smile. The first place we went to was a local restaurant. No one had told me about the barbecue house owned by a Black woman. No one had told me about the Mississippi Black women, period. These women were running the Movement while their husbands were working. There is more to a movement than having a rally when ABC and CBS are there. Local movements were going on every day, and it was the Black women out there when those news stations were gone. Stranger than anything I saw when I first arrived in Mississippi was the White police officer having to protect us. I realized on this first trip that there were two Mississippis, and they were worlds apart.

While I had gone to many rallies at the invitation of various civil rights leaders, going to Mississippi was different. Maybe it had something to do with the NAACP office being on Lynch Street. Whatever it was, it did not affect Medgar Evers. After dinner we drove to an auditorium in Jackson, Mississippi. We talked on the way, and I found him to be as personable as he had been on the phone. Medgar, Roy Wilkins, the president of the NAACP, some local leaders, and I were scheduled to speak. The place was packed with local citizens fighting for the right to vote. I noticed a man sitting in the front row who had so much pain on his face that he frightened me worse than Mississippi. I leaned over to Medgar:

"Man, keep your eye on that old man up there." There had been several threats on Medgar's life, and I thought the old man might just mow us down like they would do Malcolm years later. Medgar leaned back over to me and smiled.

"He's all right," Medgar whispered. "He's on the program. Just sit tight and listen to what he has to say; he's the next speaker."

There are few moments in my life that I can say rendered me speechless, but this was one of them. That old man had just been released from prison after serving one year for murder. He had been involved in Black voter registration and a White man had tried to burn down his house. The old man had gunned him down in self-defense. This old Black man only got one year in jail for two reasons. He was a member of the NAACP and they provided him a lawyer. Otherwise I can't image what would have happened to him for killing a White man, even if it was self-defense. When he hung his head and told his story, he broke every heart in that room, including mine.

"I'm seventy-five years old," he said. "And I got married when I was sixteen years old. My wife was only thirteen when I married her, and we never spent a night away from each other. When I went to prison, I knew that I was going for a righteous reason, but leaving my wife was hard."

I sat there thinking about how lonely his wife must have been without him. How sad she must have been when dinnertime came and she couldn't fix him a warm plate of food. Then I realized that that was only half of his story.

He continued, "She died the second night I was away."

I was now a part of the Movement. This seventy-five-year-old man had gone to jail at the end of his life to fight for all the Emmett Tills; he was fighting for my unborn child. I knew there was no amount of money that would erase his pain or bring back his wife. I was almost ashamed that all I could do was make a monetary offer. I asked him if he had family he'd like to visit for Christmas and he told me that he had relatives in California, so I gave Medgar money and a train ticket for the old man's trip.

Medgar knew that the old man's story had affected me, and he wasn't letting me off the hook with just a train ticket. As we were leaving the auditorium, he introduced me to a lady named Leona Smith. He told me she was "Clyde Kennard's mother." I stood there thinking, *Who in the hell is Clyde Kennard?* Medgar explained that Kennard was a name conveniently left out of the history books because they didn't want the world to know just how mean Mississippi was back then. Kennard was a native of Mississippi who was a paratrooper in the Korean War. When he returned home after the war, he purchased a chicken farm for his mother and stepfather, then moved to Chicago to complete his education. In 1959, his stepfather became ill and Clyde returned to Mississippi to take care of his family and the farm. Determined to finish college, he attempted to enroll at Mississippi Southern College (now the University of Southern Mississippi). He was the first Black person to enroll there and it was the beginning of the end for him. He and his family were harassed daily, but Clyde pushed forward.

This, Medgar told me, is where Mississippi gets mean. Five bags of stolen chicken feed were planted on Kennard's farm while he was at the college for his admission interview. Clyde was arrested and the price of the feed was raised to make the theft a felony offense. The chicken feed had actually been stolen from a warehouse and placed on the Kennard farm by a Black teenager who was told to do so. Clyde was sentenced to seven years at Parchman State Penitentiary.

Medgar had succeeded in making me understand that Mississippi was the most racist state in the country, but I still didn't understand Medgar. Why wasn't he afraid of the death that I could see all around him? White Mississippians feared him more than he feared them, and they should have. Mississippi Whites were not as dumb as they were prejudiced. Blacks, even in the sixties, outnumbered Whites two to one in that state. Whites knew that if enough people followed Medgar, Blacks would one day control the politics of the state. Until two years ago, there were more Black elected officials in Mississippi than in any state in the country.

Before Clyde's horrible ordeal, there was a man named Clennon King, a professor who had attempted to enroll at the University of Mississippi in 1958. But Clennon King was not jailed as Clyde had been; instead, he was declared legally insane and railroaded into Whitfield Asylum. Before Clyde and before Clennon King, there was Medgar. Very few people know that Medgar had applied to the University of Mississippi in 1954. He was, of course, denied entrance, but he was the first to try. Medgar understood this state that killed Black people as a hobby, and he wanted me to understand it as well. As I said before, many civil rights leaders were talking the talk, but Medgar was walking the walk. He changed things; he changed Mississippi; he changed me.

I thought about Medgar and the people I had met in Mississippi. I thought about the old man whose wife died while he was in prison. I kept thinking about the conditions in which they had to live to survive. I can only compare those White folks who mistreated Black folks to roaches. You see, roaches only come out in darkness and they run when you turn the light on. Well, Medgar was the light; that old man was the light. Men like the late Aaron Henry, who owned the only Black pharmacy in Clarkdale, Mississippi, in the earlier sixties, was the light. He wasn't just selling medicine; his store was a place where we met, planned, and prayed. We also ran there when we had been chased by the roaches, aka the Klan. Now, there is another way to get rid of roaches, and that is to clean house. That's what Medgar and men like Henry Aaron were doing 95 percent of the time: cleaning house. I was in and out of the South, but they were there every day, cleaning up the crumbs of racism.

There was a third light in Mississippi and all over the South, and it consisted of the old lady or old man whose families had been sharecroppers for four generations and had never made a profit. Now think about who they were and how they had little or no money. After sharecropping all year and getting most of their clothes and food on credit, then to have old White Mr. Johnson tell them that their bill at the corner grocery store is the same amount they owe him for paying their bills all year. So they have no way out, and here they thought old Mr. Johnson was doing them a favor by letting them stay on until things got better. Well, things never got better for most of those Black folks, and this went on for generations. Then we came into town and told them we were going to help them register to vote. We showed up and told them we wanted them to come off the White boy's farm that was feeding them. We asked them to go and register to vote, not at the Black church, but downtown at the courthouse. And later that evening they had to return to Mr. Johnson's farm, because we had no place for them to go. Remember, they left home unregistered boys or girls and went back registered men and women.

If you could have just been there when old brother and sister so-and-so were marching with us to the courthouse and Mr. Johnson walked up to them.

"I can't believe you are doing this to me. You have worked on my farm all your life and so did your daddy and your daddy's daddy." He would look at that old lady or man and say, "How could you do this to me? How could you follow these communists from the north?"

That's when the light would come on. That Black woman, that Black man would turn to Mr. Johnson and say, "I ain't doing it for them. I'm doing it for Jesus." Blinded by the light, old Mr. Johnson would be furious. But you have to understand the Mr. Johnsons of Mississippi. Those old illiterate Negroes were all the White folks had to validate who they were. Can you imagine being Mr. Johnson, a redneck who knew he was an illiterate cracker, and who knew that, as White as he was, he could never be president of the United States of America? As White as he was, he was never going to drive a Mercedes or go to Paris. So the only thing old Mr. Johnson had to play with was niggers. And we went down there and took them. That's what I couldn't wait to get home to tell Lil.

When I went back to Chicago, I told Lil all that I had seen. I told her about the old man and about his wife dying. I told her about Clyde Kennard and how he was still in prison. I told her that I wanted to help Clyde, and for the first time in my life, I made a New Year's resolution: "Free Clyde Kennard!"

Everywhere I went I talked about Clyde. Finally a reporter from UPI who was interviewing me became interested in the story and did some research on Clyde's case. He found out that things were worse for Clyde than we had thought: he had colon cancer. Columnist Irv Kupcinet, a writer for *The Chicago Sun Times*, broke the story and released all of Clyde's medical records. We challenged racist Mississippi and, out of shame, the prison transferred Clyde to the hospital unit, and later, Governor Ross Barnett ordered his release. We brought Clyde to Chicago for medical treatment at the University of Chicago. They could not refuse him treatment because they had a special machine owned by the government that is used to treat cancer patients. If you don't take patients in, you can lose the machine. We used that strategy to force the hospital to admit him. But, like the wife of that poor old man, it was too late. On July 14, 1963, Clyde Kennard died at the age of thirty-six. It is a crime that a young person died because he wanted to go to college. Clyde didn't get a chance to go to Mississippi Southern, but like Medgar and Clennon before him, he helped plant a seed that would not die.

James Meredith proved that the seed was growing when he broke down the walls of Ole Miss a few years later. History should revisit the life and contribution of James Meredith. It's one remarkable feat to be Black and enroll in the University of Mississippi, but quite another to have the courage to stay. I've always wondered how James managed to focus on his classes, knowing that at any moment, some racist's bullet might rip through his body. Clyde, Medgar, and James all had to live with the daily and very real threat of sudden death. No one wants to die, and I would like to believe that Medgar and Clyde's deaths were not in vain. I would like to believe that their deaths angered America enough to listen when James Meredith decided he was going to continue their journey.

Clyde Kennard was the first person I knew personally in the

Movement to die. But the bigots of Mississippi were alive and well, and I was about to return. I was performing in Chicago when a guy I didn't know came up to me and asked if I would sign a petition from the SNCC (Student Non-Violent Coordinating Committee) and make a donation to a fundraising campaign for the people of Leflore County, Mississippi. It seemed that the government had cut off food relief to the entire county. The government was hardly short of funds; they were just angry as hell that the people of Greenwood (the county seat) and SNCC were heading one of the largest voter registration drives in history. The hidden agenda was that two senators, Senator James Eastland and Senator John Stennis, both owned farms and they had thousands of Black folks sharecropping for them. Remember that those food stamps programs were federal programs provided under federal laws, yet these two senators still had them discontinued. And they did so with John F. Kennedy sitting in the White House. They knew if these people had food stamps and other aid from the government, they wouldn't need old master anymore. That's what it was really about. It only cost thirty-seven thousand dollars per year to store the relief food, but they still refused to reinstate the program. The people of Greenwood were hungry, but they were pressing on.

I signed the petition and gave the stranger a check for one hundred dollars. Word got out in Greenwood that I signed the petition and they wanted more. Not money, but my support. They invited me to a press conference in Chicago, then asked me to come to Mississippi. I decided that I would go, but not empty-handed. If the government would not feed the people, then I would. I knew they just wanted the people to beg, like Momma used to, but I wasn't going to let that happen. I went through the streets of Chicago with a disc jockey named Daddy-o-Dailey, and we collected fourteen thousand pounds of food. People gave all kinds of food, but mostly canned vegetables and fruit. We chartered a plane, and my friend Jim Sanders and I flew back to Mississippi, a place I still feared.

Jim Sanders was a brilliant young writer, and he traveled with me for years. He had one of the finest comic minds on this planet and he was really brave. His life was always in danger as long as he was with me, but he continued to travel with me anyway. We arrived in Greenwood on February 11, 1963, and Jim and I, along with several members of the SNCC, including H. Rap Brown and Stokely Carmichael, distributed the fourteen thousand pounds of food. SNCC was planning a big demonstration for the right to vote and they wanted me to stay. I was too ashamed to tell them that I had intentionally arrived on the eleventh because I was due at a White House reception on the twelfth; it was my excuse to stay only one night. No one questioned me about it, and Jim and I flew back to Chicago to pick up Lil for the trip to Washington, D.C. But I knew the SNCC members in Greenwood were fed up with the nonviolent movement. And soon their days of waiting would be over.

8 Move On, Niggers

By now I was one of the most popular comics in the country and we received invitations to everything. Lil never did like attending a lot of affairs, but she wanted to go to a dinner that the White House was hosting for Negro leaders from around the country on February 12, 1963, to celebrate the one-hundredth anniversary of the signing of the Emancipation Proclamation. My wife was almost nine months pregnant, but she went out and purchased the most beautiful dress I had ever seen. When we arrived at the White House, the scene looked like the March on Washington that would be held months later. All the men of the Movement were there — Dr. King, A. Philip Randolph, Harry Belafonte, Whitney Young, Ralph Abernathy, and Ralph Bunche. Lil looked stunning when I introduced her to President John F. Kennedy.

"This is my wife, Lillian Gregory," I said.

"I know," Kennedy said, "we have talked several times on the telephone."

It was kind of funny. I knew a lot of people — celebrities, heads of state, you name it, but Lil knew them better than I did, and she still does. From day one, she has always taken care of my affairs. Anyone who talks to me has always talked to Lil first. We talked to everyone at the reception and they all knew my pregnant wife. I was mad, though.

Not because they knew her, but because she didn't have the baby that night. That's right, I wanted Lil to have that baby right there on the floor in front of all the people who had mistreated Black folks. It would have been Momma's revenge for having to give birth to all of us at the city hospital. I also knew that was the only way to get a Negro in the White House was to have him or her born there. (But Lil, being the lady she is, waited until we got home. She gave birth to our first son, Richard, Junior, two weeks later.) A strange thing happened that night in Washington. I didn't realize how strange until thirty-five years later when I saw the picture of Monica Lewinsky hugging President Clinton. I was getting ready to say something to President Kennedy and reached to hit him on the rear, the way track guys say "hello."

"Hey, Jack," I said. Then all hell broke loose. Every Secret Service agent in the room dropped their glasses and rushed towards me.

"No one can raise a hand to the president of the United States in public. Not you, not me, not even the First Lady." When you see the Clintons in public, they are holding hands, not hugging. I was a friend to Kennedy. If I couldn't touch him to say "hello" without being attacked, how is it that he was murdered in the middle of the day? Where were all those agents who dropped their glasses and were ready to kill me? Some of the women in cocktail dresses were damn agents, ready to take me down if they had to. Where were they that day in Dallas? I ask myself that every time I think about Kennedy's death. I ask myself that every time I see that clip of Monica hugging President Clinton on the White House Lawn and no one stopping her. And why did Monica have on a winter coat and her famous beret, when everyone else in the picture wore White, short-sleeved summer T-shirts? Maybe it's called digital technology. Look at that picture again, people. That picture was damaging, but how did it happen in the first place, America?

While I was drinking champagne with President Kennedy, the good White folks of Mississippi were shooting at students and local registration workers in Greenwood. They burned down the SNCC headquarters and beat many of the local people. Momma had taught me the importance of keeping my word, and I knew I had to return to Mississippi.

Scared as hell, Jim Sanders and I got on a plane on March 31, 1963, and flew to Memphis, Tennessee. Though it is a different state, Memphis's airport is closer to Greenwood than the airports in Mississippi. From Memphis, an SNCC student picked us up and drove us to Greenwood. The plane was full and I joked with Jim about how many people suddenly wanted to go to racist Mississippi. But it was no laughing matter. The plane was full of White boys in dark suits from the Justice Department who were on the plane because I was. Many of them didn't care if I died; frankly, many of them could care less if one of those rednecks hung me from a tree. They just didn't want it to happen in Mississippi, because then they would have to take the heat when they got back to Washington. The press would be all over those Justice boys if something bad were to happen to a celebrity. We arrived in Mississippi and not even the Justice Department could stop the events that would occur over the next few days.

The press was waiting for me, but I was ready for them. They wanted to challenge what had happened in Leflore County, Mississippi, weeks before. While they knew it was wrong to take relief food away from the people of Greenwood, they hated me for helping. But those people needed to eat. As much as I disliked being on relief as a child, I know life would have been even harder for Momma without it.

"Mr. Gregory, is it true that you brought food to Mississippi for the media attention?" Journalist after journalist tried to provoke and insult me.

"Mr. Gregory, is it true that it wasn't really fourteen thousand pounds of food?" Now, I had ignored them until they started calling me a liar.

At that point I thought about Momma and my childhood. I thought about how I had learned to be quick on the streets so that people wouldn't bother me. I tried it on the media: "Why don't you check with Delta Air Lines? They had to weigh every pound of that food." The harassing went on for hours.

After being harassed by the media, we were taken to a meeting to prepare for the next march. I may have been ready for the press, but not for the old Black man who asked me, "What are you going to do if they spit in your face, if they hit you, if they knock you down? You going to hit back?"

"I'm going to try not to," I answered honestly.

"We can't use you," he told me.

Those were his exact words. He didn't give a damn who I was! These people truly believed in nonviolence. We went to our hotel rooms and the local people went home, and I thought about that old man all night.

Whatever fear I had, I left it at the hotel the next morning. The people of Greenwood were fighting back, and I wasn't going to let my own fear or the racist system run me out of town. We went to the burned-out SNCC headquarters where people were gathering for the march. The same old man from the day before approached me. He was back up in my face with the same attitude.

"We're ready to go, Mr. Gregory. What do you think?" I knew what he was asking me.

"Okay," I said. "I'll do it."

He was showing me the true spirit of nonviolence. This uneducated Black man, with no food at home, looked at me man to man and said with his eyes: "There is a price to be free, son." I was ready to pay that price.

We had only walked one block when the police came over and told us to leave.

"Move on, nigger!"

"Thanks a million!" I answered back.

"Thanks for what?"

"Up North, police don't escort me across the street against a red light."

"I said move on, nigger!"

Well, this went on for hours as we tried to make our stand. Eventually, we dispersed to get a little rest and food and to discuss the next march that afternoon. The police really didn't care what we said to them because they had won that day. They were vicious enough to close the courthouse early so we couldn't register to vote after the march. We held a rally and I spoke in Greenwood for the first time.

"We will march through your dogs. If you get some elephants, we'll march through them. And bring on your tigers, we'll march through them." Then I joked with the marchers about the phrase "survival kit.""I love that expression, 'survival kit.' Up until recently, we used to have survival kits in Mississippi. They included ten 'Yassuh, bosses' and a shuffle."

That night after the rally I called Lil. She had just arrived home from the hospital with our new son, Richard Junior. I asked her to come to Mississippi. I wanted her to see the light that I had seen. It was important for her to come. I wanted her to see the ugliness and the beauty of the place. She has always been there for me and this was no exception. As soon as we hung up, she was on her way to Greenwood. We marched together a few days and then we went back to Chicago. We left only after we made a deal with the local authorities that the demonstrators would be released from jail and the city would supply a bus for the Black folks to the courthouse so that they would vote. That way they wouldn't have to walk through town in order to register to vote. I was very afraid for the people we left behind, because I knew they would continue to march even when I was back on a plane. As long as I was there, the cameras and the Justice Department would be there, too. Once I left, it wouldn't take long for the police to start harassing them again.

When we got back to Chicago, Dr. Martin Luther King Jr. called and asked me to come to Birmingham. I said yes and started packing again. Then President Kennedy called. The same president I couldn't touch a few weeks earlier was calling me at home. I was out when he called, and Lil insisted that I call him back before I went to bed. I had been out drinking most of the night and I tried to wait until morning, but Lil would not let me go to bed until I made the call. The message he'd left said to call Operator 18, and I did so. An operator answered, and the next voice I heard was John Kennedy's.

"Oh, yes, Dick. I've been waiting for your call. I have a little problem and I wonder if you'll help me with it?"

His "little problem" was that Dr. King had made an announcement that I was coming to Birmingham.

"Dick, do me a favor and don't go down to Birmingham. I feel that

Dr. King is wrong. We have reached a settlement there and everything is going to be fine. Your going will just create problems."

I couldn't believe that President Kennedy thought we were the problem. The problem was a racist system that the government did not want to control for political reasons and couldn't control even if they wanted to.

"I know Dr. King and I know that a lot of things that are changing in the South didn't start changing until Dr. King got involved. I told him that I'm coming down and I'm going. I don't think he would have called me if he didn't need me, and the last person who is going to put me in a trick is Dr. King."

But the president was determined to change my mind.

"Well, Dick, I wish you wouldn't go. Why don't you wait seven days? I'm sure the problem will be solved."

"I told Dr. King that I'm coming on Monday," I said. "That's tomorrow, and I'm going. I want you to know that when I see on the television news what is happening to Black folks — the fire hoses and all — I know that no matter what deal has been made, the streets are where I need to be. And that's where I'm going."

President Kennedy was not at all happy with my response.

"Well, I'm sorry you feel that way, Dick. But thanks for returning my call."

We hung up, and I was off to Birmingham.

9 Turn Me Loose

After I got settled in Birmingham, I read all the papers for news about Greenwood. Some declared the Movement a failure, depending on whom they had interviewed. But in my opinion, nothing that happened in Mississippi was a failure. We marched, we were beaten, and people died for my children and yours. Promises were made and broken, but we did not fail. Some papers implied that I went to Greenwood for the publicity. It was hard to read, but I have learned over the years that you can't control or care about the press, good or bad. The truth is, I have always received more publicity from my performing than I did for marching. Forty years later they are still saying that about me and other civil rights leaders. A prime example is Jesse Jackson. As long as he goes around the world bringing America hostages back home, everyone loves him — but the minute he went to Decatur, Illinois, to deal with those Black students who were suspended from school for fighting, that same White press said he was doing it for publicity.

Not even the bad press about my intentions in Greenwood or about the march itself could stop me from going to mean Alabama to tangle with the notorious Eugene "Bull" Connor. I was glad to help in Alabama, but it was where I took my first butt kicking. Bull Connor was as bad or even worse than the press had portrayed him. But America would not see the real evil in Bull Connor until the world watched him order fire hoses turned on innocent little Black boys and girls.

Dr. King had made a move that stunned many people: he asked little children to march. His strategy was well founded; he knew that parents could not afford to take off work to march with him. He also knew that, if they did, they would be fired the next day. Being the kind spirit he was, Dr. King never imagined that Bull Connor cared as little for the children as he did for us. The whole world watched those babies holding onto poles, trees, and whatever they could to keep from drowning. It was awful.

I had been arrested several times by now. Usually they would let me out in a matter of hours, but Bull Connor was not afraid of the press. He would keep you as long as he felt like it, and he decided to keep me for five days. They arrested twenty-five hundred people that day, mostly children. I was in a jail cell made for twenty that had seventy or more people packed in it, including children. There was one little boy in there who couldn't have been more than four years old and didn't look nearly as afraid as I was.

"Why are you here, son?" I asked the little boy.

"I want my 'teedom'!"

He couldn't even pronounce "freedom," but he knew it felt good to say it. As we were talking, the police started pulling him and the other children out of the cell, and the adults tried to stop them. Remember, we had been arrested so quickly that no one had time to write down our names and the police would have easily made some of our children disappear into the night, like Emmett Till had eight years earlier. So we weren't going to let them take our children if we could help it. As we tried to stop them, one of the policemen slammed the cell door on my arm. I don't know what came over me, but I pushed the door open and started swinging. Needless to say, I lost that fight and took the worst whipping of my life. So much for nonviolence. Luckily for me, when they started whipping me with those billy clubs, I fell backward and the adults in the cell pulled me back inside. Jim Sanders couldn't see what was going on, because he was in a different cell. He could only hear the club hitting my behind. When we were released, Jim couldn't wait to tell me what he had heard down the hall.

"Man, they whipped somebody's behind earlier."

"Jim, that behind was mine!"

So Jim and I left, and I took my sore behind back to San Francisco, where I had a gig at the "hungry i" club. I had been performing there off and on all year. The hungry i was a great nightclub where all the big entertainers appeared.

But President Kennedy's worst nightmare had come true, when a picture of me beaten up went out around the world. With pictures like that out there, he had no choice but to send in the federal troops. I kept in touch with everyone in the South and learned that the deal Kennedy had mentioned to me had gone through; Bull Connor would be resigning as Birmingham's chief of police. They didn't fire him, they just passed a new law that stated that the chief of police had to pass a civil service test. Well, guess who couldn't read or write? He had no choice, he had to resign. Can you believe a man who ordered dogs on little Black boys and girls couldn't do what they did every day: READ!

While I was in San Francisco, I talked to Medgar and promised him that I would come back to Jackson, Mississippi. Before I got on the plane to Jackson, a strange and sad feeling came over me. I felt that something was going to happen to me, something really bad. *I'm not leaving Mississippi alive,* I thought to myself. I took a detour to Chicago to see Lil and the children. All kinds of things were running through my head as I held my newborn son. I thought about Momma as I played with Michelle and Lynn. Momma would have loved being a grandmother. Then I kissed Lil goodbye for what I felt would be the last time.

When Jim and I arrived in Mississippi, we went directly to the rally instead of to Medgar's house as planned, because my plane was late. We met Medgar at the auditorium. As soon as we got there I told Medgar:

"Look at these cops, man. They have this strange look on their face."

Some of the cops were almost smiling.

"Yeah, I noticed that, too," Medgar responded.

"They are going to kill us tonight, Medgar."

He didn't say anything, but he knew I was right. Just before I went onstage to speak, Medgar walked up to me. I could tell something was wrong.

"Dick, call home."

"I'll call tomorrow."

"No. Call now, Dick."

"What is it? Why can't it wait until tomorrow?"

"It's your son. He's . . . sick."

"Well," I said. "There's nothing I can do tonight. I'll call Lil after the rally."

Medgar paused for a moment. He didn't sound like the Medgar I knew.

"Dick," he said, "your son is dead."

I had been right about there being a death, but it was my son who died, not me. We didn't say anything to the audience. I quickly made my speech and left. That night, as Medgar drove us to the airport, I started to understand why I was put on this Earth. This Movement was bigger than my own flesh and blood. There was no doubt in my mind that the evil that would kill Medgar two weeks later would also have killed me if I'd gone to Medgar's house as we'd originally planned. The only thing that kept me from going to his house was the plane being late. To this day, I can still recall the tension in the air. The White cops we passed as we drove to the airport just smiled and never attempted to stop us and give us bogus speeding tickets. They had already signed Medgar's death warrant. I knew I'd never see him alive again.

"Hey man, it would have been a pleasure to die with you," I said to Medgar when we got to the airport. We hugged and I left Mississippi with Jim Sanders and took that long plane ride back to Chicago. It was just like going home from college after Momma died, but instead of having to face my distraught brothers and sisters, I had to face Lil. It was so painful, because I knew there was nothing I could do to change things, to bring my son back. When a person gets sick and you know they are dying, you have some time to prepare yourself and some time to pray. But what happened to our son was so quick, like a thief in the night.

When I arrived at home, I hardly recognized Lil. She was a woman who had just lost her newborn son to crib death. The medical term is sudden infant death syndrome. That night I learned that nature does not prepare mothers to lose their children. My Lil sat there holding Richard Junior's blanket tightly in her arms. She barely looked up when I came in. Bob Johnson, from *Ebony* and *Jet* magazines, was there, and he arranged the funeral and handled the press over the days to follow.

In the midst of our pain, I got a phone call.

"Is this Dick Gregory?"

"Yes, that's me."

"Are you that nigger comedian whose son just died?"

"Yes."

"Well, I'm glad." The evil that lived in the South had risen all the way up to Chicago to harass my grieving wife and me. Maybe I made it too easy for people to find me, because I have always had a listed number.

"You're glad? Well, me, too. I had a million-dollar life insurance policy on him, but instead of your saying that to me, would you say it to my wife?"

"I sure will," he said, like he was talking about the weather. I put the phone to Lil's ear and he repeated that same thing to her. When she heard his cruel words, she dropped that blanket she had held for hours and jumped up. Before I could stop her, she jumped on me and knocked me down. I knew Lil was hurting and I shouldn't have let her hear that White man saying those things. But I wanted her to understand that Richard Jr. had died to bring me home, so we could fight the hatred coming through that phone. If he had not died, I would have gone to Medgar's house that night after the rally. I will always believe that they would have killed Medgar, Jim, and me that night. I will always feel my son was the sacrificial lamb, who died so I could stay here and be a part of this Movement for the past forty years.

I stayed with Lil for a few days; then Jim and I left to go back to Jackson and march with Medgar and Lena Horne, who had joined the demonstrators for a few days. Then I went back to San Francisco, where I was still performing at the hungry i. I remember talking to Enrico Banducci, the owner of the hungry i. I had left several times and he had had to find a replacement for me. He just told me how much he admired what I was trying to do and told me to be careful. Maybe he had the same feeling I had, because I still couldn't shake the sensation of death in the air.

My second night back onstage, jazz great Billy Daniels came by the club. He walked up to me with this strange look on his face, and he didn't have to say a thing — I knew Medgar was gone.

"Hey, Greg, did you hear the news?"

"No, what happened?"

"They gunned down Medgar tonight."

I finished my gig and left for Mississippi the next morning.

Lil was still mourning Richard Jr., so she didn't go to Medgar's funeral. Jim Sanders flew back to Mississippi with me, and I remember how hot it was as we made our way through the crowds of people outside the church. As soon as the plane landed, I could feel that light come on again. The light that said "Our one shining candle is brighter than the one billion lights you White folks are trying to blow out. When you blow out one of God's lights, the remaining lights will only get brighter, with no fear. The White folks who killed Medgar saw that light the day of his funeral. They had no idea that people would come out by the thousands the way they did. But the young, old, crippled, and blind were there. So were Bobby Kennedy, Roy Wilkins, Ralph Abernathy, and Dr. King. I had to smile as I watched the White people looking at us. They acted like they didn't recognize us. Then I realized that they didn't; they had treated the Black people of Mississippi so inhumanely for so long that they didn't know who we were when we got all dressed up. I was so proud of Medgar that day. Although he was gone, his spirit was alive and he had done what he had died for: he'd made White folks see how truly beautiful we were.

At one point there was some bottle throwing, but Medgar's spirit stepped in and things calmed down. You just couldn't escape who and what Medgar was that day. Nor could you ignore how strong and beautiful his wife, Myrlie, was. At one point the whole church held its breath when a photographer almost stood in Medgar's casket to take a picture of Myrlie. But that picture of her with a single teardrop rolling down her face on the cover of *Life* magazine will forever be in my mind. I will always admire the wife she was to Medgar until the day he drew his last breath.

Medgar had died like the soldier he was. On June 12, 1963, the night of his murder, his family was watching President Kennedy deliver a speech while they waited for Medgar to come home. Medgar was returning from a NAACP meeting in his '62 Oldsmobile. As his children waited, so did that coward, Byron De La Beckwith. He hid in the bushes in front of the Evers's house with a high-powered deer-hunting rifle. Medgar must have been very tired, because he normally got out of his car on the passenger side under the carport so that the door would protect him until he was in the house. But on that night, Medgar stepped out of his car on the driver's side with his "Jim Crow Must Go" signs under his arm. He never stood a chance. De La Beckwith pulled the trigger and changed America with one cowardly shot. The children did as they'd been taught, grabbing one another and diving for cover. Myrlie ran to the door as Medgar held his keys and pulled his strong body towards the house. The children jumped up and ran to the door. Medgar's neighbors ran over to help and one of them, Houston Wells, fired a shot into the air. I suspect that that is when De La Beckwith dropped his rifle and ran. They put my friend on a mattress, placed him in the back of a station wagon, and rushed him to the hospital. Myrlie stayed home to comfort the children, while a neighbor named Willie Quinn rode with Houston Wells to the hospital.

Myrlie fought for over thirty years to put Medgar's murderer behind bars, and I will always admire her for that. I barely knew her second husband, Walter Williams, but I also admire him for being so supportive of Myrlie's efforts to bring Medgar's killer to justice. Only God knows what the wives of the Movement have been through. Myrlie said goodbye to Medgar only after she'd brought Mississippi to its knees. She sat through two trials that ended with a hung jury. But on February 5, 1994, De La Beckwith was found guilty and sentenced to life in prison. And it was only then that I, too, was able to say goodbye to Medgar. I know that on that day in 1994 when justice was finally done, Medgar rose from his grave at Arlington Cemetery. I thought about his last words as he was bleeding to death on his daughter's mattress, thirty-some years before.

"Sit me up," he told them. They sat him up. He didn't die until he reached the hospital. This hell of a man — this man I knew would never die lying down — sat up and said his final words:

"Turn me loose."

10 Bombingham

It's eerie knowing that De La Beckwith was lurking in the bushes waiting to kill Medgar while President John F. Kennedy was addressing the nation about racism. I doubt that De La Beckwith knew or cared that the president was speaking. His knowing would not have prolonged Medgar's life anyway; many in White Mississippi had decided it was time for Medgar to die. It never mattered to me who fired the shot — racism pulled the trigger. If De La Beckwith had not killed Medgar, someone else would have.

I got crazy after Medgar died. I was no longer afraid of anything, not even my own death. I was no longer afraid of Mississippi, neither the stories I'd heard as a child, nor the events I'd witnessed myself. I knew I had to continue the fight for Medgar. Maybe we all worked a little harder after his death. We wanted the world to know that he did not die in vain.

A. Philip Randolph began planning a march on Washington that would become the largest march ever to be held in the capital before Louis Farrakhan repeated history with his Million Man March in October 1995. Although it was not planned, the March on Washington was held on the eighth anniversary of Emmett Till's death, August 28, 1963.

This was not the first time Randolph had threatened a march on Washington. During the Roosevelt years, he had threatened to bring thousands of Negroes to the capital to force concessions from politicians and pressure them to keep their word. This time, an estimated 250,000 people joined in the march. People were sick and tired of being sick and tired. The old, young, blind, and crippled came by bus, car, train, and plane.

People all around the world listened to our leaders speak, among them Dr. Martin Luther King Jr. His "I have a dream" speech went out all over the world. It was the first time people heard him speak internationally. People who were at that march or those who listened to the speech carefully got his real message, but others even today don't understand what he really talked about that day. His famous line, "I have a dream," was actually a closing remark that the press picked up on and has held onto for the past thirty-seven years. They held onto that phrase because it was the safe part of King's speech. Everyone in America should go out and get a copy of that speech. I was there, and what he clearly said was that it was the one-hundredth anniversary of the Emancipation Proclamation and America had written Black folks a bad check. King had come to Washington to cash that one-hundred-year-old check. He wanted to collect for all of Black America, not discuss a dream. The press entitled his speech "I Have a Dream," and he copyrighted the speech with that title to prevent people from doing whatever they wanted to do with it. But he should have called it "America's Bad Check," because that was his message.

John Lewis also made a great speech that day. He had intended to include in his speech the question, "Which side is the federal government on?" I didn't understand why this upset people since that was a part of the reason we were all there. But so much controversy surrounded Lewis's original speech that the organizers of the march threatened to remove him from the program if he didn't modify it. Cardinal Patrick Boyle assured them that he would not deliver the eulogy as he'd been requested to do unless the speech was altered. Sitting behind the Lincoln Monument, Lewis, James Foreman, Joyce Ladner (who eventually became an interim president of Howard University), and Courtland Cox rewrote parts of Lewis's historic message, and he was brilliant that day.

Lil came with me to the March on Washington, and she brought the children along. They were too young to understand why they were there, but this was their history in the making and I wanted them to be a part of it. The whole event was beautiful, colored sadly by the loss of W.E.B. DuBois the day before the march. Someone got on the microphone around noon and announced his death. That announcement somehow helped set the tone for that special day. It was almost as if his spirit traveled across the Atlantic Ocean from Africa, where he had lived for many years. We left Washington, D.C., feeling very hopeful. For the first time in years, many leaders felt some validation of their work. The good feelings didn't last long.

On September 15, 1963, only three weeks after the March on Washington, many Black folks in Birmingham, Alabama, were in their homes, getting dressed up for Sunday school at the Sixteenth Street Baptist Church. Just as De La Beckwith waited in the bushes for Medgar, someone planted a bomb that would kill Denise McNair, age eleven; Addie Mae Collins, age fourteen; Cynthia Wesley, age fourteen; and Carole Robertson, age fourteen. The girls came to church wearing white dresses and ribbons in their hair as planned for "Youth Sunday." They were all in the church basement brushing their hair and filling the room with laughter when their young lives prematurely and violently ended. No one knows which child died first. It was a horrible experience to listen to the reports about one little girl's decapitated body and Denise McNair's precious little head embedded with a rock from the blast. As sad as it was to lose those little girls, we silently said thank God it was only four. Because one thing people must understand is that bomb was put there to blow up the entire church and everyone in it, not just four innocent little girls. Some said there was a loud noise — like a firecracker going off — and the girls were dead. Twenty-two others were injured. The nation went into mourning and the whole world reeled from the shock of that bomb blast. I will never forget when Bob Lipsyte, who was cowriting my first autobiography, *Nigger,* at the time, came to my hotel room in New York and broke the news. He woke me up and I just remember lying there crying. By now there were few things that you could tell me about a White racist system in the South that could stun me. But that stunned me, because even I was naïve enough to believe that the church was safe. I couldn't help thinking that even the people who killed Jesus Christ didn't tamper with the sanctity of the church. Folks had thought that the church was a safe place until that day. I don't know why I believed it myself; Black folks in the South had known for years that churches had been burned and bombed. The difference was there had been no cameras before that sad day in Birmingham to show the evil in America to the world.

There was a mass funeral for all the girls except Carole Robertson, whose parents wanted a private service for their daughter. Lil and I went to the mass funeral. Those little girls were the ages of the children I had marched with months earlier. The funeral was by invitation only; it had to be, to control the crowd and to ensure everyone's safety. But people came anyway. The rich, the poor, people from all over the world came. That's who those little girls died for: all of us.

When Lil and I left the funeral, we decided to go over and take a look at Sixteenth Street Baptist Church where the carnage had occurred. There was a stained-glass window portraying Jesus Christ and the window had been blown out from the head up. What a sight. Jesus with no eyes. That was a symbol to me of where America was going. The blind leading the blind. It was also a depiction of the hundreds of years of hatred that have been inflicted upon people of color.

Before that sad feeling could take hold of my heart, I spotted a White police officer standing across the street from the church leaning on a red, white, and blue mailbox. He was watching us. The look on his face clearly said that he didn't care if every little Black girl in the world was murdered. It would take sixteen years for the police to try anyone for that bombing.

In 1977, a White supremacist named Robert Cambliss, nicknamed "Dynamite Bob," was tried and convicted of the murders of the four girls in Birmingham. Witnesses said that they saw him standing around the church for days after the murders, just looking and smiling. Cambliss died in prison in 1985, but few people believed he was the lone assassin. The case was reopened in 1998, and on May 17, 2000, as we finished this book, Thomas Blanton Jr. and Bobby Frank Cherry were indicted. The fourth suspect, Henry Frank Cash, was never indicted and died in 1994.

God, I pray that one day those four little girls' families will be able to see justice for their children, as Myrlie did for Medgar.

The more lives we lost, the harder it was for me to ignore what was happening to Black people in the South. Being a comedian was fine: flying first class, staying in four-star hotels. But things had changed — I wanted Black and oppressed people to be free. The press had begun singing a new tune about me. They started writing that my demonstrating was interfering with my career. My response was that my career was interfering with my demonstrating. The freedom of Black folks has always outweighed my life as a comic. Civil rights leaders knew that, and called upon me more and more. It was around that time that I first met my man Malcolm X.

I was performing at the Basin Street East in New York the first time Malcolm called me at my hotel room.

"Brother Greg? This is Brother Malcolm."

"Hello, Brother Malcolm."

"Brother Greg, I understand that you have been marching down South."

"That's right. I have."

"Well, I would like to invite you to come down to the mosque."

"Send a car to pick me up. I will come right now," I said.

Malcolm was speechless. I feel he didn't expect me to say yes. He had called upon many entertainers who were in fear of jeopardizing their public image. Only a few, like the great Ossie Davis, put dignity over image and supported Malcolm 100 percent.

"Brother Malcolm," I added, "there is one condition. You must sit beside me and arrange to have a photographer there to take our picture. Then I want you to guarantee me that the picture will appear on the cover of *Muhammad Speaks*." *Muhammad Speaks* was and still is one of the best papers in this country pertaining to Black folks.

"I'll call you right back." Malcolm was still stunned as he hung up the phone. A few minutes later he called me back.

"Brother Greg, have you been drinking? You know I can't let you come down here. The press will have a field day with you if you come down here."

Now understand, Malcolm was fearless, but he was also a protector of his family and friends. But I didn't know much about him at the time. I didn't know his call was just a test. But he was testing me because he knew it was safe to go and march and protest in the South with all the other civil rights leaders, but it wasn't safe in terms of one's public image to associate with a Black Muslim. He sent a car to pick me up and I went to meet with him, and that was the beginning of our friendship.

My brother Presley knew Malcolm before I did, back when he was known as "Detroit Red," a two-bit hustler, living the gangster life in Detroit. It was Detroit Red who was sent to prison and became transformed into Malcolm X, one of the most beautiful cats ever to walk this planet.

Our friendship blossomed as Malcolm began to receive death threats. The breaking point came for Malcolm when Kennedy was killed.

11 Sad November

Like most others, I will never forget November 22, 1963. I was on tour at the time and Jim Sanders was traveling with me. He was not only a great writer, he was also a master astrologist and often made predictions based on his knowledge of that science. We were sitting watching TV one night, as we often did. Kennedy was in San Antonio, Texas, speaking to a crowd of people in Spanish and they loved it. The following night we were watching TV again and the news reported that Kennedy was going to be in Dallas, Texas, the next day and they showed his picture.

"Look at him," Jim said, pointing to Kennedy on TV "They're going to blow him away if he goes to Dallas on Friday."

"How do you know that?" I asked.

"Just look at the position of the planets. I'm telling you it's not a good time for Kennedy."

I wasn't much of a believer in astrology at the time, so I decided to play what turned out to be the worst joke of my life on Jim.

"Well," I told him, "if something bad is going to happen to the president, I'm canceling our trip to the University of Pittsburgh, because it's going to be canceled anyway."

We were supposed to be on our way to the University of Pittsburgh at the time, but I called Lil and told her to reroute Jim and me through

Chicago. She played along with the joke and I went back in to tell Jim. Of course, Jim didn't want me to do that. In fact, he was very upset with me, but I decided to play the joke out all the way to the end. I told everyone else about the joke and sent them on to Pittsburgh, and Jim and I got on a plane back to Chicago the next morning. He didn't know that I had plane reservations to Pittsburgh for that evening. I was the final act, so I didn't have to be on stage until ten, and I was going to ride this joke out. What happened next would make me a believer in astrology for the rest of my life.

When we arrived in Chicago around 12:30 P.M., we got into a taxi and were headed home. The taxi driver had the radio on, but I wasn't really paying any attention. I was busy messing with Jim's head about his prediction. Then I heard the words "shot in Dallas" on the radio. The president was shot at 12:33 P.M., but since we had gone directly from the plane to the taxi, we hadn't heard any news reports.

"Brother," I said to the driver, "what did they just say about Dallas?"

"Man, haven't you heard? They shot the president this afternoon!"

My mind just started going in all directions. I kept thinking about the day President Kennedy was inaugurated. I could still picture him walking down Pennsylvania Avenue on that cold day without a hat. That was a big deal, because he was the first president in history not to wear a hat on Inauguration Day. The hat industry went crazy. Then I thought about the night Kennedy called me and asked me not to go to Birmingham and I went anyway. And my mind flashed back to the night at the White House a few months earlier. The Secret Service stopped me in seconds from touching him. *Where were they today?* I asked myself.

Then my mind raced from Kennedy to the fact that this guy sitting beside me had just predicted the night before that the president would be killed in Dallas. *Who is this guy?* I wondered. *Who is Jim Sanders?* I turned to him. "Can you teach me astrology?"

When we got home, I rushed to my room and turned on all three of my TVs and my tape recorders. I was thinking about how valuable the tapes would have been if they had had tape recorders one hundred years earlier when President Lincoln was assassinated and someone had recorded all the reports. They would not have been worth anything then, but they would have been priceless later. On all the channels, witnesses were telling their stories. Then a strange thing happened on the evening news. All those people who had given their stories earlier in the day changed them. These people had one thing in common: they had all talked to the Secret Service. I couldn't believe it. To this day, I regret that I got so upset that I turned off all my tape recorders. It was that day that I started to understand and believe in conspiracy. That day I began to understand that we could not trust the government or the press.

One key piece of evidence that is public knowledge proves that Lee Harvey Oswald was part of a conspiracy to kill Kennedy. The car the president was riding in went down Elm Street in Dallas. But that was not the original plan and the car was rerouted to go down Elm Street only thirty minutes before the shooting. So how did Oswald know about the route change if he was acting alone? He started his job at the book depository one month before the shooting. The president's route through Dallas was clearly changed to put President Kennedy in front of that book depository where Oswald worked. Elm Street is very important here, because the corner where he was shot is so sharp that you have to slow down to less than thirty miles per hour to make the turn. You are therefore driving slow enough for someone to take a clear shot at you.

Lil and I went to Kennedy's funeral. It was such a sad and cold day. Dignitaries from all over the world were there. Thousands stood in line to view the casket at the Capitol's rotunda and bid farewell to their president. Lil and I stood in line, too, and waited like everyone else until U.S. Marshall Luke Moore insisted that we not stand outside. Luke later became a federal judge. But he will be remembered forever as the brave marshall who guarded James Meredith as he walked the halls of Ole Miss. His life, too, was in danger every day and he, like James, never wavered. Luke escorted us into the Capitol. It seemed like the world had stopped that day. I guess for many people, it did.

The day of President Kennedy's funeral was also the day everyone learned who the most powerful person in the world was: the Emperor

Haile Selassie. A Black man. When the dignitaries, including Queen Elizabeth, lined up for the funeral procession, they lined up by protocol and Emperor Haile Selassie, the Lion of Judah, the descendant of the Queen of Sheba, was first in line, representing what people of Ethiopia already knew and we didn't. People were stunned.

Things that happened during Kennedy's funeral upset me. People around the world saw the funeral televised and thought that John Junior saluting his father was a special moment in history. But when I saw Jackie Kennedy lean over and tell her son to make that gesture, I thought it was coldhearted for a mother to tell her child to do something so staged during a time of profound grief. But that gesture worked; the press made it work.

More disturbing than that to me was the riderless horse that walked ahead of the hearse. In the horse's stirrups were a pair of boots turned backwards, which is a Mason's symbol used only when one of their soldiers has died in battle. Kennedy was a Catholic, and Catholics are not supposed to be Masons. So why was that symbol used?

I was still thinking about that symbol at the final farewell at Arlington Cemetery. My thoughts were interrupted when a cluster of leaves went swirling above our heads. I only pointed this strange and beautiful phenomenon out to Lil.

"Lil, I don't know what that means, but it must mean something."

Then I thought about Momma and how she sent us to church on Sunday, even when she couldn't go, and I remembered the words of the prophet Hosea: "For they have sown the wind, and they shall reap the whirlwind."

12 With His Armor On

The nation continued to mourn President Kennedy through 1963. The Movement seemed at a temporary standstill, and many civil rights leaders were even more afraid for their lives. If the president could be murdered in cold blood in front of millions of people in the middle of the day, surely Black leaders were sitting ducks. But as for me, I wasn't just thinking about who would be next. I had begun to realize that we were dealing with a conspiracy against anyone who was trying to help the Civil Rights Movement.

My friend Jim had felt the president's death. I wondered now if he could see all the other lives that would eventually become casualties of the Movement. Just think how sincere Jim was in his prediction and compare that to the predictions of Jeanne Dixon. After Kennedy's death, she became famous worldwide for having predicted, eighteen months before the assassination, that Kennedy should not go to Dallas because she saw dark clouds around him. Well, well, on December 29, 1999, the *New York Daily News* reported that Jeanne Dixon had worked secretly for the FBI in the sixties, using bureau secrets when she spoke on the radio making predictions. So her dark clouds were Hoover and the FBI. We now know through the Freedom of Information Act that Jeanne Dixon was assigned to write articles to undermine the Civil Rights and anti-war movements, according to her FBI file. Because of the Jeanne Dixons of the world, we must not take the government's word for anything that they say happened to our leaders.

I had to stifle my own fears of being killed soon after, however, when I received a call from SNCC members in Atlanta, Georgia. They were attempting to integrate restaurants and other public accommodations, but were being blocked by a state law that allowed authorities to arrest anyone who wouldn't leave when an owner asked them to in the presence of a law enforcement officer. People in Atlanta, the city that's too busy to hate, are still bragging that they were the first city in the South to pass a public accommodation bill. But they forget to mention that state law took precedence over their city law. They knew that they could have us arrested at any time, not for integration, but for trespassing. They tried to keep their hands clean by having every demonstrator who tried to integrate a place in Atlanta arrested under the Georgia state law. So SNCC wanted me to come down and be arrested. I had, of course, been arrested many times, and I thought it would send a more powerful message if Lil, pregnant with twins, was jailed instead of me. Lil agreed and was arrested her first day in Atlanta at Dobbs House. It was Christmas Day. I called a press conference and read part of the telegram that I had sent to Lil in jail: "If they had found as much room in the inn two thousand years ago for a pregnant woman named Mary as the Atlanta police found in their jail for you, maybe none of us would be celebrating Christmas today."

As the demonstrations continued, I went down and joined them. I was informed that Dobbs House and Toddle House were both on the New York Stock Exchange. I had my friend Arthur Steuer, a talented young writer, buy two shares of stock in each restaurant and mail them to me in Atlanta. I took the two shares and went to Dobbs House. As soon as we arrived and started demonstrating, in the presence of a cop the manager asked us to leave the premises. I stepped in front of the other demonstrators. "I happen to own stock in this business. Do you?" I didn't tell him it was only two shares and I'm sure they thought I owned more. The manager said no, he didn't have stock. And I used that as my trump card.

"Well, under these circumstances it appears that I represent more ownership than you do. So I'll have to ask you to leave my premises."

I turned to the cop and said, "Officer, arrest this man!"

Needless to say the manager called the corporate officer and they sent a representative out to speak with us immediately. He tried to explain that there were restaurants across the street that were not integrated and if he let us in, White folks would boycott his place and go across the street. I wasn't buying that reasoning and I told him we would deal with the other restaurants later. We refused to leave and we integrated those two restaurants and the Holiday Inn the same way. Afterward Lil and I went back to Chicago to await the birth of our twins.

On March 18, 1964, one year and three days after Richard Jr., was born, Lil gave birth to Paula and Pam. We gave them the middle names of Inte and Gration so they would always remember the sacrifice their mother had made while they were still in her womb.

In fact, Atlanta was not the first time that Lil had gone to jail pregnant with the twins. In the fall of 1963, while I was performing in New York, I received an unbelievable call from Jim Clark, the sheriff of Selma, Alabama. Just when I had gotten over my fear of Mississippi and Birmingham, here came the racism of Selma, compliments of Sheriff Clark.

"Dick Gregory? This is Jim Clark. I understand a sheriff just ain't a sheriff until he's tangled with you, boy. Why don't you come on down here to Selma?"

"Can't come right now," I responded. "But I tell you what, I will send my wife."

This was incredible! I called Lil. She dropped everything she was doing and went to Selma, knowing she was going to jail. When I finished performing at the Apollo in New York, I went down there and bailed her out. When I met old, dumb Sheriff Clark, he was already under the spell of Lil Gregory. The Lilly of the Valley had touched his racist spirit. Because then-Attorney General Bobby Kennedy was sending an FBI agent to check on Lil, the sheriff tried to give her special treatment while she was in jail, but she always refused. If she were given one 7-Up, she would take a cup and give every other woman in the cell a small sip.

So the Movement continued, even in the dark shadow of Kennedy's death. All the marching, praying, and protesting we were doing was not changing things for our people. The press continued to dog our every move. They still accused me of using the Movement to get publicity. In addition to that, the White press started calling me a communist. At first the rednecks were calling me a "millionaire nigger," but now I was a communist or an outside agitator. It made me as curious about communism as I had been in high school when the FBI labeled me a communist. Can you image being in high school and having the FBI go to your house in the ghetto to tell your Momma her son is a communist? My curiosity, plus an evolving understanding that the Movement was much larger than American Black folks, led me to Russia to explore international racism.

I traveled to Moscow with Art Steuer, who was writing a story on me for *Esquire* magazine at the time. In Russia, I discovered the same problems that we were facing in America: racism was rampant, even in their school system. Not even the world's largest university, the University of Moscow, admitted Black folks. African people who wanted to go to college in Russia went to Lumumba University, named after the great Patrice Lumumba. Art and I were planning a demonstration in Red Square on the night we arrived to protest the murder of a young African student who attended Lumumba University. The student had been found frozen in the snow, and his friends believed that he was killed because he was dating a Russian girl.

The morning before the protest, however, a reporter from United Press International brought us the terrible news that three young freedom riders, Mickey Schwerner, Andrew Goodman, and James Chaney, had disappeared in Philadelphia, Mississippi. They had gone to Longdale, Mississippi, to investigate the burning of Mt. Zion African Methodist Episcopal Church. Like Sixteenth Street Baptist Church in Birmingham, Mt. Zion was what we called a "civil rights church"; it was a church that opened its door to people from the Movement to sleep, eat, and hold meetings.

The Klan had beaten several church members and burned the church to the ground on June 16, 1964, after the church had agreed to host a freedom school. On June 21, 1964, Goodman, age twenty; Chaney, age twenty-one; and Schwerner, age twenty-four, drove to the scene of the arson and never made it back. They were arrested on bogus charges in Philadelphia, Mississippi, then released at 10:30 that night by Deputy Sheriff Cecil Price. When I heard that the boys had not come home, I knew they were dead. They were young in age, but they were veteran civil rights workers who would never have left the main road unless they were forced to.

Art and I got a plane and headed back to the States immediately. James Farmer of the Congress of Racial Equality (CORE) met me at the airport in Meridian, Mississippi, and we went to Philadelphia to do our own investigation. We gathered a caravan of people to make sure no one else disappeared. On the way, we stopped by the COFO (Council of Federated Organizations) office where the three boys worked. Their coworkers also knew by now that they were dead.

It was a long, lonely drive to Philadelphia, Mississippi, knowing that each mile could be our last. We also knew that somewhere out there lay the bodies of Chaney, Schwerner, and Goodman. I couldn't help thinking about their parents, who were sure by now as well that their sons were dead. So many parents lost their children to the Movement. Along the way, the State Police stopped us and I got out of my car to see what was going on. When I got to the front of the caravan the police were telling some of the younger members of COFO that they couldn't go any further because there was an investigation going on. I told them that we were not leaving so they made an agreement with us. A few of us could go and talk to Deputy Sheriff Price and Sheriff Rainey if the others agreed to stay behind. So James Farmer, John Lewis, a few others, and I got in two cars and drove into town after they radioed Sheriff Rainey and Deputy Sheriff Price. They also said we had only thirty minutes to talk to them. I laughed in their faces. I didn't need thirty minutes to say the word "murderers."

When I walked into the sheriff's office, I did so on the shoulders of Medgar Evers, those four little Birmingham girls, John F. Kennedy, and many others. I couldn't allow myself to be afraid. They were killing our children. At first they tried to feed us some lie about those boys driving seventy-five miles an hour when they picked them up.

"As little as this town is, if they were driving seventy-five, they would have been in another county in a matter of seconds," I said. "You couldn't have stopped them."

That really pissed off old Rainey. One thing a redneck can't stand is a Northerner making fun of his little town, but we talked long enough for him to piss me off, too.

"Look," I said, "I know you killed those boys!" Rainey responded by offering me a Coke.

"Give it to your momma," I said.

We left within ten minutes, instead of the thirty minutes we'd been allowed. We now had to prove that they killed those young men. On the drive back, I told James Farmer that we should post a one-hundred-thousand-dollar reward for information that would lead to the recovery of the bodies. To my surprise, James Farmer told me that CORE was broke. I later learned that most of the Movement's organizations were operating on a zero budget. My own funds were limited because I'd spent more time fighting for equal rights than performing, and my gigs were fading away. So I called Hugh Hefner. I asked him for a twenty-five-thousand-dollar advance against my next gig at the hungry i in San Francisco. Hugh didn't think twice before loaning me the money we needed.

My next move was to make an announcement that the reward had been posted, and guess what happened next? The FBI topped my reward with their own thirty-thousand-dollar reward. It was the first time in history that the FBI had posted a reward, but it was not for the same reason I had posted one. They posted a higher reward to make sure that I didn't receive the information first.

A few days later I received a call from a man in Mississippi who said he knew where the boys were buried. He sent me a tape and a map that told me everything. My next move was a bad one: I called Bobby Kennedy and told him what I knew. Bobby sent some of his boys to retrieve the tape, and I thought some immediate action would be taken. But nothing happened for three weeks, and I had to fly to Honolulu to do a gig. I called a press conference and told them that I knew where the bodies were and so did the FBI. I also told them that if those bodies were not found, I was going to do some digging myself.

What I didn't know was that the man who sent me the tape and the map had also contacted the FBI. Within two days of that press conference, something happened that deepened my mistrust of the FBI even more than John Kennedy's murder. On August 4, 1964, the FBI conveniently found the burned bodies of Chaney, Schwerner, and Goodman in a dam on Old Jolly Farm outside Philadelphia, Mississippi. On that same day, President Lyndon Johnson ordered the bombing of North Vietnam in retaliation for an earlier attack on the United States. That second event really blew me away. The headlines in every newspaper in the country were about the bombing, not about the same-day discovery of the three civil rights workers' bodies. *How convenient,* I thought. People thought I was crazy when I suggested that the president had dropped those bombs when he did to downplay the discovery of the freedom riders' bodies. But no one thought it was crazy thirty-five years later when President Clinton was accused of doing the same thing to cover up the Monica Lewinsky sex scandal.

I don't know if the informant received his reward from the FBI, but he never claimed the one I offered and I never heard from him again. The state of Mississippi was so vicious in 1964 that it denied the request of the parents of Schwerner and Chaney that they be buried together. Blacks and Whites could not be buried together then, and even today it rarely happens. The funeral program for Chaney read: "He died with his armor on." All those boys had.

Many years later, a movie was made about the murders of Chaney, Goodman, and Schwerner called *Mississippi Burning.* The title came from the FBI code words for their so-called investigation of the case. If they had done a real investigation, they would have found those boys the day after they disappeared, not two days after my press conference, three months after the murders. We know now that nineteen people were involved in those murders. We also know that the FBI arrested twenty people, including one suspect who was in jail in Louisiana at the time of the murders. Therefore, we know that his arrest was a government trick designed to get the whole case thrown out. If his arrest was made to appear an accident, then they could make the world believe that the others were wrongfully arrested as well. After many delay tactics, the deaths of Chaney, Schwerner, and Goodman eventually resulted in the very first federal conviction for racially motivated violence in the State of Mississippi. Seven Klansmen were found guilty of the murders, including the Imperial Wizard of the White Knights who served six years in federal prison, Deputy Sheriff Cecil Price. However, Price's boss, Sheriff Rainey, was acquitted of the charges.

Nineteen sixty-four was really a sad year of murders, church bombings, and the beating of children. I was doing as much marching as entertaining. I no longer waited to be called; I did my own research and made sure I went where I was needed, when I was needed.

The first protest I did alone was to challenge the fact we didn't even have our public accommodation bill passed here in the United States. I flew to St. Louis where the AAU was holding national track and field championships and selecting a team to compete in Moscow. I was asking the Black athletes there not to go. They didn't understand that they were representing a country overseas and they were not free at home. The press was there from all over the world. I stood there alone, but not afraid. Everyone walked by me and ignored me, even the Black folks. One coach even spat at me. I got on the plane and went back to San Francisco where I was again at the hungry i. I left feeling defeated, alone and hurt. It took four years for that hurt to dissipate.

At the 1968 Olympics in Mexico, two Black track and field athletes, Tommy Smith and John Carlos, came in first and second for the United States in the 200-meter dash. As they were presented with their medals, they each raised a Black-gloved fist in the air in front of the whole world in solidarity with the Black Power Movement. The world was never the same. A year later when I was in Thailand, the number one-selling souvenir was a Black fist attached to a key chain. When a reporter asked Harry Edwards, the professor at San Jose University who had engineered Smith and Carlos's demonstration, where he got the idea, his response shocked me: "I saw Dick Gregory protest the try-outs of the Olympics in St. Louis."

When I read that, I felt more humiliated than I had in St. Louis. I felt humiliated because I realized that all God had been doing at those Olympic tryouts was planting a seed, like the farmer planting his crop. He didn't need me; He just chose me. He was saying to me: "This is my crop, this is my sun, this is my rain, this is my cool evening, this is my morning dew. You don't determine when it is harvest time. Only I determine that." I was trying to make harvest time come and I had no right to do that. All I was doing was planting God's seed.

13 In the Snake's Mouth

It seemed that no matter how much we struggled, people in the Movement continued to die. The country was painfully slow in changing, and I knew more men and women would be killed. In early 1965, I was back at the hungri i in between marching. When I finished there, I went to New York, where I was performing at the Basin Street East. I had been there for three weeks when I received a call at 6 A.M. from Malcolm, asking me if I was coming to the Audubon Ballroom that day, which was Sunday, February 21. It was also my last night performing at Basin Street East. I told Malcolm I couldn't come because Lil had booked me in Chicago; I had asked her to book me there. I had told Lil weeks before that tragic day that I was sure they would kill Malcolm if he spoke at the Audubon Ballroom. I told her to have George O'Hare, who arranged my engagements in Chicago, book me there at a college close to the airport. I wasn't afraid of being shot, and I expressed that to Malcolm: "Malcolm, I'm so sure they are going to kill you today, I don't want them to get two for the price of one."

"Well, Brother Greg, I'm sorry that you feel that way."

"Not only that Malcolm, I'm going to call Adam Clayton Powell and tell him not to come to that ballroom when he finishes preaching today." I did, and Adam said he would think about it. He eventually decided not to go.

George had scheduled me to appear at Elmhurst College in Chicago. I was performing there when he slipped me the note: "Malcolm has been shot." George and I left immediately after my engagement. When I arrived at the airport, the press was already there.

"What do you have to say about the murder of Malcolm X?" a reporter asked me.

"Who did it?" I asked him back.

"Muslims," he replied.

I was not surprised at all by Malcolm's murder. I knew it had been planned down to his last breath and that once planned, nothing was going to stop the killers. The press gave me the same lie they would feed to the American public for the next thirty-four years. I disagreed then, and I still disagree. I knew that day I got the news that Malcolm's assassination was a government hit. Even after Malcolm was shot, they had their men in place to make sure he was dead. The man who gave Malcolm mouth-to-mouth resuscitation was an undercover cop. When we finally got a copy of Malcolm's autopsy report, it showed air bubbles in his lungs. It is fatal to give a person mouth to mouth when they have chest wounds, because you pull air bubbles into the lungs. Strangely enough, Malcolm's autopsy report showed the same cause of death as Lee Harvey Oswald's, showing gunshot wounds to the chest and air bubbles in the lung. Another key piece of evidence from Malcolm's autopsy report clearly showed that the bullets in his body were fired from above him, yet the men who allegedly shot Malcolm were standing in the audience below him. So the brothers that the government paid to kill Malcolm were given blanks and they didn't even know it. The government didn't trust that they would do the job, so they had agents in the ceiling of that building to take care of him themselves. Under the Freedom of Information Act, we now know that the CIA rented the Audubon Ballroom the week before Malcolm was murdered. Now, people must ask themselves why would the CIA rent the Audubon Ballroom and what did they do while they were there? I know what they did and one day the world will know the truth.

They showed Malcolm's funeral on national television. It was the first time a Black man's funeral was ever televised on national TV in its entirety on all three networks. The press didn't care about Malcolm or his family; they showed it because they thought there would be more bloodshed because of the conflict between the Muslims and Malcolm. I didn't think there was going to be any problem between Malcolm's friends and the Muslims; I just sat there thinking that the government would blow that church up at any moment and blame it on the Muslims. But Malcolm's life was not about bloodshed. Thank God nothing happened, because Malcolm really was a man of peace who refused to be pushed around, and he refused to allow his people to be pushed around.

Three pictures that have stayed in my mind over the years are Myrlie Evers-Williams, Betty Shabazz, and Coretta Scott King at their husbands' funerals. At Malcolm's funeral, I had a vision of my own funeral: I saw an image of Lil sitting with our children, as Betty sat that day with their children. I reflected back on all the years of struggle and thought about my own children. Poor baby Michelle had almost fallen through the floorboards of my car while I was struggling to become a comedian; Lynn had integrated the family history by becoming the first Gregory born in a private hospital. Richard Junior was taken to bring me home, away from the evil of Mississippi; and the twins, Pam and Paula, had twice gone to jail in Lil's belly. I thought about the women of the Movement and their children, and how hard it was for them.

I sat at Malcolm's funeral and watched Betty take that same long journey that Myrlie had taken just two years before. Ossie Davis delivered the eulogy and it was beautiful. The real beauty was Ossie being there in deed and not just in words, because he was at the height of his career. Most entertainers were afraid to attend Malcolm's funeral, and they definitely would not have given the eulogy. Ossie Davis summed Malcolm's life up and he described the man better than anyone ever has. He said Malcolm was a beautiful prince. He was. I think the only thing more painful than Malcolm's funeral was Betty's thirty-two years later.

It would take me a long time to get over Malcolm's murder. I was amazed at the boldness of the people who were killing our leaders. They no longer hid behind the bushes like De La Beckwith did when he murdered Medgar. President Kennedy and Malcolm X were just mowed down in front of the world.

I didn't know what to do with myself in early 1965. I was glad when my agent called me soon after Malcolm's death about starring in a movie. It would be my first acting job. It took a lot out of me, but it also took my mind off Malcolm. The movie was called *Sweet Love, Bitter* and it was a story about jazz great Charlie Parker. The other stars were Robert Hooks, Diane Varsi, and Don Murray. Woodie King Jr., who is now the producer of the Federal Theatre in New York, was my acting coach. Both Woodie and the director of the movie, Herb Danska, were very patient with me, but I don't think they knew what they were getting into when they hired me. Not even my first movie could keep me away from the Civil Rights Movement.

I had only been on the set for a few days when the Edmund Pettus Bridge in Selma, Alabama, became the site of a bloodbath. John Lewis of SNCC, Hosea Williams, and Albert Turner were leading a march that Sunday in protest of the recent shooting of young Jimmy Lee Jackson on February 18, 1965. (Jimmy died eight days later at Good Samaritan Hospital in Selma.)

The events that led up to Bloody Sunday began when members of the Rising Star Association, the SNCC, and the SCLC (Southern Christian Leadership Conference), led by Albert Turner, took a major stand in an attempt to register people to vote in Marion, Alabama. It was a cold winter night when the organizations held a rally at Zion United Methodist Church, where the Reverend C. T. Vivian spoke. Vivian was and still is a fine spiritual force on this planet. Following the rally they marched to the courthouse in protest of jailed SCLC activist, James Orange. Though it was a peaceful march, there were accusations from the police that the march was actually an attempt to break James Orange out of jail. All the streetlights were shot out and the police beat every Black person in sight, including people who were just walking home from work. The marchers began to run and most of them ran back to Zion United Methodist Church. Jimmy Lee Jackson was trying to protect his mother and his grandfather when he was shot in the stomach. No one is sure who fired the fatal shot, but Al Lingo, Alabama's public safety director, admitted in court that the bullet was from a state trooper's gun.

Dr. King spoke at the memorial service at Zion United Methodist Church and led seven hundred people to the cemetery to bury Jimmy Lee beside his father, who had died six months earlier in a car accident. As they walked in the rain to the burial ground, it was decided that they would return the next week and march in protest of Jimmy Lee's murder.

Many people don't know about the activist Albert Turner, but one day he will receive his rightful place in the history books. Albert had a B.A. in History and Mechanical Arts, but he spent most of his years not working in his field, but working in the fields of the Movement. He hid the fact that he had a degree so that he could touch the people at the bottom. Three years after Bloody Sunday, Albert would help to lead another march, the funeral procession for Dr. King, in which he held one of the two mules pulling the coffin. He died in April 2000, and at his funeral was Governor Donald Siegelman of Alabama, the governor of the same state that George Wallace governed on that Bloody Sunday. Governor Siegelman didn't just pass through and say a few words; he was there like all of us to say farewell to a great civil rights leader. I had met him the month before at the thirty-fifth anniversary of Bloody Sunday. What a moment when he met us at that bridge and greeted President Bill Clinton with a handshake.

Led by Williams, Lewis, and Turner, more than five hundred people lined up in front of Brown's Chapel Church to start the march on March 7, 1965. When they approached the bridge, all they could see, according to John Lewis, was "a sea of blue." That sea of blue was the state troopers waiting for them. When Lewis and the others refused to turn around, the state troopers and "volunteers" started to beat the marchers back across the bridge. Can you believe that the authorities would actually recruit volunteers to help them beat Black folks? The marchers were beaten with billy clubs and guns all the way back to Brown's Chapel. I can still see the images of those rabid troopers beating the marchers — some of whom were carrying little children — as they ran away from the tear gas.

When I learned what had happened on the Edmund Pettus Bridge, I knew two things: first, I had to go to Alabama; and second, I knew I could never be an actor. When you are on a movie set, every minute counts and every minute costs. You can't schedule filming around the Movement. It would be several decades before I would act again because I was no more willing to sacrifice the Movement to be an actor than I was to be a comedian. I explained to the director that I might have to leave for Selma at some point, and he understood. He began to shoot the movie in a manner that would allow me to leave at any time. I sent Jim McGraw, one of my writers, to Alabama, and he kept in touch with me hourly by telephone.

Everyone was on hold, waiting to see what would happen next. Dr. King flew into Selma and started planning a second march. People from all walks of life were there to support the cause. On Tuesday, March 9, 1965, with a federal injunction hanging over their heads, they started to march, then they turned around at the bridge and went back to Brown's Chapel. What we now know as "Turnaround Tuesday" ended in the death of one of our White supporters. After the march, James Reeb, a minister, and two others ate at the Silver Moon Café. There, James Reeb was attacked by some local Whites. Only after James Reeb died did President Lyndon Johnson intervene, even sending flowers to his widow.

We appreciate all of the White people who marched, fought, and died with us. But how could the president send flowers to Reeb's wife and not send flowers to Jimmy Lee Jackson's family? Didn't he realize that James Reeb would have been alive if Jimmy Lee Jackson had not been killed? If Jackson were alive, Reeb would not have been marching in Selma. After Reeb's death, even more people came to Selma for the five-day march to Montgomery. Only then were we able to get a permit for the march, despite Judge Frank Johnson's restraining order prohibiting it.

On March 21, I left Philadelphia, Pennsylvania, where the movie was being shot, to join Dr. King and the others. On the night before the march, we all gathered at Brown's Chapel where a number of people, including myself and Dr. King, spoke to the crowd. The next morning, Dr. King delivered a glorious speech on the steps of Brown's Chapel. Then the march began. When we reached the Edmund Pettus Bridge, we were met by law enforcement officers from all over the state. But we crossed that bridge and wrote a victorious chapter in history that day. After crossing the bridge, we walked day and night, trying to show the world that all the Jimmy Lee Jacksons we had lost during the Movement had not died in vain. We walked in all kinds of weather, but we also walked with a fear that the camera couldn't see. There were White folks and Black folks, just standing on the side of the road, giving us water that we couldn't drink, because we didn't know if it had poison in it. We didn't know if a bullet would come from behind one of those old oak trees or a bomb from a rooftop. Although President Johnson sent in the FBI, federal marshals, and the National Guard, there was no one to really protect us. Those who were supposed to protect us had beaten innocent people on national TV the week before. We were living in the mightiest country in the world, yet we had a government that we couldn't call on to protect us. We still can't. So we called on God. We knew every step could have been our last step, but we had to trust Him and we made it through. A few celebrities stayed the entire week, and on that final night before reaching the capital everyone came back. We entertained those who had marched. Everybody was there: Sammy Davis Jr., Alan King, Tony Bennett, Nipsey Russell, Chad Mitchell Trio, James Baldwin, Floyd Patterson, Marlon Brando, Peter, Paul and Mary, Mahalia Jackson, Harry Belafonte, and many others.

Harry Belafonte was always there. He put his career and his life on the line, and he still does. He deserves his proper day in court and he will receive it one day. When I think of Harry, I think of a line in Rudyard

Kipling's poem "If" that reads, "If you can talk with crowds and keep your virtue, / Or walk with kings — nor lose the common touch, / . . . you'll be a Man, my son!" That's Harry; he understands the world and its politics and yet he understands the poorest child. He is always there when he is needed without compromise. He came to Selma along with the other celebrities, not as actors and singers, but as men and women fighting for their human rights.

On March 25, 1965, we walked hand in hand, arm in arm, heart to heart all the way to the Capitol in Montgomery, right into the snake's mouth, with their Confederate flag flying above us. We had walked the roads of death for Black folks, but there we were. Dr. King was the final speaker as the day came to an end. More than fifty thousand people were there. The last time we had gathered in a large number was the March on Washington, and three weeks after that, four little girls in Birmingham were dead. This latest march would be no different, but the racism of Alabama wasn't going to wait three weeks this time.

As beautiful as the day was, it ended on a sad note when a White housewife from Detroit, Viola Liuzzo, was shot and killed as she and a Black SCLC volunteer, Leroy Morton, returned to Montgomery from Selma after driving some of the marchers home. Leroy escaped death by pretending he was dead when the Klansmen came to the car after the shooting. Before it was all over, this march that had been in protest of the murder of one innocent Black man would claim the lives of three White people, including a young minister named Jonathan Daniels who stayed behind after the march to help with voter registration. Daniels was murdered five months later as he left a restaurant.

Liuzzo, Daniels, and Reeb are a prime example of the White folks who put their lives on the line for our freedom. As far back as the Underground Railroad, some White folks have tried to help, and one day we will have to talk about them in the same breath as the many Black folks who have sacrificed.

With the blood of Jimmy Lee Jackson, Viola Liuzzo, Jonathan

Daniels, James Reeb, and countless others on it, the Voting Rights Act went into effect on August 6, 1965.

14 A Bullet of My Own

After the march on Selma, I went back to Philadelphia to finish filming *Sweet Love, Bitter*, which was completed on schedule. I didn't appear in another movie until 1990, when my good friend Melvin Van Peebles asked me to portray a local civil rights leader in his film *Panther*. Even if I hadn't known Melvin, because of the dignity of his work as a filmmaker and the respect I have for him, I still would have said yes.

After we wrapped *Sweet Love, Bitter*, I went back to marching. When the press learned that I had temporarily left the production to participate in the march on Selma, they hit me with the same old questions. "Was I risking my career as an entertainer for the Movement?" "Would demonstrating interfere with my nightclub gigs?" The answer was as clear then as it is now. Few people may remember a movie called *Sweet Love, Bitter*, but that historic day we marched through racist Alabama is recorded in every book around the world that mentions the Civil Rights Movement. Yes, I was losing money, but the stakes were just too high to turn back.

Many people around the country were getting tired of all the marching and demonstrating and protesting. It was yielding too little, too slowly, at too high a price. Riots began breaking out around the country. I don't remember where I was when I first saw the Rodney

King videotape, but I know exactly where I was when the same thing happened in Watts, California, decades earlier.

In December 1965, the lovely, talented Sarah Vaughan and I were billed together at The Royal Tahitian Club in Ontario, California. One night, we were on our way back to our hotel when we heard the news that riots had broken out in Watts in South Central Los Angeles. A group of White cops had beaten a Black man, and though it was not caught on tape like the Rodney King incident, word got out on the streets and all hell broke loose. The residents of Watts were fed up and they were angry. They began throwing bottles and interfering with commerce to the point that the National Guard was sent in to keep them confined to the South Central area. The riotous destruction would continue throughout the next day and well into the night. Fires were burning everywhere and people were dying.

After the driver dropped Sarah off at the hotel, I decided to head up to Watts and try to help in any way I could. The first thing I saw when I got there was a little Black boy standing over a body, crying. As I got closer to the scene, I found out that the little boy was crying over the headless body of his father. The police and the National Guard were everywhere, and they were ready to shoot on sight.

I don't know exactly how it happened, but at some point I found myself right between riot-helmeted police and a group of very angry, armed Black men. This confrontation was happening in a housing project; clearly, innocent people were going to die in this standoff if someone did not stop them. I walked between the two groups and tried to calm things down, but after I'd walked about one hundred feet, bullets started to fly. I kept walking, even when I felt a burning pain in my leg. It took me a few more minutes to realize that I had been shot.

I couldn't believe it! After all the marching I'd done in the South, after all the times I'd been arrested by redneck deputies in the past four years, here I was shot by a Black man in California! But the face of that little boy crying over his father's corpse, and the faces of all the little children of Watts who were in the line of fire, overshadowed any physical pain. I kept walking. Either side could have easily killed me, but I think the brothers were as shocked as I was that I'd been hit. When I yelled at them, "Alright, goddamn it. You shot me, now go home!" They turned and started going back into their homes.

The tension was defused, but I realized that Black people all over the country would learn that I'd been wounded and assume that a White cop did it. I would have to set the record straight immediately. Before I could be treated for my gunshot wound, I'd have to stay on the streets and spread the word that a Black man had *accidentally* shot me. The next morning, I woke up in the hospital and read all about the incident. The headline was "Dick Gregory Shot in Watts," which sounded a whole lot better than "Dick Gregory Murdered by a Black Man," which most people wouldn't believe anyway.

I didn't stay in the hospital long, maybe a few days. Soon I was back doing my gigs and marching. Times were changing, and I felt like I was marching to a different drum than I had heard in the past. I realized, once and for all, that I was no longer just a comedian — I was a celebrity with a responsibility to be more than just funny. I also began to change my eating habits. I had stopped eating meat in 1964 when Lil and I were marching in Alabama. She had been pregnant with the twins at the time, and I guess she wasn't walking fast enough, so a White sheriff kicked her. I did nothing for two reasons. First, the sheriff who kicked Lil was six-foot, five-inches tall with a gun, so, yes, I was scared as hell. Second, we were supposed to be nonviolent, so how could I justify hitting that sheriff back even if he was four feet tall? When I thought about what nonviolence really meant, I decided that if I would not hit a man who kicked my pregnant wife, then I could no longer participate in the destruction of any animal that has never harmed me.

As the years went by, I not only researched the destruction of animals for the purpose of food, but the mistreatment of animals for pleasure. Under the leadership of Dr. King, I became totally committed to nonviolence. I took it a step farther, becoming convinced that nonviolence meant opposition to killing in any form, including the practice of killing animals for food and sport.

My resolve deepened thirty years later when I started to read about the mistreatment of animals in some of the circuses. When I think of animals held captive by circuses, I think of slavery. They are shackled and chained like our ancestors, and they represent the domination and oppression we suffered for hundreds of years. But I didn't understand the whole truth about the condition of circus animals until I got involved with PETA, People for the Ethical Treatment of Animals, which was founded in 1980 in Norfolk, Virginia. They have over six hundred thousand members and operate under the simple principle that animals are not ours to eat, wear, experiment on, or use for entertainment.

One of the things that I was most disturbed by was the treatment of elephants. Did you know that elephants have extended families just like people: nephews, nieces, the whole nine yards? PETA informed me once of a particular situation with an elephant named Kenny. Kenny died after the Ringling Brothers and Barnum & Bailey Circus forced him to perform sick. In the wild, elephants stay with their mothers until they are fifteen years old. But Ringling took Kenny from his mother at age two and sent him on the road. I don't see any difference between taking Kenny away from his parents and taking human children away from their parents. After that I became a member of PETA.

When I stopped eating meat, I came to look at the whole concept of nutrition differently. I had suffered from sinus problems most of my life. When I stopped eating meat, I began to feel better within weeks, and within a few months my sinuses had totally cleared up. I am really glad that I did not stop smoking and drinking at the same time that I stopped eating meat, because I would have thought that the drinking and the smoking were the major cause of the sinus problems. Even so, it would be two more years before I truly understood the importance of changing my diet and fifteen years before I would create Formula Four X.

15 Black Power

Nineteen sixty-five had been a year of change and a year of devastating loss, but 1966 started off on a much happier note. Our newest daughter, Stephanie, was six months old and healthy. *Sweet Love, Bitter* premiered at Carnegie Hall on January 30, 1966. What a fabulous evening! Lil looked beautiful as we stood and posed for pictures before the screening. The new mayor of New York, John Lindsay, a Republican, was there because I'd endorsed him in 1965. I remember watching this film that I starred in and thinking about all the nights Boo and I had sat in the balcony in St. Louis watching Clark Gable. Now I was on the big screen.

It seemed no matter where the Movement took me, I always ended up back in Mississippi, where it had all begun for me. The 1966 call to Mississippi came when James Meredith was shot during his March Against Fear. He had been gunned down on Highway 51, outside of Fernando, Mississippi, but thank God, he was still alive. Just as he had sat alone at Ole Miss, James decided to march alone on June 5, 1966, to demonstrate that Black people could vote, walk freely, and live without fear. James was shot in the back the day after he crossed the border from Memphis, Tennessee, into Mississippi and he was rushed to William F. Bowld Hospital in Memphis. I knew the moment I got the news that I would have to go. I asked Lil to come with me. Even with all of our kids, I knew she would come; Lil never said no.

We sent a telegram to President Johnson and to Attorney General Nicholas Katzenbach to inform them of our intentions. I also called my good friend James Allen, who lives in Mississippi, and told him to meet me at the airport. We released a statement to the press about the shooting, then left for Mississippi to continue the march that James had started. I felt indebted to him — we all were. He had walked the treacherous halls of Ole Miss for the benefit of all our children. All of my kids went to predominantly Black colleges, except my oldest daughter, Michelle — but it was good to know that because of James Meredith, they could have enrolled in Ole Miss if they'd wanted to. Michelle attended Louisiana State University so that she could play basketball. If she had gone to a Black university she would have been deprived of playing on a team, because, in the days before Title IX, Black colleges didn't have female teams. If not for James Meredith, she would not have had that choice.

The scene when we arrived at the airport in Chicago was one I will never forget. The airport was filled with well-wishers who had heard about our trip beacuse of the press conference. People yelled out, "Good luck, Mr. Gregory," "Good luck, Mrs. Gregory," "We love you!" It was beautiful. Those Black people at the airport understood that they, too, were indebted to James Meredith. At that point they didn't know if James was going to live or die, and I'm sure a lot of those people were afraid that we would be hurt or killed also. After that heartwarming send-off, Lil and I boarded yet another plane to the state that, in my mind, epitomized many White men's hatred for Black folks.

Along with James Allen, two other men met us at the airport in Mississippi: Stanley Branch and Frank Ditto from Chicago. Stanley and Frank were two young men from the North who had to deal with a different type of racism. In the South, the police would put dogs and water hoses on you in front of the camera. In the North, the police would kill you in an alley in the middle of the night and say you were resisting arrest. They would plant drugs on you and frame you for crimes you didn't commit. These two men said enough is enough, and became a part of the Movement.

Whenever there was a call for action, you could count on a certain group of people, like Stanley and Frank, being there, along with women such as Gloria Richardson. Gloria played a large role in organizing the Movement on the Eastern Shore of Maryland, and she always came to the South when she was needed. Another Northerner who was always there was a White Catholic priest named Father Groppi from Milwaukee. I marched with him several times when he was fighting for fair housing laws in his state. You talk about a man who was dedicated, he marched against his own mother for the righteousness of Black and oppressed people. Groppi's mother owned a corner store and she wouldn't serve Black folks. Well, guess who led a demonstration in front of her store? Her son! I couldn't resist joking about him at the Playboy one night. "Just when I had decided that I didn't like any White folks, Father Groppi comes along. Now I have to postpone it for another month." He, like Branch, Ditto, and Richardson, was always there. You didn't even have to call them — there was just that group of people that, if there was a march or a funeral, you knew they would be there. Their presence said, "If death comes tonight, then let it come." The press didn't write enough about those unsung heroes. But the press isn't important when you know that there is a God, and there is a bigger book and those heroes' names are all in it. When the police would tell us, "You demonstrators can't march until tomorrow because we don't have enough officers to protect you tonight," one of them would say, "Fine, we will march without protection."

So I was not surprised when Ditto and Branch were at the airport to pick me up. They drove us to the spot where James had been shot. I thought it would be hard to find the exact location on that long stretch of highway, but it wasn't. The blood was still there. Thirty-two years later, the horrible story of James Byrd being dragged to his death in Jasper, Texas, and his body being found in seventy-two pieces reminded me of that scene. The difference between what happened to James Byrd and what happened to James Meredith is that the Movement has forced them to have to catch the people who commit these crimes against us now. Also the media is covering their every move, including the trial.

Every now and then the media works to our advantage, and it did in the case of James Byrd. Most people don't realize that those three White guys were arrested before James Byrd was officially identified. Just think about the way the case was handled; they had a Black foreman read the verdict of the death penalty. That is a long journey from the way they handled the Klansmen who shot James Meredith. They had to punish the men who killed James Byrd immediately and they knew it. That verdict benefited more than Black folks — it was more political than anything else. Just look at who the governor of that state is: George W. Bush, who is running for president as this book is being written. The murderers were taken care of so quickly that the crime they committed has not come up one time during his campaign.

As we parked our cars off the bloodstained highway where they shot James Meredith, we heard the state trooper talking on the radio. As I approached him, I was afraid that I might be joining James in the hospital.

"Dick Gregory and his party just arrived," he said into the radio.

"How are you going to handle it?" the voice on the radio asked.

"The same way we handled James Meredith," the trooper said.

I thought they were getting ready to shoot me.

Instead, the trooper shook my hand and thanked me for coming. I guess the attorney general had received my telegram!

We began the march, and I remember Lil was marching so strong and determined, as if it was her duty. All along the highway, people were running out of the cotton fields with big smiles on their faces, offering us water. Like in Selma, it was water that we knew we couldn't drink, for fear that someone would try to poison us. While we were marching, civil rights leaders by the dozen were visiting James in the hospital. When we, too, had a chance to visit him, we learned that the other leaders planned to join the effort we had started. They did and the March Against Fear continued without James. When James was well enough to be released from the hospital, he went home to rest and I went back to Chicago for a few days while Dr. King, Stokely Carmichael, and many others continued to march.

James and I talked daily, and we planned to join the other marchers over the weekend for the final leg of the march. But when we got back to Mississippi, we found out that the leaders had canceled the final days and were off in Tugaloo, Mississippi, for another march unrelated to James's. But James was determined to finish what he'd started, and so we continued from the point where they had stopped. When Dr. King and the others finished demonstrating in Tugaloo, they rejoined us. We marched all the way to the Mississippi Capitol and laid our weary bodies on those steps. We had proven once again that with the help of God we could live without fear. Not just for America, but for the whole world to see. We were just determined. All of us, including Stokely Carmichael, aka Kwame Ture, whose voice was beginning to be heard around the world.

Stokely was a Howard University student who had come down from Washington, D.C., with the Freedom Riders. He had also succeeded John Lewis as president of SNCC, though he would only serve one year, with H. Rap Brown succeeding him. On the steps of the Capitol, at the end of the March Against Fear, I witnessed Stokely Carmichael raise his fist and yell "Black Power!" And things would never be the same. It was 1966 and Stokely was part of a new generation that saw nonviolence as a tired and ineffective philosophy.

I'm sure their reasoning was that they had seen so much death and despair that was never reported. The beauty of Stokely and those young folks was that, after all the federal protection and the press were gone, they were still there, sleeping in ditches and eating pork and beans out of a can. Those guys would get up at four o'clock in the morning and visit the Black funeral parlors to make sure no Black bodies had been taken there in the middle of the night after being lynched or shot to death. In those days it was nothing for many in law enforcement to kill a Black person and take his body to a Black undertaker in the middle of the night. They would demand that the undertaker bury them before daylight, by threatening to kill the undertaker and his family.

As militantly as the White press always portrayed Stokely, he only got in one fight during the entire Movement. As much as he and Dr. King differed, the only physical altercation Stokely ever had was when someone pushed Dr. King during a demonstration. Stokely really was a good brother, and the government kept him under surveillance until the day he died. Stokely passed away before this book was finished, but I am so glad I had an opportunity to visit with him in New York during some of the last days of his life. He eventually left New York for Miami to spend some time with his mother and family before going to Africa for his final trip. He also went to Washington, D.C., for an event in his honor, and it was like a Movement reunion. I was out of the country and unable to attend, but some of our mutual friends told me that Stokely was really happy that night. I teased him about the money they raised for him. When I got back in the country I told him that if he got well, he was going to have to give all the money back.

He was in so much pain as he raced against time, trying to get his autobiography and other documents completed. Those documents will be very important one day. They were not important to Stokely for the money; they were important for history and he knew that. You see, Stokely understood not just the immediate problems that oppressed people were facing, but the politics of this whole Movement; he understood international affairs, the whole nine yards. He understood the role the emerging new Africa would play in the faith and destiny of the entire planet, because of its raw and natural resources. It was so important for him to go home to Africa to die and to be buried there. It is my hope that young people will learn to understand who Stokely Carmichael was. What he and guys like James Meredith did will never happen again. Not in this lifetime.

16 Code Name "Zorro"

While major demonstrations were being held all over the South, Los Angeles's Watts and other major urban areas outside of the South were venting their anger as well. The good people of Chicago had their own political movement for civil rights going on. Northern racism was, and still is, very different from Southern racism. In the South, racism looks like Bull Connor; in the North, racism looks like racism. And I decided it was time to face it head on.

Don't be afraid — that's what I was saying to the people of Chicago in 1967, when I ran for mayor of their city. Richard Daley was the current mayor and he was holding the city hostage with fear. We called him "Master Daley," and I thought it would be nice to take his job.

Columnist Drew Pearson wrote in the *Chicago Tribune*, "Two knock-down, drag-out political battles in Illinois are scheduled to attract attention. One is between the Negro comedian-civil rights scrapper, Dick Gregory, and veteran Mayor Richard Daley to rule the second largest city in the United States. Dick is almost certain to run for mayor." That mention in Pearson's column was the kick-off for our mayoral campaign. I was going to be a write-in candidate.

My candidacy made people nervous. They remembered what happened to the last Black man who disobeyed Master Daley and his vicious political machine; Ben Lewis, an alderman in Chicago, boldly took on "the Master" once by running for mayor. He was gunned down in his campaign office on the eve of the election. But death threats had never stopped me before. We opened the campaign office at 1251 Sixty-third Street. The race was on.

I ran against "Master" Daley in the same spirit that I used the word "nigger" in my comedy acts. I used that word so that White folks couldn't find power in it, and I ran against Master Daley to take away the power he had over Black and oppressed folks in Chicago. At that time, he controlled many of the Black churches; he told the press to kiss his ass; and he would let the cops beat a Black man in a New York second. I quickly recognized the power he had over rich and poor Black folks alike, and I knew that I had to show Black folks that we didn't have to be afraid. It was like James Meredith walking in Mississippi to show Black folks that even in the shadow of death, we would not have to fear evil.

Some of my best friends came into my life during my run for mayor. Attorney Rudy Burrows wasted no time resigning from her job with the EEOC in Washington, D.C., to become my campaign manager. This brilliant sister was up for the task; she had recently worked on Teddy Kennedy's successful campaign for the Senate. Also Attorney Jean Williams, who represented me each time I was arrested during the sixties, was my attorney during the campaign. She later became a judge in Arizona.

And, of course, there was Mike Watley. When God referred to "my brother's keeper," he was talking about Mike Watley. "Big Mike," as my kids renamed him, was a skycap I had first met at the San Francisco International Airport. He always took care of Jim Sanders and me when I was in San Francisco for gigs at the hungry i. I offered Big Mike a job in my campaign and he moved to Chicago. Mike was like the apostles in the Bible, who responded when Jesus said, "Stop what you are doing and follow me." He stopped what he was doing and worked with me on the campaign and just became a part of our family. Lil loved Big Mike immediately. She really didn't campaign a lot because she was pregnant with our son Gregory, who was born on May 28, 1967.

The other person who was always there for me was my driver when I was in the Bay Area, a student at San Francisco State at the time and mayor of San Francisco now, Willie Brown. God, I love it.

Another important person I met during the campaign was Dr. Alvenia Fulton. Not only did she come into my life, she saved my life. Dr. Fulton had owned a health food store in Chicago for more than fifty years. She had one of the best nutritional minds on this planet, but I didn't realize it the first time our paths crossed. When I announced that I was running for mayor, she sent me an unsolicited container of funny-looking salad that I promptly threw in the trash. I thought the lettuce could have been laced with arsenic. (Running against Mayor Daley, you knew you couldn't eat anything that was delivered to your headquarters unsolicited; he had a political machine that would stop at nothing.) Dr. Fulton later taught me not only that the body needs nutrition, but also about what nutrition and herbs are; she would teach me how badly the body needs raw foods. It was Dr. Alvenia Fulton who planted the seed in my mind that would grow into Formula Four X fifteen years later.

But for the moment, the only seed I wanted to plant was on Master Daley's plantation. I knew it was going to take a lot to beat Master. So I decided to solicit the help of my old friend, the grand master of politics, Adam Clayton Powell. I found out that he was in self-imposed exile on an island in Bimini. I went to visit him. The powers that be had conspired to strip Powell of his chairmanship of the House Committee on Education and eventually barred him from resuming his seat in Congress. But Adam still had the power to bring our people together. He could simply walk down the streets of Harlem for any cause he believed in, and people would follow him like Jesus. I fantasized about the two of us going to church in Chicago on Palm Sunday, then releasing hundreds of white doves and marching through the streets with signs that read, "Dick Gregory for Mayor."

I guess I had watched too many movies. Adam was a far cry from my Palm Sunday fantasy when I found him living comfortably in Bimini. I heard the sound of his beautiful laughter as he spiked his milk with scotch, and I felt the peacefulness of his spirit. I knew then not to ask him to be involved in my campaign. He had put in his time — and then some — and was now experiencing a well-deserved life of comfort that few of our warriors had lived to enjoy. I joined him for a glass of scotch and never mentioned his coming back with me.

Now, Muhammad Ali was a different story. After winning the world heavyweight championship in 1967, he shocked the world — and me — by walking over to the mic and saying, "I want to ask folks to vote for Dick Gregory for mayor of Chicago." What a moment!

That support really upset Master Daley. After that, his staff began watching our every move. Daley was so desperate that he had someone in his camp send two guys by my house one night to offer me a payoff. It wasn't a payoff to drop out of the election; it was to get me officially on the ballot. When I declined, the White guy turned to the Black guy and said, "Give me my money."

The Black guy had bet the White guy that I would take the money, and the White guy had bet him that I would not. The Black guy was so ashamed over the bet that he asked me if I would meet him at the Tiger Lounge, a Black-owned tavern in Chicago, so that we could talk. When I met him, he took me to a warehouse where they kept the voting machines. He showed me something that night that changed my views on our so-called democracy. The Black guy unscrewed the back of a voting machine and showed me that you could tamper with it.

"The reason Daley wants you on the ballot," he said, "is he is worried about being humiliated by you in the Hyde Park / Kenwood area." Daley knew that the people living in that area were sophisticated enough to know all about write-in voting. The guard continued, "They want your name to appear on line four and Daley's name would be on line five. They are planning to take a wire and hook it around line four and line five, so that when people vote for you it will register to Daley."

I left that warehouse wiser and remained a write-in candidate.

I learned so much about the corruption in government during my run for mayor. On Election Day, the Master's poll watchers listed the names of everyone who wrote in "Dick Gregory" for mayor on their ballot. You see, the pencils they used to write me in with were attached to strings that hung below the poll booth curtains. Every time the pencils were raised, the watchers knew that the occupant of the booth was writing my name on his or her ballot. The poll watchers would then write down the names of those who were voting for me and they harassed some of them for months after that. We should have instructed people to bring their own pencils.

We lost the election, but we had planted another seed in the minds of the people. Black folks in Chicago knew that it was now okay not to obey Master; I guess you could say Old Master and I became official enemies that year. I kept thinking about how Daley had given me a key to the city of Chicago back in 1961 when I first hit it big. He gave me a key — then changed the lock after he realized I was not a good little nigger. Round One of our twenty-year fight was over.

Big Mike packed up the campaign office, and things got back to normal . . . well, not quite, because I was broke. Thank God I had met Bob Walker of the American Program Bureau in Boston around that same time. He kept me busy by arranging speaking engagements for me. But it was summertime; I had to deal with the reality that my new means of generating funds — the college circuit — was not lucrative in the summer months.

Around that time I got deeply involved in the protest against the Vietnam War. I vowed not to cut my hair until the war ended. That was in 1967, and I still have not cut my hair thirty-three years later. I also vowed to fast until the war ended, starting with a thirty-day fast. But I was putting the cart before the horse, because I knew nothing about fasting safely. The day after I announced my intention to fast, I ran across an ad in the paper about the person who had sent me the salad — Dr. Alvenia Fulton. I cut the ad out of the paper and showed it to Lil. The next day we went to visit Dr. Fulton at her health food store and thanked her for the salad that I had actually thrown in the garbage. Dr. Fulton was a warm and brilliant woman and she already knew about my plan to fast. She agreed with my reasons for fasting and told me exactly how to do it. And, because of her own dedication to the Movement, she agreed to fast along with me.

I did everything Dr. Fulton told me to do; I drank only fresh-squeezed juice for seven days and took enemas to flush all the poisons out of my body. Once Dr. Fulton began supervising my fast, my body and my life were never the same. That first fast was the beginning of a new and healthy life. The fast lasted through the summer and into the fall semester. I was booked for fifty-seven lectures and did them all while I was fasting. The money from the speaking engagements provided for my growing family, while I worked my way back into the political arena. This time, I was going to run for president of the United States.

I would run again as a write-in candidate, but this time I would be smarter: we'd take our own pencils. *Write Me In* became the title of a book I wrote during my campaign that explained my reasons for wanting to be president of the United States. I received a one-hundred-thousand-dollar advance that I used to finance my campaign, which was very costly. The first thing I vowed to do if elected was paint the White House black.

There are only two things needed to qualify to run for president: you must be at least thirty-five years of age, and you must have been born in the United States. I met both qualifications, so the race for the highest office in the land was on. But my next move almost landed me in jail. I produced a facsimile of a one-dollar bill with my face on it instead of George Washington's. My running mate Mark Lane's name was also on these bills. Mark is a longtime friend, a respected attorney, and a former member of the New York Legislature. He authored *The Rush to Judgment* about the Kennedy assassination, a book that totally destroyed the conclusions of the Warren Report. Before the book was published, the FBI mounted a smear campaign against him. Because of J. Edgar Hoover's interference, Mark's book was initially refused by all the major publishers in the United States. His book was published in England, and it became the number-one best-selling book worldwide. I was proud to have him as my running mate and to place his name on the dollar bill.

I had gotten the idea one day when Lil and I were delivering food to some people in need in Mississippi. Another couple had driven down from Illinois to meet us to help with the food drive. A brick had been thrown through their window because, like all Illinois drivers, their license plates read "Land of Lincoln." There is a lot of hatred for Lincoln in the South because he freed the slaves. Imagine, people would throw a brick through a car window simply because it had "Land of Lincoln" written on it. But they couldn't get rid of the five-dollar bill that has his name and face on it. That's when I realized the power of money.

I thought my facsimile dollar bills were a great publicity idea, but the U.S. Treasury Department didn't agree. It made the news. And not just any news, mind you — there it was, big as day, on the *CBS Evening News*. Walter Cronkite held up one of my bills with a blown-up image of the dollar bill behind him. The Secret Service confiscated my campaign literature under direct orders from the Treasury Department. They claimed the bills were working in change machines all over the country and they were. But Cronkite said on the air that the money was tested at the CBS news station in the snack-room canteen, and it did not work. Now if Cronkite said it, then "that's the way it is."

Eventually, the Feds had to return our money, because we found out that there was a federal law that said any facsimile of American money was a violation of the law. Well, our answer to that was, until you put a Black person's face on American money, nothing that has my picture on it is a facsimile of American money. So they gave us the money back and we continued our campaign.

My bid for the presidency came to an abrupt halt at 6:00 P.M. on April 4, 1968, when Martin Luther King Jr. leaned over a balcony at the Lorraine Motel in Memphis, Tennessee. He was talking to some of his supporters below when the assassin pulled the trigger and gunned him down. I think the heart of America stopped beating for a moment that day. Ralph Abernathy was in his room at the hotel, putting on cologne, when he heard the noise outside. He ran to the side of his longtime friend and comrade, calling him by his birth name: "Michael, Michael, it's me, Ralph!" But it was too late. Michael was gone.

Martin's father, Martin Luther King Sr. (Daddy King), changed both their names to Martin when his son was six years old. Before that both their names had been Michael. According to the Bible, Michael is the one who will be the leader in the war between God and Satan. Surely, King had lived up to his name.

The only comfort I have ever had over the murders of Martin, Malcolm, and Medgar is that they all died suddenly. None of them lived to make deathbed statements from the hospital; no one had a chance to prolong the agony of the families as their loved ones hovered near death; there were no comas, no useless surgeries. They all died just as they had lived: bravely, like true soldiers and real men. I think it would have broken my heart to see them suffer.

I did not accept the government's theory on Martin's assassination any more than I had accepted it for John Kennedy's, Malcolm's, or Medgar's. I was Martin's friend, but knowing immediately that a conspiracy was behind his murder prevented me from mourning too much. But no matter who the assassin was or what the reason was behind Martin's death, the impact was something I will never forget. Violence erupted following the sad news of King's death. Black people were so angry and hurt and, yes, riots broke out in some of the Northern states. But not as much as I believe the FBI had hoped, and not as much as they reported.

I was being driven to Hartnell College in Salinas, California, to deliver a lecture when the news of Martin's assassination came over the radio. The newscaster said, "Dr. Martin Luther King has just been shot in Memphis by a White man. We have no further information." That is when I knew it was a conspiracy and they were trying to promote riots. They didn't know if he was dead; they didn't know anything except he had been shot. They simply didn't have enough information to make that kind of announcement.

I must have thought of a million things about dear Martin when I heard the news, but I did not cry. I didn't shed a tear when Malcolm and Medgar were killed, either. The Movement had a way of taking away your ability to cry. The next thing I knew, I was at Hartnell College. I don't remember the car moving, I don't remember making any turns. I just remember the driver saying that we had arrived.

I decided to go ahead with my lecture that night, and I wish I had a videotape of that evening now so I could once again see the faces of those youngsters. Everyone looked the same to me: they were in shock. I went to my room and turned on the TV before going to the auditorium and there was then-Governor Ronald Reagan, crying as he talked to the people of California. A few minutes after that, my phone started to ring. It was the press calling to get my reaction to Dr. King's death. I don't even remember what I said to them. I just remember the pain, the same pain the rest of those who loved Martin were feeling. I still remember that hurt and pain.

When I arrived at the auditorium, the place was packed. Most of them were White and they were very angry. They didn't buy J. Edgar Hoover's lies about Martin. I don't remember my exact words, but I know it was good for me to be in a situation where I could talk about what a fine man Martin was to people who wanted and needed to listen.

I left California for Atlanta to take that last march with Dr. King. Lil and Jim Sanders met me there. As sad as Dr. King's funeral was, I'm sure if you ask anyone who marched with him they would tell you that they were not shocked by Dr. King's assassination. After they blew up the Sixteenth Street Baptist Church in Birmingham in September 1963, we were prepared for the worst. After that, we knew that no place and no one was safe. Murdering those little girls had put us into a "who will be next" frame of mind.

Dr. King's true teaching came out when he died. With all the people who criticized and disliked Dr. King, no one said anything negative during those dark days leading up to his funeral. People from all over the world, rich and poor, lined the streets of Atlanta to bid farewell to our King. Bobby Kennedy, Andy Young, Eartha Kitt, Nancy Wilson, Sidney Poitier, the little Black lady on welfare; they were all there. One day, when historians write the honest history about America, one of the shames will be that the president of the United States, Lyndon Johnson, did not attend Dr. King's funeral.

Dr. Benjamin Mays delivered the eulogy; he had been Dr. King's mentor while King was a student at Morehouse College. As president of Morehouse, Dr. Mays touched the lives of every student he came in contact with. It was one of the great moments of my own life when I met Dr. Mays. At Martin's funeral, he talked to us about Martin and tried to make us feel better, like we were all his students. Just hearing his voice helped. I regret that my children didn't get to know Dr. Mays and never got to sit at the master's feet and listen to his brilliance. But I did, as often as I could. He even remarried Lil and me in 1979. (Dr. Mays was so special and such a child of God that when he died, a hurricane erupted thirty miles from his birthplace in South Carolina and traveled all the way to Maine, where he attended Bates College.)

After Dr. Mays finished the eulogy, God opened the gates of Heaven and Mahalia Jackson's voice came out. She sang like an angel. Mahalia loved Martin, she loved the Movement and Black folks. She sang wherever she was needed and never charged a dime. Her voice should be a national treasure. We needed everything she had that day as she sang to us, to Martin, to the world.

After the funeral Lil and I went back to Chicago, and my running mate Mark Lane and I started our campaign again. We also started investigating who really assassinated Dr. King. Mark and I shared a belief in the conspiracy theory behind Kennedy's and King's deaths. I will always believe that the primary reason Dr. King was killed was because he was the first Black person in the history of America in a position to determine public policy.

Mark is one of the few people on this planet who understands why great men like Kennedy, Malcolm, Medgar, and Martin were really killed. We agreed that the assassinations were not just related to their roles in the Civil Rights Movement. These men had gone the extra mile to show how beautiful America wasn't. They fought not only for civil rights; they fought for human rights. All of their assassinations were planned very carefully, including Medgar Evers's. People want to believe that Byron De La Beckwith was just another redneck who wanted to kill a nigger. If that was true, why, then, did the government protect him? They not only protected him, but as far as I'm concerned, they even paid him off when they purchased land from him to build a U.S. Post Office location in Mississippi. De La Beckwith used that money for his legal defense. The same government that was supposed to protect our leaders paid an accused murderer for land. Why?

God only knows what else those who were supposed to protect Medgar, Dr. King, and all the others did to them and their families. An FBI agent in Atlanta told Mark Lane how excited the Atlanta agents were when they received the news of Dr. King's death. What's scary about that is they are the ones who later went to Memphis to take over the investigation. Mark was told that one agent was so happy when he got the news that he yelled, "They got Zorro! The son of a bitch is dead!"

"Zorro," the Spanish word for fox, was the code name the FBI and Hoover used in their ongoing investigation of Dr. King. No matter what Hoover called him, there will never be another Dr. King, nor does there need to be.

17 Nothing but Grace

Mark Lane and I worked on Martin's murder for so long and uncovered so much information that we eventually wrote a book about it called *Code Name Zorro.* (The title of the book was eventually changed to *Murder in Memphis.*) The release of this book brought out a lot of information that many people were unaware of and eventually led to the Kennedy/King assassination investigation. Most people don't know that King was never supposed to go back to Memphis; he only planned to go once to support the garbage collectors. However, while he was there, a little group of thugs called the Invaders created a riot. King had a problem with that, and rightfully so. The Senate and Congress were trying to block King's Poor People's Campaign that was scheduled for June 1968. They were trying to stop the Poor People's Campaign by saying that Dr. King could not control the violence if we came to Washington. Yet look at all of his marches in the past — the only violence during them was the police beating us. The March on Washington in 1963 definitely was not violent, so they had no reason to believe the Poor People's Campaign would be any different. Therefore, they created violence to force Dr. King to come back to Memphis to prove that he could still conduct a nonviolent march. It was nothing more than a trap to get him back in Memphis and to the Lorraine Motel.

Now, turn to page 151 in this book and look at that famous picture of Dr. King lying on the balcony of the Lorraine Motel, dying, with a Black man kneeling next to him and supposedly helping him. That man was Marrell McCullough. We know now that he was an undercover cop for the City of Memphis. He also was a part of the group the Invaders, which had started the riots the first time King came to Memphis. All the riots in the past were started when the police attacked us. Well, no one attacked the Invaders that day. They started throwing bottles, breaking windows, and looting as the march progressed, so the police would respond. Marrell McCullough was one of the people instructing the Invaders. We know all of this now, but back then he was so undercover that his paychecks came from the Memphis utilities company. He now works for the CIA. As you are reading this book in the year 2000, he still works there. That's right, call there and ask for him.

All of this information came out during the King conspiracy trial in Memphis in December 1999. God, what it meant to the people who really loved King to have their day in court. It was not about winning or losing; it was about public record, one hundred years from now. I went to the trial one day and sat there and listened to people one by one give testimony about things many of us have been saying for thirty-two years. More important than hearing this information was watching that court reporter transcribe word after word about what really happened in Memphis on April 4, 1968. People like Mark Lane and I knew that the real assassin of Dr. King was not James Earl Ray, but a Memphis police lieutenant named Earl Clark.

The impetus for this new trial had started six years before when a man named Lloyd Jowers came forward. He owned a restaurant, Jim's Grill, beside the flophouse where the shot came from, across the parking lot from the Lorraine Motel. Jowers went to ABC and said that in 1968 he received one hundred thousand dollars from Frank LiBerto (who ran the Memphis Mafia for the New Orleans Mafia). Jowers admitted giving the money to the killer and said that the killer was not James Earl Ray. He admitted that after Earl Clark shot Dr. King, Clark handed him the gun though the window of his restaurant. After Clark handed Jowers the gun, another important set of events happened just a few minutes away from Jim's Grill. In Cab 58 sat a driver named Paul Butler, who was waiting for his next pickup when he heard a shot ring out. He got out of his cab to see what was going on. At that point he saw Earl Clark jumping over an embankment. Butler followed him and watched Clark jump into a police car and drive away. Once he realized that Dr. King had been murdered, Butler went to the Memphis police and the press and reported what he saw. A few hours later, Paul Butler was pushed out of a moving car and was dead.

Jowers took all of his information about Clark and his involvement in King's murder to ABC and they did nothing, so he went to the King family. He told them that when he was meeting with the assassin, there had been a Black man present as well. He said that the Black man was the same person in one of the famous pictures that went around the world of a man pointing upward, a pose that led people to look the wrong way. Again, Marrell McCullough. The bullet came from down below, not from above.

So the King family filed a wrongful death suit for one hundred dollars against Jowers. Lloyd Jowers's defense was that sure, he was part of a conspiracy to kill someone, but he didn't know that that person was Dr. Martin Luther King, and the King family had no right to file a wrongful death suit against him. Neither his defense nor the money were important. What was important to Dr. King's family and many others was for this information about Earl Clark and others to be recorded in a court document.

During the trial, Earl Clark's wife tried to clean up her husband's name. In my opinion, she should have been jailed for perjury after her testimony. William Pepper was the attorney representing the King family. He has invested his time, and, I'm sure, his money into trying to find out what really happened on April 4, 1968. Attorney Pepper questioned Clark's wife as follows:

"Where was your husband on April 4, 1968, the day that King was killed?" Pepper asked.

"He had been at home sick that day and he didn't go to work," she responded.

"How did he find out that King had been murdered?"

"He heard it on his police radio."

"What did he do then?"

"He said he should go in because he knew there was going to be trouble."

"Then what happened?" Pepper continued.

"I had to go to the cleaners and pick up my husband's clothes, because all of his uniforms were dirty."

"Mrs. Clark, do you know what time Dr. King was shot?"

"Yes, I do, 6 P.M."

"Do you know what time the cleaners close, Mrs. Clark?"

She didn't answer. Attorney Pepper turned to the jury. "Let the record show that the cleaners close every day at 5 P.M."

That was what the jurors heard that day. She may have come to clear her husband's name, but she didn't; she just confirmed what we already knew. And I believe she should have been arrested for perjury.

Other important testimony was that of Carthel Weeden, a retired White Memphis fireman who was a captain at firehouse No. 2 across from the Lorraine at the time King was killed. I sat there in a Black judge's courtroom and watched a jury that consisted of six Blacks and six Whites and thought about all that had changed in thirty-one years. The testimony I heard that day from Weeden never could have happened immediately after King was killed. He testified that on the morning of Dr. King's murder, a group of White men showed up at the station and identified themselves as military intelligence agents. They told him they needed to go up on the roof of the building to run reconnaissance on Dr. King, who was staying at the Lorraine Motel.

Then his testimony goes as follows:

"Did they have anything with them?"

"Yes, containers."

"What did the containers look like?"

"Some were long and some were short."

"Could they have been high-powered rifles?"

"Yes."

"Could they have been filming equipment?"

"Yes."

"Were you there later that day when the shots rang out at the Lorraine Motel?"

"Yes."

"Were the men still on the roof of the fire station?"

"Yes."

"What did you do after that?"

"I went over to the Lorraine Motel and helped them put Dr. King on the stretcher."

"Did you see the wound in Dr. King's neck?"

"Yes," he said.

"Would you describe the wound?"

"Well, the bullet was in an upward projective position."

That statement alone proved what the people standing in the parking lot below Dr. King have always said: that the shot and smoke came from the ground, not from the second floor of the flophouse as suggested. Weeden's testimony also proves that the men on the roof who described themselves as military intelligence agents had been there to take King out if Earl Clark missed. It further suggests that, if they were indeed filming, not only did they get a picture of King being killed, but they got a shot of the killer as well. Even without his testimony, we have proof that military intelligence was there that day. Under the Freedom of Information Act, John Judge obtained a copy of the entire operation, called Lantern Spike. This document is a telling thirty-eight pages describing the entire operation from March 28 to April 12, 1968.

There is also a woman whom the world should know about who witnessed something crucial on April 4, 1968. She is a poor, toothless, White woman named Grace Walden Stephens. Mark Lane was told about Grace by a man named Renfro Hays, who was the original defense investigator for James Earl Ray. Grace had been living in the flophouse across from the Lorraine Motel at the time of the murder. Her testimony is important because her common-law husband, Charles Stephens, told the FBI and the Memphis police that he saw James Earl

Ray leaving the hotel bathroom where the shot was supposed to have been fired from.

As Grace Stephens lay in her bed on the evening of April 4, 1968, she heard a shot and within seconds a man ran past her door and she looked directly in his face. When he got outside, he dropped a blanket that contained a rifle with James Earl Ray's fingerprints on it, the rifle police claim was used to kill Dr. King. This blanket also held an empty beer can that had Ray's finger prints on it, along with a radio. The radio had Ray's name and serial number on it from the Missouri State Penitentiary, from which he had escaped on April 27, 1967. I believe that they had planned to kill Ray, and the case would then have been open and shut. But Ray — who thought that all he was doing was running guns for some thugs out of Canada — noticed a few hours before King was shot that his rear tire was getting flat and left the flophouse to have it repaired. That means he was not even there when King was shot.

When Ray was arrested, he had five passports. Now we know Ray didn't have the intelligence or the connections to pull that off by himself. When he was arrested he was charged not with the assassination of Dr. King, but for being a fugitive from justice from the Missouri State Penitentiary in Jefferson City, Missouri. Britain has a law that states you can only try a person extradited from Britain for what they were arrested for. In order to try James Earl Ray for King's murder, they had to present evidence that there was a witness placing him at the scene of the crime.

That is where Grace Stephens comes into the picture. The FBI and the Memphis police needed Grace Stephens's testimony to place James Earl Ray at the scene of the crime and to have him brought back from England. They went to Grace and showed her a picture of Ray and told her they wanted her to identify the man who killed Dr. Martin Luther King. She told them that was not the man she saw. They in turn told her that they were not asking her, they were telling her to identify him. When she still could not identify him, they informed her that there was a ninety-thousand-dollar reward and that it was hers if she identified James Earl Ray as the killer. All she had to do, they told her, was say this is the man.

She still could not identify Ray as the killer. So the FBI and the Memphis police went to her common-law husband Charles Stephens and told him that because Grace had not identified the man who killed Dr. King, she would not get the ninety-thousand-dollar reward. They told him that he should go upstairs and persuade Grace so that they would get the money. At that point Charles went upstairs and showed her the picture of Ray, and she told Charles that that was not the man. Charles then beat Grace. A few days later, the Memphis police and some FBI agents showed up at her door and said, "Grace Stephens, get your coat. You have to come with us." They then took a sane woman to Bolivar Mental Institution in Bolivar, Tennessee, and told the authorities there that she suffered from high and low depressions and that she was suicidal. They told the authorities that Grace was so out of it she thought she had witnessed the murder of Dr. Martin Luther King. The authorities had no reason to question the FBI and they admitted her. She would stay there for eleven years.

After the FBI succeeded in having Grace committed, they went back to Charles Stephens and told him that he would get the ninety-thousand-dollar reward money if he said he was the person who saw Ray leaving the flophouse. He then identified Ray, believing he would get the money, even signing an affidavit. When they didn't give him the money, he filed a lawsuit against the FBI. That lawsuit is a sealed document in the state of Tennessee that should be released so that the American public will know what Charles Stephens told them is a lie and James Earl Ray was framed.

On November 12, 1977, Mark Lane interviewed Grace Stephens at the Bolivar Mental Institution, where she was held against her will. Mark said when he first met her, she sat silently for a moment and then said, "I knew this day would come. I did not know it would be you. But I knew this day would come and this case would get on track for the first time. And I'm ready, I've been ready." When Mark asked her if she remembered what had happened on April 4, 1968, she said "sure."

Lane: What happened that day?

Stephens: I was lying in bed reading. Then my husband came in and said that he couldn't get into the bathroom. He had to go around to the other side to the other bathroom. So he went off. I don't remember exactly how long he was gone. Then I heard this shot.

Lane: You heard a shot?

Stephens: Yes. I recognized it as a shot. My father was a great hunter. He taught me all about guns. In fact, two of my husbands collected guns.

Lane: After you heard the shot, what happened?

Stephens: In a few minutes the bathroom door opened. I could see that. My door was partially opened and I was propped up in bed, as I said, reading.

Lane: You could see out into the corridor?

Stephens: Yes, and the bathroom was right next to us.

Lane: Did you see anyone come out of the bathroom?

Stephens: Yes, I saw this man come out. He had something in his hand, but I couldn't see what it was because he was carrying it next to the railing.

The railing she referred to was to the right of the man leaving the bathroom. It was near the bathroom at the top of the stairwell that provides a rear exit to the rooming house. It was that staircase that Charles Stephens had used in his search for an unoccupied bathroom. The room that the Stephenses occupied was across the corridor from the stairwell. Consequently, Mrs. Stephens did not have an unobstructed view of the object carried by the man, since his body came between her and the object. Mrs. Stephens described the physical layout of the building to Mark with absolute accuracy, remembering some of the details that Mark had forgotten. He had seen the interior of the building on several occasions earlier that year. Mrs. Stephens had spent a great deal more time there than Mark had, but she had not been there for nine years.

Lane: Since then have you seen pictures of James Earl Ray?

Stephens: I've seen pictures of James Earl Ray, but never saw that man in person.

Lane: Was the man who you saw come out of the bathroom James Earl Ray?

Stephens: No, it wasn't James Earl Ray I saw. It didn't look anything at all like him.

Lane: Did anyone from the police talk to you afterwards?

Stephens: Yes, we had police, reporters, and more reporters. It was a mess.

The police showed her a series of pictures to see if she could identify the man she had seen.

Stephens: There was a picture that looked like the man I had seen. I pointed it out to the police, but they never did pay any attention.

She said that the picture she picked out was not a picture of James Earl Ray.

Later, after Ray became known as a suspect, she said the police tried to get her to say that she had seen Ray leave the bathroom. She consistently refused to make a false identification, she said.

Lane: Is there any doubt in your mind that the man you saw was not James Earl Ray?

Stephens: There is no doubt in my mind. That wasn't James Earl Ray. It was an entirely different man. He was older, had dark hair, he was brunette.

Lane: Do you remember what he was wearing?

Stephens: A windbreaker. I called it a hunting coat then. And under the coat he had on a checkered shirt, a loud, checkered shirt. The coat was open.

Lane: Did your husband Charlie ever see that man?

Stephens: I don't think he did. He couldn't see without his glasses, anyway. He didn't have his glasses on, they were on the bed, in the room.

She went on to explain that her husband left the glasses in the bedroom while he went looking for the other bathroom. He then returned a few minutes after the shot was fired.

Lane: When he returned, did you tell him what you saw?

Stephens: Yes, I told him the man went down the hall, and he [Charles] went down to look down the stairs. He motioned me to come down there and look, but I was afraid that he might take a pot shot at me, and I wouldn't go.

The point about his glasses is very important, because Mr. Stephens clearly didn't see well without them and could not make an accurate observation, yet his testimony was the only one the state uncovered to point the finger at James Earl Ray.

Grace continued telling Mark her story until they were interrupted by the staff at the mental hospital and he was forced to leave. The staff tried to take the tape recorder from Mark, but they were unsuccessful. What you just read is that recorded conversation.

When Mark left Bolivar, he went to the American Civil Liberties Union, but no one there was able to help him in the release of Grace Stephens. She was only let go after Reverend James Lawson, who had worked with Mark Lane, organized a meeting of representatives of all religious faiths in Memphis and they demanded her release. If Mark Lane and I knew about Grace Stephens, the FBI and Hoover certainly knew about her and knew the truth.

Grace Stephens's testimony proved that there was a conspiracy to kill Dr. King, along with all the other testimonies we heard in that courtroom in 1999. But if those testimonies are not enough to convince the American public that it was indeed a conspiracy, then everyone should take a look at the following transcript of a letter from James Earl Ray's attorney Percy Foreman.

March 9, 1969

Mr. James Earl Ray,
Shelby County Jail,
Memphis, Texas.

Dear James Earl:

You have asked that I advance to Jerry Ray five ($500.00) of the "$5,000.00", referring to the first five thousand dollars paid by Wm. Bradford Huie. On January 29th, Mr. Huie advanced an additional $5,000.00. At that time I had spent in excess of $9,500.00 on your case. Since then, I have spent in excess of $4,000.00 additional.

But I am willing to advance Jerry $500.00 and add it to the $165,000.00 mentioned in my other letter to you today. In other words, I would receive the first $165,000.00. But I would not make any other advances — just this one $500.00.

And this advance, also, is contingent upon the plea of guilty and sentence going through on March 10, 1969, without any unseemly conduct on your part in court.

Yours truly,
Percy Foreman

P.S. The rifle and the white mustang are tied up in the suit filed by Renfro Hays. Court costs and attorneys fees will be necessary, perhaps, to get them released. I will credit the $165,500.00 with whatever they bring over the cost of obtaining them, if any.

That is the kind of evidence the State of Tennessee, the FBI, and J. Edgar Hoover knew about, in addition to their knowledge of Grace Stephens.

When I think of Hoover and how people accept what he did to our leaders, I can only compare him to Hitler. If you were in Germany and saw a new building named after Adolf Hitler, wouldn't you know that there was something evil going on inside that building? In the nation's capital, they have a brand-new FBI headquarters, the J. Edgar Hoover Building. We should all suspect that something evil goes on inside there. And can you imagine what went on at FBI headquarters while Hoover was alive? When Hoover was alive, he believed he had real power. Never in his wildest, sick imagination would he have thought that his own death would be brought about the same way as Medgar's, Malcolm's, Martin's, Jack's, and Bobby's. I got it from good authority that Hoover was found dead on the toilet in his bathroom with the same type of expression on his face as a person poisoned. His house was ransacked, and all the files he had kept on people from the Movement, celebrities, and gays whom he hated were all stolen. He never imagined that in the nineties there would be a documentary made about his life saying he was gay and showing a picture of him in New York in a dress.

I think about Dr. King all the time, even thirty-two years later. I will never forget one of the last conversations I had with him as we sat together on an airplane. I had received several death threats and Dr. King knew about them.

"Dick," Dr. King said, "I understand you have received several death threats and I want you to be careful."

"I will, Doc, but if I am killed, would you preach my funeral?"

"Sure," he said. Then we laughed and talked about other things.

Before the wounds could heal from Dr. King's assassination, they killed Bobby Kennedy, too. The news of all their deaths are just etched in my mind. You hear so much about the Kennedy family, but I knew Bobby personally and much better than I did John. He was probably one of the most powerful, ethical people for righteousness that ever lived on this planet.

I remember June 5, 1968, as if it was yesterday. I was at home in Chicago watching television coverage of the California primary. I just remember getting up to go to the bathroom and before I could reach the bathroom door, I heard this voice on the TV say "They shot him, they shot him!" I turned around and saw my friend Bobby lying on the floor of the Ambassador Hotel's kitchen in a pool of blood. I had predicted on a Irv Kupcinet television talk show in Chicago that if Bobby Kennedy won the presidential primary in California, he would never leave that state alive. Bobby and I were among the guests on the show, and he had been asking me to support him. I had not given Bobby or his staff an answer. So when Bobby and I were on the show together, he said, "Are you going to come out to California and help me with the primary? It's very important."

"No," I said, "and give me my dollar," referring to a private bet I had made with Bobby weeks earlier.

Irv turned to me and said, "What is this about?"

I replied, "He owes me a dollar, because as sure as he goes to California and wins the primary, he will never leave California alive."

Three days after Bobby was murdered, I received a call from Irv.

"Dick, are you all right?"

"Yes."

"Are you sure?" he asked.

"Yes, what are you talking about?"

"Bobby Kennedy, I know he was your friend. You can talk to me."

"Man, I'm fine. Bobby was a friend, but I'm okay."

Then he said, "No, no, I'm talking about the FBI. Didn't they come by your house? They came by and ransacked my place and took that tape where you mentioned Bobby not leaving California alive." I couldn't believe it.

Bobby's assassination was broadcast live on national television, just as his brother John's had been. But one key piece of evidence in Bobby's murder, just as in his brother's, proves there was a conspiracy: Rosey Grier grabbed Sirhan Sirhan when he was six feet in front of Bobby. That's as close as Sirhan Sirhan ever got, six feet in front of Bobby. All three bullets entered Bobby's body from behind. Two were around the shoulder blade and the one that killed him entered his body through the back of his head at a point-blank range of less than one-quarter of an inch. More bullets were found in the panel behind Bobby than the gun that Sirhan Sirhan allegedly used could hold. But we can never prove that, because the FBI went in and took out the wall panel. We also have to look at the fact that Rosey Grier grabbed Sirhan Sirhan, not anyone from the Secret Service who was supposed to protect Bobby.

The fact that the Kennedys were killed in front of the cameras bothers me much more than the cowardly act of Medgar's killer. De La Beckwith just hid in the bushes and shot an unarmed man who had no Secret Service men to protect him. But the Kennedys' murders are fascinating, disappointing, and unexplained; and one would assume it is out of just plain fear that with all the money and power the Kennedys have, they have never bothered to find out who killed their family members. I guess it was best explained at a conspiracy convention I attended in the early eighties. The question was raised that if there was a conspiracy to kill off the Kennedys, why hadn't the family done something about it? Why did they remain silent? One of the attendees at the convention stood up and made a profound statement: "Don't judge the evidence by the Kennedys' silence. Judge their silence by our evidence."

The King family is not wealthy, but they were not afraid to challenge the system, to at least have it recorded in a court of law what really happened to our friend Martin. The very people who were supposed to protect Dr. Martin Luther King Jr. gave him the code name "Zorro," and I have no doubt that they assassinated him. But they did not kill the spirit of Dr. King or the King family's will to find out the truth.

My momma, Lucille Gregory.

My daddy, Presley Gregory ("Big Prez"), leaving St. Louis.

SHELIA P. MOSES

The apartment building where my siblings and I grew up, at 1803 N. Taylor Street. My brothers and I planted that tree.

SHELIA P. MOSES

Sumner High School in St. Louis.

SUMNER HIGH SCHOOL ARCHIVES

Me running track at Sumner in 1951.

SUMNER HIGH SCHOOL ARCHIVES

That's me (the third guy from the right) at Sumner High in 1951.

ERNEST C. WITHERS

We unloaded food all day for the people in Clarkdale, Mississippi, 1961.

JET MAGAZINE, JOHNSON PUBLISHING COMPANY

Dr. King and I at Medgar Evers's funeral in June 1963.

A photo taken during an August 1964 Playboy *interview.*

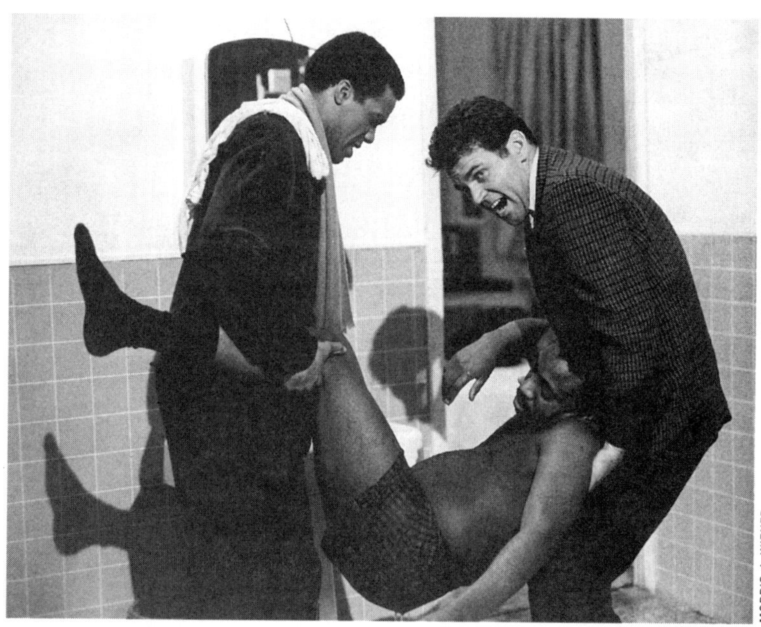

Robert Hooks, me, and Don Murray filming Sweet Love, Bitter *in 1965.*

In the kitchen during my first fast, 1967.

With Lil at the inauguration for Dick Hatcher.

Big Mike and his guest at Dick Hatcher's inauguration.

The one-dollar bill we used for my 1968 campaign for president.

JOSEPH LOUW / LIFE / TIMEPIX

Moments after King's assassination, April 4, 1968.

DOLORES GREGORY HILL

During my run against hunger in 1976.
With Muhammed Ali and my brother Ron.

REGGIE TORAN

With Walter Hudson at his home in 1988.

DOLORES GREGORY HILL

My brother Ronald and I the
day they named a street after me.
(Dick Gregory Place)

FERDY BANKS

Giving Nelson Mandela a can of my Formula Four X in 1990.

FERDY BANKS

With Richard's daughter Rain Pryor and director and friend Melvin Van Peebles, while filming Panther *in 1990.*

CHRISTIAN GREGORY

With Reggie Toran, Stevie Wonder, and Jesse Buggs.

With George O'Hare, Dr. Alvenia Fulton, and Herbert Jubirt.

With Roseanne Barr in her studio after appearing on her show in August 1998.

The Reverend Al Sharpton and I.

BILLINGSLEY CAMERA

With Reverend Randel Osburn, Martin Luther King III,
Barbara Skinner, and Walter Fauntroy.

FERDY BANKS

Me speaking at Ebenezer Baptist Church at the 1996 King Celebration.

BARBARA SKINNER

With C. Delores Tucker and Dr. Betty Shabazz.

FERDY BANKS

With Maxine Waters and Gerald Busby at the Black Caucus.

My nephew Ferdy Banks (Dolores's son), Dr. Joseph Lowery, and I.

LIL GREGORY

With my siblings the day I received my star on the St. Louis Walk of Fame. Ronald, Presley, me, Garland, Dolores, and Pauline.

DOLORES GREGORY HILL

With Lil the day I received my star on the St. Louis Walk of Fame.

FERDY BANKS

My return to Broadway in December 1995 with Dolores, her husband Roland, and Lil.

ARDIS GRAHAM

Above: My family on November 6, 1999.
(left to right) Gregory, Miss, Lynne, Pamela, Dick, Lillian, Paula, Ayanna, Yohance, Michelle, Zenobia (formerly Stephanie), Christian.

ARDIS GRAHAM

With five of my grandchildren at Paula and Roger's wedding on November 6, 1999. (left to right) Joshua, Sikani, me, Afrika, Shayla, Eusi.

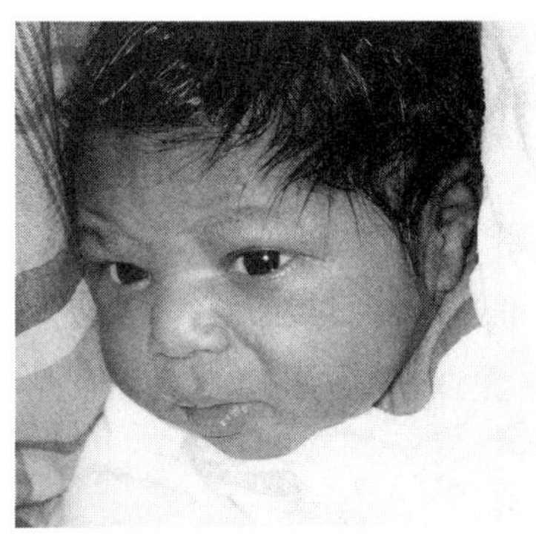

My other two grandchildren, Hodori Gregory and Julian Gregory Vivian Cenac, the newest addition to the Gregory family.

Me at Marla Gibb's Theatre in 1995 in Los Angeles.

18 Redskins

I did not go to Bobby Kennedy's funeral; I went to jail instead. I was at home in Chicago listening to the radio when I heard that I had lost my appeal and had been sentenced to ninety days for a 1966 arrest for illegal fishing in Washington State. I knew that I would have to serve the sentence because in the Movement, you cannot let your attorneys bail you out of every situation — you have to serve your time and by doing that, you give oppressed people, poor people, and people at the bottom strength. It was rare that any of us stayed in jail for longer than a few days, but there was no way out of this one. I would have to do the whole ninety days. It was worth it to me then and now.

I had been performing at the Edgewater Inn in Seattle, Washington, in January 1966 when some very beautiful people had come into my life and changed my perspective on the Movement. I had actually been there because Marlon Brando, who was supposed to speak that night, had to cancel. He called me and asked me to fill in for him. I was glad to go for Marlon, because he is a man who was out there marching in the line of fire with us many times. I had no idea that filling in for Marlon would lead to a lifelong friendship with American Indian people all over the country. In my act I told jokes about the Nisqually Indians' legal battles, but I quickly learned that it was no joking matter. After my show, some Indians came backstage to talk to me about their concern over changes in a one hundred-year-old treaty that gave them the right to fish by any means. The Indians used nets to catch fish, and the law had been changed to outlaw the use of nets. What the government was trying to do was simply cut off their source of income and send them back to the reservation. The Indians continued to fish with nets, and I went with them. Many people were angry that I was helping the Indians, especially the judge who sentenced me to ninety days in jail in 1968. But my colleagues from the Movement were very happy that I was taking a stand for the Indians. They all, including Dr. King, called Lil to check on me or wrote me in jail. I left Seattle on bail and left my attorney, Jack Tanner (who later became a federal judge), there to file my appeal. After that incident I began to work harder for human rights, not just civil rights.

Today I meet with the Indians twice a year. One day the Justice Department must investigate the violent attacks against Indians from outsiders on their reservations, not to mention the poor quality of the schools provided to them.

The only people on this earth who have been treated worse by this White racist system than we Blacks have been treated are the Indians. One example of this is the football team in your nation's capital called the Washington Redskins. I mean, I cannot believe that Black folks even go to their games, let alone play on their team. To name a football team the Washington Redskins as if the Indians are animals is so inhuman. We Black folks who attend the games show a lack of sensitivity.

Maybe folks just don't know where the word *redskin* came from. In the old days, there used to be a bounty on the Indians, and the White folks' motto was "a good Indian is a dead Indian." Because the bounty hunters were bringing in so many Indian bodies, the U.S. government had to stop them, telling them to just bring in their heads. After that they brought in so many heads that the government had to stop and tell them just to bring the hair. Well, then White folks started killing each other for their hair and the government said, "No, no, the hair has to have red skin on it." There you have it, the name *redskins.*

The Washington Redskins were sold not too long ago for eight hundred million dollars, and I was hoping that some of the Indians would use their casino money and buy the team. Then I was hoping they would rename the team the Nigger Honkies.

But such racism was going on before the Redskins football team. When I was a little boy, the images I had of Indians from movies were that they were savages. Every time a White person killed one of them, the White person was a hero. So even as a child you are programmed to cheer for the White boys. Do you remember the show *The Lone Ranger*? You had two main characters, Tonto and Kemosabe. In Spanish *Tonto* means the stupid one and *Kemosabe* means the learned one. We cheered for the White man to always win the war, and we watched him call Tonto stupid for decades.

It would be nice if some of the decent White organizations and organizations like the Black Caucus took up their cause and defended our Indian brothers and sisters. I believe if Indians started their own movement today it would be as powerful as the Civil Rights Movement was in the sixties. First, the young people today do not have the same images of Indians that we had. Second, the media today allows us to really see the way they are treated.

What makes many White people uncomfortable is knowing Indians have powers that are unexplainable. They proved that when they put the curse on the president of the United States, also known as the curse on the White man. The president's curse is believed to have begun in 1811 during the Battle of Tippecanoe, when American troops led by William Henry Harrison defeated the Indians. The Indian chief Tecumseh was later killed in another battle in 1813. It is believed that as Chief Tecumseh lay dying on the battlefield, he cursed Harrison, promising that any president elected in a year ending in zero would die in office. You can call it curse or coincidence, but every president elected thereafter in a year ending in zero, with the exception of Ronald Reagan, has died in office:

- Harrison: Elected in 1840. Died of pneumonia after serving only thirty-one days.

- Abraham Lincoln: Elected in 1860. Assassinated.
- McKinley: Elected to a second term in 1900. Assassinated.
- Harding: Elected in 1920. Died of a stroke in 1923.
- Roosevelt: Elected to a third term in 1940. Died of cerebral hemorrhage in 1945.
- Kennedy: Elected in 1960. Assassinated.

Some believe that President Reagan broke Tecumseh's curse when he survived the assassination attempt by John Hinckley in 1982. But the Indians know that that is not true. They also knew that whoever was elected president in 1980 would come close to dying, but would survive, because the planet Mars was not in place. We won't have to wait long to see if the curse returns, since the year 2000 is an election year. If I was a presidential candidate in the year 2000, I wouldn't be too interested in winning.

After my sentencing for the fishing violation, I turned myself over to the authorities to start serving my time. While I was in jail, I continued my presidential campaign. I figured if Eugene Debs could do it, so could I. Debs ran for president in 1920 while he was serving time in jail for his antiwar activities. He ran as a Socialist and received 3 percent of the vote. I also started a fast that I intended to stay on until my release from jail. In 1968, in the state of Washington, you could feed an inmate three meals a day for thirty-two cents. It cost them eighty-two cents per gallon to supply me with the distilled water I needed for my fast. My incarceration and the cost of my water each day made headlines and the people of Washington State were outraged — not because I was in jail, but because the government was using the taxpayers' money to supply the distilled water. I had beaten the press again with my fast, because I didn't care about the fast making headlines; I was happy that it was bringing attention to our mistreated American Indian brothers and sisters. On the fortieth day of the fast, I was released. They said it was because I might starve myself to death, but the truth was they hated the attention my fast and incarceration were giving the government's mistreatment of the Indians. The forty days was not that long to me; I needed the rest. But I also needed to get back on the college circuit because I had a still-growing family, included my newest daughter, whom I had named "Miss," for Momma. I wanted Momma to know — wherever she is — that there is a Black woman in the world that White folks have to address as "Miss Gregory."

When I was released from the Thurston County Jail, I went back home for a few days before I got back on the college circuit and the campaign trail. The candidates for president in 1968 were Richard Nixon, Hubert Humphrey, George Wallace, and me. The press was as clever then as they are now, and that worked to my advantage. The media was calling me daily asking for interviews. They really did not want to hear about my desire to paint the White House black, let alone any of the more serious issues on my platform — it was all about equal-time regulations. They knew that George Wallace and other candidates would demand equal time if I were to appear on their shows.

I lost the war, but I won the battle. My campaign had given me the opportunity and forum to discuss issues that affected Black and oppressed people, and that was more important to me than winning. After the election of Richard Nixon, I declared myself "President in Exile," and we planned two inaugural balls in Washington, D.C. One ball was held at the Hilton and the second at American University. Several weeks before the ball George Wilkins, president of American University, abruptly canceled our ball because, he said, there was insufficient parking available. God stepped in, and so did the faculty and staff at American University. The American Association of University Professors and the Organization of Afro-American Students openly supported me. The chairman of the student group wrote: "In specific terms, the question is Gregory, but generally, it is whether students will be trusted with themselves. This university is racist. We feel that Gregory is important to the nation. We're talking about the hunger right here in Washington. What if the people were to eat up everything in sight? What if they became human locusts? This time they might come up past Connecticut Avenue."

The articles written about the American University cancellation had the same effect on my visibility as the interviews had on my campaign. We finally received permission to have the ball. And what a ball we had! My "Vice President-in-Exile," Mark Lane, wasn't able to attend because he was in New Orleans working with District Attorney Jim Garrison on the Clay Shaw case. Shaw had been charged with conspiracy in the assassination of President Kennedy. Mark couldn't leave New Orleans, so attorney Jean Williams swore in Lane via telephone. I was sworn in by attorney Rudy Barrow at the ball. We thought about calling Billy Graham, but it was Reverend Jim McGraw who opened our ball with a prayer. After the swearing-in ceremony, we went over to the Hilton where the second ball was in full swing.

The crowd at the Hilton cheered as their president-in-exile took the stage. Lil and I danced all night, shuttling back and forth between the two balls. The evening was so perfect, I almost forgot that it wasn't real. I wondered what Momma was thinking as she watched the ball from heaven. She now knew that Richard and Dick were the same person, her son. The next morning when I looked in the newspaper, there we were — Lil and I — on the fourth page of the afternoon paper.

I guess Ol' Master Daley in Chicago had also read about the balls. Within weeks, I was back in Chicago in a jail cell for allegedly biting two police officers two years earlier during a demonstration. I served forty-five days and fasted the entire time. When they let me out of jail, each of the two cops sued me. Shortly after the suit was filed, I was invited to appear on a talk show with Governor Claude Kirk of Florida and famed attorney F. Lee Bailey. Bailey and I talked after the show and he agreed to represent me in the cop-biting case. Thanks to columnist Irv Kupcinet, my new attorney Bailey and I made national headlines and both suits were dropped two weeks later. I guess Ol' Master wasn't up to tangling with F. Lee Bailey. The next time I heard about those two cops, they were being indicted for shaking down restaurant and tavern owners in Chicago.

F. Lee Bailey and I became friends and later neighbors after he moved to Massachusetts. My kids always got a kick out of him landing his helicopter on our farm to visit instead of driving.

After my court ordeal, Lil and I decided to attend the World Assembly for Peace in Berlin. We stopped in London to meet some friends from North Vietnam. They had a "home movie" they wanted us to see. Lil and I were sickened as we sat and watched the film. It showed proud American soldiers murdering innocent women and children in a North Vietnamese village. These soldiers were not defending their country. One scene showed footage of the soldiers drinking and posing for the camera just before they blew off a child's head. We went back to Chicago horrified by what we had seen.

It took me a couple of days to decide what to do. I told Lil that I was going to show her how to make a tapped phone pay off. When she asked me how I was going to do that, I picked up the phone and started calling people:

"Hey, man. I'm going to pick up a tape that I know will get this war cut in half."

When they asked what I was talking about, I let loose.

"Well, Lil and I saw this tape of American soldiers laughing while they killed Vietnamese women and children."

I stayed on the phone all day telling people the same story, just to make sure the government people bugging my phone would know that we were going to London. When we got to the airport in New York, it didn't take long to locate the agent assigned to follow us. Once we arrived in London, we started playing cloak-and-dagger with him immediately. First we arranged a secret rendezvous with our friends from North Vietnam; then we went to the movie theater, with the agent following. We sat in the movie theater a few minutes and then we lost the agent by slipping out the back door. From there we picked up the tapes and walked the streets all night.

Our agent eventually caught up with us, but he had no idea we already had the film in our bags. We would now need to get through customs in Paris. My good friend and attorney Adam Bourgeois got there a week before me and arranged to get us through customs with the tapes. Adam has been my attorney and friend for almost forty years, and he has taken many risks to help me in situations like the one in Paris. The agent was still trailing us when I just walked up to him. "Look, I know who you are. You've been following us all the way from the States. But now you need me for protection. What you were supposed to keep us from getting, we've already got. It's already been dealt with."

Then I pointed out Adam to him.

"See that Black cat over there? He's an agent, too. I know him from Chicago. I'm almost positive that he's the one sent here to take care of you if you messed up. But I tell you what, I will keep an eye on him in the interest of your own personal security."

The fellow was so confused that he went with us to dinner that night. Adam went by the hotel earlier and tipped the maitre d' one hundred dollars, explaining to him who I was. In the meantime, I was back at the hotel talking to the agent in my room. As we were leaving the room I picked up my briefcase that contained the My Lai tapes. The agent didn't question me about carrying my briefcase to dinner, because I always carried it with me. When we arrived at the restaurant, they treated us like royalty. After dinner we all got up and left, and I purposely left the briefcase under the dinner table. When I got back to my hotel room, I called the maitre d' and told him that I had forgotten my briefcase. He started insisting that he would bring the briefcase to my room. I had to lie and tell him that it had pornography tapes in it that I didn't want my wife to see. He agreed to hold the briefcase until the next morning. In the meantime, Adam and I arranged for Lil to leave the country the next morning. We slipped out of the hotel early, stopped at the restaurant to pick up the tapes, gave them to Lil, and we were off to the airport. Under her maiden name, Lil flew from Paris to Montreal, Montreal to Toronto, Toronto to Chicago, with the package in tow.

As Lil's plane took off from Paris, the agent ran into the airport thinking that I was trying to get away from him. Luckily for me, I was standing at the newsstand. The moment I saw him, I looked down and saw a *New York Times* and I grabbed it like I was there to buy papers, which would not have been unusual. He came running over.

"Where's your wife?" he demanded.

"Hey man, I just came out to get a *New York Times*. You must have known I was a news freak. I'm just picking up the paper. My wife's back at the hotel."

"No she ain't, I went by her room."

"She's there man, you know she goes jogging every morning. Didn't your people tell you that?"

When I called Lil after she'd arrived back home, she was hysterical. She was screaming and crying simultaneously. "Don't you ever ask me to leave my children again! No more leaving my children!"

Lil had found out that working against the Vietnam War was more dangerous than fighting for civil rights. She wasn't afraid of dying, but she was afraid of never seeing her children again. After she calmed down, I gave the government that I knew was listening with their wire taps one more message. "Well, fellas, you're really in trouble now. That My Lai mess has got to come out."

We gave the tape to Irv Kupcinet, but I will always believe that before he could do anything with it, the U.S. government broke the story that we know today as the My Lai massacre. But it was the courage of Lillian Smith Gregory that lay behind the headlines declaring the court martial of Lieutenant William Calley for his involvement in what our new president called the "abhorrent" massacre. President Nixon promised justice for all those involved.

Whatever Lil's fears were, she had kept her commitment that the Movement would always come first.

19 Going Home

Every Black person in America should go home at least once in his or her lifetime. I made my first journey to Africa in 1970 with my friend the Reverend Jim McGraw. Lil didn't go because she was pregnant at the time.

My friend Bob Lecky had arranged for me to speak in Australia at an event sponsored by the Aquarian Foundation, of which he was the current chairman. After my lecture, I wanted to attend a summit conference of nonaligned nations in Lusaka, Zambia. Bob arranged for Jim and me to have two tickets on to Africa after leaving Australia, and Jim was handling our visas and passports. I thought everything was just fine until Jim called and said our visas to Australia had been denied. It didn't register with me that anything major was wrong, so I told Jim to go ahead and pick up our passports; I figured we could get our visas at the Australian Embassy in London.

The situation proved to be a prime example of how far the American government would go to get what they wanted or to stop what they did not want. We were met by the press when we arrived at the Australian Embassy. Thanks to the CIA, the Australian government believed our visit would be disruptive. It was no secret that I was opposed to the Vietnam War; I talked about it everywhere I went. Based on my antiwar sentiments and the fact that Australia had fighting forces in Vietnam, they refused to issue us visas. *This,* I thought, *was going too far.* Nothing I said convinced them that I was merely touring. We had no choice but to leave. Our visas were similarly denied at the Australian embassies in Paris, then Rome. I finally gave up and we were off to the Motherland.

My anger about the denied visas eased as the plane flew over the ocean toward Africa. I thought about all the Black folks who had died on the journey to America. I thought about my ancestors being shackled to the bottom of ships for months, with no way out but to jump to their own deaths. I thought of their tears for the families they had left behind. God, we will never know how many long-forgotten bodies are at the bottom of that ocean. I will always remember the feeling of going home as the plane landed in Nairobi, Kenya. Since that journey I try to return home every year, just to be in touch with the voices of the past.

The CIA had contacted every Australian embassy in Europe to make sure we were not granted visas, and we were tired of trying to outrun them. Once we realized that we would never be allowed to tour in Australia, we relaxed and enjoyed the beauty and warmth of Africa and the African people. There were so many good things to focus on in Kenya and too many bad things still happening back home to let our first trip to the Motherland be spoiled.

After weeks of having a great time, we went home. My son, Christian, was born soon after my return. I guess Big Prez and I had one thing in common: I was constantly traveling and it seemed as if every time I went home, Lil got pregnant. Fourteen months after Christian's birth, our youngest daughter was born on October 20, 1971. I was still high from my trip to Africa, so we named her Ayanna, which means beautiful flower.

Two years later we would have our last child, Yohance. He was born two months after I retired from the nightclub scene. On May 23, 1973, a Saturday night, I walked onto the stage of Paul's Mall nightclub in Boston for what would be my last night in show business.

"I want to thank President Richard Nixon for not appointing any Black folks to his cabinet. Now he can't blame us for Watergate."

That joke brought down the house as the curtain fell on that chapter of my life. For the past fourteen years I had walked into rooms and tickled thousands of funny bones at nightclubs around the world. I had been speaking at three hundred colleges a year, sometimes two per day. I also had about four club dates a year, each lasting approximately two weeks. I decided to leave the club scene because, due to my focus on nutrition, I now had a problem performing anywhere that encouraged people to consume alcohol or anything else that was damaging to the body.

I thoroughly enjoyed my last night in that smoke-filled, liquor-soaked room packed with people, Black and White, who had come to say good-bye. I had flashbacks to my years of chasing down gigs with baby Michelle resting precariously on the floorboards of my old car, to the Playboy Club and beyond. And between each and every gig, I had protested, been arrested, marched, and/or fasted. Not only was I leaving the nightclub scene, I was months away from leaving Chicago.

When Yohance was born on July 25, 1973, he filled the last empty space in our apartment in Hyde Park. We needed a bigger place, even if it meant leaving Chicago. For months Big Mike and I looked for a new home for my family, and finally found a farmhouse in Plymouth, Massachusetts. But leaving Chicago was not so easy. As crowded as our apartment was, Lil and the children liked it there — it was the only home they knew. Against their will, I packed them up and we were off to our new house. My family was mad as hell at me. The children missed their friends, and Lil missed the convenience of Chicago living.

Big Mike went with us, and I think that made it easier for the children. I am the first to admit that Big Mike was like a second father to them. He loved them dearly and they thought he was a big, wonderful toy; he could ride three children on his back at one time. In addition to the large farmhouse, we had a twelve-room boathouse near a pond on the property. Big Mike turned the boathouse into a wonderful home for himself and for our occasional guests. My family's anger eventually turned into laughter and acceptance, and Big Mike and I were no longer the house enemies.

On December 2, 1973, Lil and I returned to Chicago for a farewell celebration in our honor sponsored by the Chicago Society of Writers and Editors at the Orchestra Hall. The date had been declared "Dick Gregory Day" by then-Illinois Governor Daniel Walker. The sponsors had petitioned Ol' Master Daley to celebrate "Dick Gregory Day" in the City of Chicago. Daley refused and issued a statement through his spokesperson, Frank Sullivan, that said, "There will be no Dick Gregory Day proclamation." Talk about having a long memory! Other than using Daley's statement in jokes, I did not respond. The young people of Chicago responded for me.

I will be forever grateful to columnist Vernon Jarrett who wrote an article in *The Chicago Tribune* entitled "Gregory Tribute Won't Need Daley." It was a beautiful article that not only defended my right to have a day in my honor in Chicago, but also defended the community's right to celebrate any Black person they wanted to celebrate. Jarrett's article basically stated that we are no longer on the plantation and don't need the master's permission to honor anyone we choose. At the farewell celebration, I sat back and listened to everyone from Jesse Jackson to my good friend George O'Hare tickle *my* funnybone for a change. Lil and I had a ball. Then we got on a plane and returned to our new home in Plymouth, leaving behind a place that had given me everything I needed: Lil, fame, ten children, and my dear friend Herb Jubirt.

With my family all settled in on the farm and happy again, I was able to go out and start fighting once more. The war in Vietnam was slowly coming to an end, and I began waging a new war that may never be over: the war against poverty. I had brought international attention to many causes through my fasting and praying, and it seemed appropriate to go on a hunger strike for the poor people of the nation.

The year before we moved to Massachusetts, I ran the Boston Marathon. I had been fasting for a month in protest of the Vietnam War and I felt that running the marathon would take my protest to another level for world hunger. I was training daily and when the day of the marathon arrived, I was ready. As usual, Lil was there to support me. Steve Jaffe, Coach St. James, and Dr. Alvenia Fulton were also there. Many people doubted my ability to run this famous race, but I made it twenty-five miles before my legs gave out. I cramped in the last mile and fell to the sidelines. I remember people standing over me as I lay on the ground. Their faces all looked the same, except for the judge who told me I had almost finished the *twenty-six-mile* race. "Twenty-five miles!" he screamed. I couldn't believe it. I had dedicated myself to running twenty-five miles, but the Boston Marathon is twenty-six miles. I didn't know anything about marathons at the time and I just set my mind to run twenty-five miles. I didn't finish their race, but I had finished mine. That race proved to me that once you set your mind to achieve something you can do it.

The Boston Marathon gave me the idea to start my own run across the country as part of my war against poverty and hunger. Steve Jaffe and I planned a thousand-mile cross country run from Chicago to Washington, D.C. But first, we had to raise enough money to sponsor the race. Many of the people we approached didn't understand why we needed money to run. The average person thought that all we had to do was get out there and start running, but we needed everything from running shoes to hotel rooms.

Steve Jaffe arranged for me to meet with Barbra Streisand and her boyfriend at the time, Jon Peters. They wanted to talk to me about nutrition, and I wanted to talk to them about sponsoring my run. Steve and I drove out to their house in Malibu and spent hours talking about everything except the money we needed. Somehow it just didn't feel right. They were really nice people, but I didn't feel comfortable asking them to sponsor my run across the country.

So instead, I went for a run through their lovely neighborhood. But it seemed like every dog in Malibu chased me; I had to turn around and head back to Barbra's with the dogs still on my heels. I told Jon Peters about the dogs and he pointed out a better trail. I ran for miles and kept hearing this funny noise under my feet. After a while, I looked up and saw Jon on horseback riding toward me like he was Matt Dillon.

"Man," he said, almost out of breath. "Didn't you hear all those snakes under your feet?"

"Hell, they weren't barking," I told him, "so they didn't bother me."

I jogged back to their house with a stunned Jon Peters following me on horseback. I was so tired from the dog and snake run that Steve and I left and drove back to his place.

The next day I went jogging in peace in Beverly Hills. When I stopped running, I found myself in front of Michael Stewart's office at United Talent Agency. He had been responsible for my last album, *Caught in the Act.* Michael Stewart was one of those people who helped the Movement without marching. He wrote me a check for twenty thousand dollars before I could even finish telling him about my plan to run across country.

During the run, I planned to test my new "Formula Four X." It was a nutritional supplement that I had been working on for years which consisted of a combination of kelp — that little green seaweed you see growing in the ocean — and a few other ingredients.

In the first few days I ran from Chicago to Gary, Indiana, where I received a warm welcome from Gary's first Black mayor, Dick Hatcher. His welcome was a real boost to the run. No matter how right you think your cause is, it's always good to have the support of a man like Hatcher.

There were several other people who helped me get through the run. Big Mike was important to the success of this race because he handled the logistics; he had to get to every city before I arrived and prepare for my stop. The moment I arrived in a city, I would talk to the press, then Big Mike would take me to my hotel. He would fill me up with juices, water, and Formula Four X. We'd get some sleep and start all over again the next day: Big Mike would drive to the next stop and I would start running again.

I don't know what we would have done without John Bellamy. I met John in 1974 in Chicago when he was a volunteer for the Society of Writers and Editors and I was on its board of directors. John was working at the post office at the time, but he took a leave of absence from his job to come on the road with me. For twenty-nine days, John would drive from town to town just ahead of me. He would stay about a quarter of a mile in front of me to make sure the press was waiting in the next city.

Dr. Roger Holt from Chicago was also there along the way to care for my feet. Dr. Holt is a good friend and one of the best foot doctors in the country. He would massage my sore feet and treat any problems to get me ready for the next day's run. Each of these men was incredibly supportive.

In Detroit, Ralph Abernathy, C. T. Vivian, and my good friend Muhammad Ali joined me for a few miles. Ralph and C. T. ran a few miles as promised. Ali lasted the longest, but he, too, gave up after five miles. He wrote a poem for me that I loved: "Dick Gregory has speed, Dick Gregory has endurance. But if you're going to run with him, increase your insurance." Some famous people would have joined the run to get publicity for themselves, but Muhammad Ali certainly didn't need the press. He joined the marathon to get us the publicity that our cause needed.

I thought about Momma as I ran from city to city, state to state. Sometimes I would run all day without seeing a tree, a house, or even a bird, just open lonely highways. I wondered if she could see me on those lonely roads. Almost all of her life, Momma had walked the streets of St. Louis trying to feed her babies. There I was, twenty-two years later, running across America for all the poor children like me. I understood the sound of hunger coming from their little stomachs; I understood Momma.

It was the thought of Momma and all those nights that we went to bed hungry that made me keep running. I ran in hopes that no other child would have to go through what my brothers and sisters and I had gone through. I just kept running and praying — I couldn't give up even if I'd wanted to. King had been dead for six years, and a part of the Movement died with him. Many poor people just gave up. I wanted people to know we were still fighting for them; I wanted them to know that they were not forgotten and that they were not alone.

One of the things I discovered on my trip to Africa, and in other countries I had visited, was that America deals with poverty in a unique and inhumane way. In America, the poor are treated as outcasts, criminals, as though the disease of poverty was something they wished upon themselves. Every effort is made to exclude them from the mainstream and to make them nearly invisible.

In Africa and other countries, people learn to coexist with the less fortunate. You see all these beautiful sisters from the poor villages in Africa walking in the finest neighborhoods with baskets on their heads. In Mexico you might be confronted by five poor people selling something before you can get from your expensive hotel to your car. If you're poor in America, stand in front of a four-star hotel trying to sell something and you will most likely be treated as a criminal and arrested. Very little effort is made in this country to end poverty, but there is endless legislation to criminalize it.

I thought about the plight of poor folks in this country as I ran. I thought about Momma as my feet swelled, just like hers used to. *Keep running, Flagpole,* I thought to myself. "Flagpole" had been my nickname in high school because every time I won a race at the public school stadium, I'd salute the American flag. I didn't know that the flag wasn't for me. *You ran your way out of St. Louis,* I'd say to myself. *You ran all the way to college. You ran from college to Chicago and from Chicago to being a celebrity comedian. Keep running, Flagpole!* I figured that if I kept running, maybe someone would stop and listen. Maybe they would understand this disease called hunger and maybe they would help make a change.

20 The Greatest

One person who truly understood what I was trying to do was Muhammad Ali. The way Ali affects people is both profound and universal. Ali's power over people is some reparation for the treatment of boxer Joe Louis. When you look back at Joe Louis, you can gauge the progress we've made and better understand the importance of Muhammad Ali's position in the world.

When White people looked at Joe Louis and recognized his talent and his potential, they had no doubt that he was the greatest fighter in the history of boxing at that time. But his White handlers also understood racism, and they trained Louis never to raise his hand in victory; they understood that White folks would never tolerate that after his knocking out a White boy. All he would say in his distinctive Alabama drawl, arms at his side, was, "Momma, I shoo am glad I win." Regardless of how the White racist system tried to demean him, the effect that Joe Louis had on Black folks was beautiful. In the 1940s, Black folks would crowd into one room and listen to the radio, as if Joe Louis was right there in the room with us. The power he had over a race of people who were fighting for human dignity made him a true champion.

Children loved the Joe Louis fights as much as the adults did. The one thing we knew was we were going to get all the candy and peanuts we could eat that night. The amazing thing about Black folks is that when something big is happening, like a Joe Louis fight, there was no such thing as poverty. Everyone was going to have a radio to listen to and the peanuts just weren't going to run out. During his fights no one was in the streets; it was as quiet as Christmas morning. When the fight was over, it was as noisy as New Year's Eve; we would even make drums out of washtubs and march around the block.

There was something about a Joe Louis fight that said to White folks, don't mess with Black folks tonight. It was that whole African spirit thing coming back. White folks had seen it before during slavery, on Pensacola Sunday. On that weekend, the masters knew they couldn't control their slaves. Slaves could leave the plantation and travel miles away, and their master wouldn't even look for them.

That's what a Joe Louis fight did to us. Something so beautiful, so powerful came over us that White folks just knew not to bother Black folks the night of a fight. In the forties, there was no Civil Rights Movement as we know it today. We heard about men like Adam Clayton Powell and A. Philip Randolph, but we didn't have the media that we have today to tell us what they were really doing. But we had Joe Louis on that radio. You couldn't see him, but we knew he was In your face, Mr. White Boy; he was In your face, Mr. White World. He was saying it and representing all of us, and he got us over that bridge for a minute. After the Joe Louis era, along came a seamstress in Montgomery, Alabama, named Rosa Parks, who would start a revolution and the world changed that day. Changed to the point that a Movement arose and freed Joe Louis's hand and in stepped Muhammad Ali.

When Ali raised that powerful fist in victory, it had thank you written all over it from Black folks to Joe Louis. But Ali not only raised his hands in joyous victory and proclaimed himself "the greatest"; he also praised his God. No athlete before Ali had talked about God. You might see Notre Dame football players or prize fighters make a symbolic gesture acknowledging God, but you never heard them say the words. Ali was the first athlete with enough power to speak about his God. "First," he'd say, "I want to give honor to the great power of

Allah." The White boys may not have liked it, but they soon realized that they couldn't talk to Ali unless they first listened to him praise his God.

The powers that be attempted to destroy Ali at least twice. They took his title when he refused on religious grounds to be inducted into the U.S. Army. Then they created the great White movie hero, Rocky. They took a well-muscled little White boy, Sylvester Stallone, and created a fictitious champion boxer who could knock out any Black boxer on the big screen. The first Rocky movie made more money than all of Ali's fights combined. When you go in remote areas of the world and ask little children who's the greatest, they say, "Rocky, Rocky!"

But not even Hollywood could shut Ali down. Without his title, he stood his ground and fought back for all the oppressed people of the world. When he supported our cross-country run for the hungry, he was standing tall for hungry people around the world. Every place we stopped on the run, Ali was there — either in person, via television, or in spirit. Even if he was in training for a fight, he would come if we needed him.

While I was running across the country, a young Black man — Marcus Chenault — was riding a bus from Dayton, Ohio, to Atlanta. Once he arrived in Atlanta, he walked into Ebenezer Baptist Church and killed Mrs. Alberta King, Martin Luther King Jr.'s mother. He also shot and killed Deacon Edward Boykin and wounded Mrs. Jimmie Mitchell. Chenault also had a list of civil rights leaders whom he intended to kill, but the press reported that it was a random shooting by a man who had gone berserk. I didn't think he was crazy; I thought he was part of the same conspiracy that had killed Dr. King six years earlier. The only thing "berserk" about that incident was that people believed Chenault was berserk.

In the midst of our sorrow for the King family, I made it to Washington, D.C., on July 10, 1974, in time for the unveiling of the Mary McLeod Bethune Memorial. Dorothy Height and Secretary of the Interior Rogers C. B. Morton unveiled the impressive statue of Ms. Bethune. C. Delores Tucker and Cicely Tyson read, and Barbara Jordan and Vice President Gerald Ford also attended. After the ceremony, I met with Dr. Dorothy

Height concerning my run across country and why it was necessary. As president of the National Council of Negro Women, she had set up a miniconference to educate people across the country about the food crisis among the poor. She helped people understand why Dick Gregory was running across America.

Dr. Height never cared about fame, and she has never compromised the causes for which she works. She had enough faith in the Black community to start the Black Family Reunion, which is held annually in different cities across the country, at a time when violence was running rampant. This event features booths set up to educate Black folks on everything from lupus to financial workshops. The great thing about the Reunion is that it's free and open to everyone, and tens of thousands of people show up in each city every year. Now, if you charge five hundred dollars a ticket to an event, you can control who is coming. But the Black Family Reunions are free because Dr. Height had enough trust and faith in Black folks to say "come as you are." This event has been a success for years. Never a fight, no bad press. This beautiful woman has an admirable strength of conviction and has earned the respect of everyone who knows her. That spirit enhanced my run across country and diluted criticism from the press.

I finished the last mile of my run on August 4, 1974, when Louis Stokes, Walter Fauntroy, Andrew Young, and I ran right up the steps of the Capitol in Washington, D.C. Mayor Walter Washington was also by my side. The momentum we had built across the country for one thousand miles, with the help of so many committed individuals, should have climaxed on those Capitol steps. But the American public and the press were preoccupied with another major event: President Richard Nixon was in the process of moving out of the White House. Nothing else mattered to the press for the entire week; certainly a thousand-mile marathon to bring awareness to the plight of the poor and disenfranchised was back-page news compared to Watergate. While Nixon leaving Washington with his tail between his legs got all the press, we had still accomplished our mission, and, we hoped, the hungry folks of

America realized that they, too, were important.

By November 1974, nothing much had changed except that America had a new president. The worldwide food crisis still existed, and I was still committed to the promise I had made before the press a year earlier at the United Nations World Food Conference in Rome. I sent a telegram to President Gerald Ford:

"Only you as President of the United States can rescue the international assembly from utter fiasco and set a positive course. Cries of overpopulation and acceptance of the inevitability of human doom are not the answer. I urge you to instruct delegates representing our nation to assert humanitarian leadership by the immediate pledge of a firm and generous commitment of food and funds to ensure that fifty million people will not have to die."

I further promised that I would picket the White House at 10:30 A.M. on Thanksgiving Day if Earl Butz, the Secretary of Agriculture, did not make a budgetary commitment of thirty million dollars to help end world hunger. He didn't, and I started my demonstration. At 10:30 A.M. on Thanksgiving Day, I stood in front of the White House with a picket sign that Willie Beal, a wonderful artist and a friend of John Bellamy's, had designed. It showed a fat turkey with Earl Butz's head just where it belonged and read, "While millions starve, are you going to swallow this?" The press went crazy taking pictures and reporting the incident. Of course, the paddy wagon was there waiting for me and for the handful of demonstrators who showed up to protest with me. The cops told us that we would be arrested if we didn't leave — I told them that they would have to arrest us to make us leave.

We never knew what was going on behind those White House doors on that Thanksgiving Day as we marched to force the hand of the most powerful man in the world. They were probably eating turkey until the press disclosed that the best turkey was on a sign right outside on Pennsylvania Avenue. I don't think Earl Butz liked being eaten alive, so he announced a $110 million budget for emergency food aid to Bangladesh and India. We had accomplished a lot that day in Washington, but our fight would continue.

One year and one month after our turkey day with Earl Butz, I started a fast at West Hunter Street Baptist Church in Atlanta, where Reverend Ralph Abernathy was pastor at the time. The fast was again to expose the food crisis around the world. While millions brought this so-called bicentennial year in with a bang, millions more would go to bed hungry on New Year's Eve. I started on Christmas Day 1975 and fasted until midnight on December 31. And I was not alone. After holding a press conference to announce my fast, to my surprise people from around the world fasted with me. Atlanta Mayor Maynard Jackson proclaimed that week "Dick Gregory Fast for Hunger Week," and Coretta Scott King, Andrew Young, and many others joined us. Stevie Wonder, who was fasting at his home in Los Angeles, called and offered his support, and I thought to myself, even Stevie Wonder can see what is happening here.

The last call of the evening was from Muhammad Ali. He talked to everyone by speakerphone. He was in training to fight Jean Pierre Coopman. As focused as Ali is when he is in training, he took the time to call us.

"The reason I canceled my training program today, Dick, was because what you are doing is so worthwhile and so great. People don't realize how far ahead of them you are. You mentioned that you all have been fasting since Christmas. The rest of them told you that they have been fasting since Christmas right along with you, but in reality, you're probably the only one who's been fasting that long."

Everyone had a good laugh when he said that, but he wasn't through.

"You have to condition yourself for that kind of suffering. I just can't believe that the average person fasted for that length of time with no prior training. But if they did, God bless them. Most of us are intoxicated with wealth and lifestyle so we no longer see the conditions facing the people around us. But if you can allow yourself to get that hungry to realize how other people feel, you have moved far beyond the average person's understanding.

"I'll do everything I can to help your program. If it weren't for this important fight I have coming up and the fact that I'm fifteen pounds overweight, I would be there with you all. But I want you to know that I'm with you in everything you want to do."

Of course I jokingly defended the others in the group when Ali said that they were cheating. He can be so funny, and I know that he got a kick out of upsetting my fellow fasters. He joked about me the same way when I ran from Chicago to Washington, D.C., and I reminded him of that.

"It's hard to believe, Dick," he responded. "I'm in training for a fight that will pay me a million dollars and I wouldn't fast three days to get that million. But you fast for twenty-nine, sometimes forty days. Now you tell me you gonna run across the world! You're a miracle man, Dick. The more I hear about you, the more I watch what you do, and the more I think about the things that you do, I figure that you must be one of the greatest men in America today. That is, if you're telling the truth. Just keep out of the boxing ring!"

Ali went on to tell everyone about how we ran together in Detroit.

"I met Dick," he said, "and I knew I was good for five miles. Five miles amounts to about forty-five minutes of continuous running. Anyone who knows anything about jogging knows that five miles is a long way. I told myself that I was gonna take this chump for five miles and see what he can do. We went four miles and Dick wasn't even breathing hard. I stepped up the next mile real fast. Dick followed me, then he got faster. By mile five, I figured he couldn't last much longer, so I jumped into the car that accompanied us, and doggone if Dick didn't run another fifteen miles. I said to myself, 'This man's crazy!'"

That call lifted everyone's spirits, and those who were thinking about big, juicy hamburgers started thinking about water and juice again. Ali has that kind of effect on people. Like Ali, that year-end fast in 1975 was the greatest!

Through most of 1975 and 1976, my good friend Jim McGraw traveled with me and completed the second installment of my autobiography, *Up from Nigger*. It's amazing to me how much the world has changed since we wrote that book. But the real problem is how much has not changed. The same world hunger I protested back then still exists today. Millions of people, millions of little children, are starving to death and going to bed hungry and the world community still turns a deaf ear to their life-threatening poverty.

But I refused to give up or give in, so I planned another run that would truly be "cross-country." I decided to run from Los Angeles to New York and fast the entire journey, taking only my new product, Formula Four X, and fresh fruit juice. I called it the "Dick Gregory Bicentennial Run Against Hunger in America." I thought I would shed some light on what we did not have to celebrate after one hundred years of so-called freedom. My agenda was real simple: We would no longer tolerate starvation and hunger in the world. And it definitely would not be tolerated in the United States of America, the richest country in the world. I also called on the government to create a new cabinet seat: the Secretary of Food and Nutrition.

I left Los Angeles on April 21, 1976, and arrived in New York on July 4, 1976, with a schoolteacher named Gordon Brooks by my side. Many people joined us for a day or two, but he ran the entire race with me. As we ran across the country, I pressed the issue of world and domestic hunger at every press conference. When I got to Arizona the stage was set when Muhammad Ali joined us. He brought out the media and got the publicity this cause so urgently needed.

I don't remember who told me about her, but the day before Ali arrived, I went to the hospital to visit a little old White woman who was dying of cancer. "Mr. Gregory, I understand that you are traveling with Ali."

"Yes, I am."

"Well, I sure would like to meet him before I die."

When Ali arrived, we were seventy-five miles from where the woman was hospitalized. I told Ali about her, and we decided to get up early the next morning and drove back to see her. She was so happy to meet Ali, and six hours after we arrived, Ali was still doing magic tricks to make this lady happy in her final days. That's the way he was then and that's the way he is now. There was never a time in his career when he did not care about other people. He became and remains to this day the darling of America and the world.

Our stop in Albuquerque, New Mexico, was another memorable moment. Muhammad Ali was in Germany getting ready for a fight. Every time he got in front of a camera, he publicized our run for world and domestic hunger. The night of the fight he said, "I just want to say hello to Dick Gregory, who is now fifty miles outside of Albuquerque, New Mexico." I was in my hotel room that evening when an Albuquerque state trooper knocked at my door and told me I had to come with him. Apparently there was a crowd of people fifty miles outside of town waiting for me. I jumped in the car with the state trooper who sped me out to the people. That was the power of Ali.

Three months later, I got a chance to reciprocate for Ali's goodwill. He was in training for his fight with Ken Norton. The bout was going to be held at New York's Yankee Stadium on September 2, 1976, and we were going to join Ali at a place in Springville, Arizona, that I had visited when I was running across the country. But Ali had found a place called "Show Low" in Arizona, and he decided that we would stay there instead. I put him on a massive nutritional program using Formula Four X, and Ali beat Norton. After the fight, Ali credited the formula with helping him win. I was glad my formula was able to help my friend; it was the least I could do, after all his generosity. His saying that Formula Four X helped him win the fight was great, but I still believe Ali would have beaten Norton without it.

What Muhammad Ali said after the Norton fight was just like reading something in *Jet* magazine; if Ali said it, then it must be so. Athletes from all over the country started calling about Formula Four X, but I was not yet ready to sell it. I was willing to use it to promote the cause of world hunger and to help strengthen athletes who were sick or injured, but I was not ready to market it.

The third time Ali joined us during our run across the country was in my hometown of St. Louis, Missouri. People back home were so excited to see him in person and newspapers around the country covered Ali's visit to St. Louis in support of our cause. When the press asked him why he had come to St. Louis, he responded with a big smile and said, "Because Greg needed me." You can always count on him to support any cause that helps people.

I wanted to take our run through St. Louis to give people at home hope. I wanted them to know I cared about them. I never understood how a city with companies as big as Anheuser Busch, McDonnell Douglas, and TWA could have so much poverty and such extraordinarily high unemployment.

That was a part of the message all the way to New York City. One of the things I learned on my run across country that I was never aware of is what a beautiful country America is. I saw the power of God on all those lonely but beautiful roads. On the highway you see no hunger folks, no beggars. No misery, no sorrow. You see the moon, the sun, and the stars. No phones ringing, no one asking you to do anything. Just to show you the power of God, we didn't see one car accident the entire time. As we approached New York, fifty miles outside of the greatest city in the world, I thought about all the people who had helped me to get to that last fifty miles. Gordon Brooks was still with me. He had run every mile of the way. Charlene Mitchell and Charlotte Fox were still handling the press and, boy, was their job hard — mainly when Ali came in, because everyone wanted to interview him.

When we got to Morristown, New Jersey, we had to swing to the right to go to New York and there it was: the greatest city in the world. After running three thousand miles, New York City was the most beautiful place in the world. It would take three more days to get there and every mile seemed like heaven. The last night before we ran into the city I got a call from my old friend Marlon Brando. He was calling to congratulate us and to see if there was anything he could do to help. After I told him that we were fifty thousand dollars in debt, I think the check reached me before I reached New York. But that's Brando.

On the morning of July 4, 1976, we had one hurdle to cross that we were not aware of. New York was having Tall Ships Day to celebrate the Bicentennial, and President Ford was there and so was an army of security. Well, when we got to the George Washington Bridge, we were stopped by the Secret Service and told we couldn't go across, the bridge was closed. Something just came over me. I turned to the top man in charge: "I don't know who you have to call, but you call someone, because we are going across this bridge." I continued to explain why we were there. They got the word to President Ford. We ran across that bridge to the sound of a horn from Gerald Ford's ship and people waving at us. The toll that run took on my body, the financial toll, the whole nine yards — who cared? It was worth it.

I was ready for my next run when I met Willie Stargell in 1979. He was playing for the Pittsburgh Pirates when I saw that they were in trouble. Willie was well aware that I had run across the country surviving basically on my Formula Four X. At Willie's request, I started working with him and his teammates, mainly by giving them my formula. By October, his team had earned a place in the World Series against the Baltimore Orioles. Baltimore jumped to an early lead, beating the Pirates three games out of the first four. The Baltimore radio stations started laughing at them and at me. They said, "We should pay Dick Gregory, because whatever he is giving the Pirates is helping us." If Baltimore won the next game, it would be over for the Pirates. So I went in and talked to Willie and the other players.

"Look guys," I told them. "There is no way you can be behind three games to one and not be stressed out. So here's what I want you to do: Come in to the dugout after every three innings and take this formula."

They did what I told them and won the next three games in a row. The rest is history.

Unfortunately, I couldn't be there when they won the World Series because I had promised Dick Hatcher, my good friend who was mayor of Gary, Indiana, that I would attend an affair with him. I asked another friend, James Allen, to take the formula I'd prepared for the team to the seventh game of the World Series. Willie Stargell was thirty-eight years old at the time and his teammates had nicknamed him "Pops." Yet Pops did what everyone thought was impossible, and the Pirates won when he knocked that ball to heaven in the sixth inning of the seventh game.

I left Mayor Hatcher's affair early and went upstairs to catch the end of the game. Baltimore is only one hour from Washington, so President Carter was there on the field with the winning team. Before anyone could speak — including President Carter — Pittsburgh Pirate Dave Parker took the mic and said, "I want to say thanks to our good friend Dick Gregory. We could not be here today if it was not for him. Dick, we can't start the parade tomorrow without you." Pops and Dave Parker told the press that they had lived off the formula I had provided and that when they needed that extra boost of strength, the formula gave it to them. I said good-bye to Dick Hatcher and flew to Pittsburgh to celebrate with the team. It was wonderful to see them so happy and to see Pops go out in style. Willie Stargell was named Most Valuable Player and retired that year.

I don't want to mislead anyone; Formula Four X will not make you a world champion if you don't already have the physical and mental ability to become one. If more athletes, coaches, and trainers would incorporate nutrition into their daily routine the way they do physical exercise, they would stand a better chance of becoming champions. Because they don't, the average life expectancy of a professional athlete is fifty-four years of age. Believe it or not, many a wino's life expectancy is longer than that. One day, when researchers stop being so awed by the game of sports, they will see a thing called sports abuse. Then athletes will learn to play sports without abusing their bodies.

The reason I wanted athletes to use my formula was to take away the stigma of it being a food "for poor, poverty-stricken people." When I was a little boy, I remember how painful it was to be labeled a child on relief. People saw being on relief as a negative, and I knew they would see Formula Four X the same way if we introduced it as a formula only to help people in poverty. The celebrity athletes definitely helped with the publicity for Formula Four X, but I mainly wanted them to take away its negative image before it was introduced to the world.

Another athlete I was able to help was Bill "Spaceman" Lee of the Boston Red Sox. Spaceman was one of the greatest pitchers of all time. After a shoulder injury, he was benched and our mutual agent, Bob Walker, gave him some material about Formula Four X. He called me and I didn't even say hello — I asked him where he was and went to visit him immediately. I gave him the same vitamin-enriched formula I had given the Pittsburgh Pirates. We continued to talk afterward on the phone for a while, but I never saw him again. Years later, I read in his autobiography what he said about using Formula Four X: "My arm came back as good as new."

By now there were others, like Houston MacTeer, a world-class sprinter using Formula Four X to give him added strength. I really enjoyed watching the difference the formula made in the performance of these athletes. Their success prompted others to start using the product, and they would invite me to their training camps to work with them. I discovered the healing properties of the formula as more and more athletes called upon us to treat everything from broken bones to arthritis. Track stars, entertainers, activists, and people from all walks of life started calling me to help them, and I prepared myself for yet another journey.

21 Give Peace a Chance

In addition to my Formula Four X, I had developed a new formula called Correction Connection to help people on drugs kick the habit. One of my clients was a man who became a very good friend, John Lennon. In the late seventies I received a call from someone telling me that John Lennon and his wife, Yoko Ono, were in a cave in Amsterdam drugged out. The person who called thought that I could help. I immediately flew to Amsterdam to see John and Yoko, and they were indeed in need of help. By using Correction Connection, praying, and fasting, they both were able to stop using drugs. I later learned from John Warren, a professor at San Diego State at that time who has written several books about John and Yoko, that they never used drugs again after our fasting and cleansing together.

I must admit, I never understood what a superstar was until I met John Lennon. John, Yoko, and I began traveling around the world together, sometimes fasting for weeks at a time for world peace. On one particular trip, we were fasting and planning a prayer vigil in London. We were standing in front of a church door, waiting to get started, when a sea of people started lining up as far as the human eye could see to get close to this one man. We were preparing to sit down and stay there all night when the people started coming towards John, and I made the mistake of putting my hands up to signal the crowd to step back. Out of respect, the front row took one step back and it was like an ocean wave, the way that crowd went backward. About thirty minutes later, that crowd started coming back towards us in slow motion. We stood at the church doors about to be crushed to death. I turned to John and said, "Man, we have got to get out of here before they crush us into this church door." We ran. Out of love and admiration, that crowd could have crushed John and the rest of us to death accidentally.

That was John Lennon's power; he could bring millions of people together. The same people who came to hear his music or just see him would have supported his peace movement. John was such a great guy, and there is no doubt in my mind that something or someone assassinated him other than a deranged fan. John was getting ready to give 10 percent of his wealth to the peace movement — that would have amounted to millions of dollars.

He was a beautiful person who tried to bring peace wherever he was. He used to hold sleep-ins all over the world and invite the press up to his hotel room to talk about world peace. When he and Yoko wrote the song "Give Peace a Chance," I was there singing along with them. It was just like John and Yoko to put my name on the label credits when it was released.

I felt John's death. On the day he was murdered, I did something that has only happened to me twice in my career: I left my brown briefcase in the hotel. When I got to the airport, I realized I had left it and I had to go back to the hotel to pick it up.

The moment that happened, I knew something was wrong. I started calling Lil. I told her to keep her eyes open, because I knew that leaving my briefcase meant something was wrong. She kept telling me that everything was fine. The last time I called, she assured me everything was okay, so I went ahead and gave my lecture that evening, and I forgot to call her afterward because I was talking to a group of students in the hotel lobby. When I got to my room, Lil had left me a message to call home. I did.

"Greg, have you heard the news?"

"No, what happened?"

"John Lennon was shot today."

I talked to Lil, then I hung up and thought about John for a minute. Then I turned on the news, trying to get more information. As I've said before, it's important to listen to the news when things first happen, because the stories change after people talk to the authorities; I learned that when President Kennedy died. A man named Mark David Chapman was later convicted of John's murder and sentenced to twenty years to life in state prison. The day John was murdered, a man in the neighborhood who was walking his dog told a reporter that at the time of John's murder he heard only two shots. He also said that he was only a few seconds away from the street John's apartment was on when he heard the shots. When he turned the corner there were at least five police cars already at the scene. So we have to ask ourselves, how did they get there so fast? And if the man walking his dog heard only two shots, why were there seven bullets in John's body when he arrived at the hospital? Where did the other five bullets come from and when were they shot? Why did the FBI have John Lennon under surveillance? As this book went to press in the year 2000, you could go on the Internet and find hundreds of pages of FBI information about John and Yoko released under the Freedom of Information Act. He was a musician and a wonderful human being using his money and his celebrity status to help bring peace and freedom to the world. Why would the FBI use our tax dollars to investigate him? The answer to that question became very clear when I learned that John and Yoko were planning a press conference the day following his murder. At that press conference they were going to announce that they would give 10 percent of their worth to the world peace movement. His murder was no longer a mystery to me. The world has had many people work on behalf of world peace, and John and Yoko are two fine examples. I grew fond of them both, and we lost a shining light when John died.

A few years later, we lost another important person who had come to me for help with his drug addiction. That person was the great Marvin Gaye. I met Marvin through a mutual friend, and we talked a lot before he confided in me about the problems he was having with drugs. Like John, we just became friends and we worked on his problems. God, Marvin was so kind. Every time I saw him he was asking about Lil and the children. Lil has never been one to go to a lot of concerts or any-place else, but boy did she love to go see Marvin Gaye perform.

One on one, Marvin and I had some wonderful times, just sitting around talking about racism, nutrition, and the power of love. One of my favorite pastimes was to be at Marvin's home and watch him and the fellows play basketball. They would actually play all day. When he wasn't playing ball, we would sit around and talk. But when it came time to clean Marvin up, it was no longer a game. I would go with him on the road and mix his vitamins and give him Correction Connection. Marvin got cleaned up and went to Europe to live for a couple of years. When he returned, he had started using drugs again. I didn't realize how bad Marvin's problem was until one morning after a concert. I was on my way to the health store to get his vitamins and I stopped by his room and told him I would be right back. When he realized I was going to the health food store, he insisted that I stop by his accountant's downstairs to pick up some money. My intuitions told me not to stop, but I didn't follow them. So I stopped by this guy's room and he opened the door. He was really nice until I told him the reason I stopped by.

"Hey, Dick Gregory, come on in, it's really nice to meet you. I didn't get a chance to say hello at the concert last night."

We had all gone to watch Marvin perform the night before in Philadelphia.

"Hey man, Marvin sent me down here to pick up some money for his vitamins."

This White boy's whole demeanor changed when I said that.

"Marvin did what? He had no right to send you down here."

And boy, did he go off on Marvin. I was very angry at Marvin for putting me in such an awkward position. But that is when I realized the power of drugs and the power that it gives the people around you. Marvin was making millions for himself and the people around him were getting their share. When I mentioned money to his accountant, it was as though Marvin was working for him, not the other way around. I had seen Marvin work so hard and I just couldn't believe this White boy. I don't know if Marvin was in debt to him because of his on-again, off-again drug problems, but whatever it was, it was ugly. So I went back to Marvin's room, where he was still in bed, and told him what happened.

"Man, how could you put me in a position like that?"

"Oh, Greg, I'm sorry."

Marvin apologized and I know he was sincere, but I couldn't shake that morning. So after that I flew with Marvin back to Los Angeles and tried to get him to go on a program to get cleaned up again. He just couldn't do it, so I left in frustration.

I called Lil later. "If Marvin Gaye calls, don't even tell me, because I don't want to deal with that relationship anymore." I meant it for that moment, because although I was over what had happened in the hotel, I was frustrated that Marvin wouldn't let me help him.

I don't know where I was when I received the call from Lil about Marvin. I just remember the pain.

"Greg, Marvin Gaye is dead. His father shot him."

Dead! I hung up with Lil and called Marvin's mother and sisters, whom I had become very close to. They were all crying and his sister asked me to come out to Los Angeles and deliver the eulogy at Marvin's funeral. So I called Felicia Coleman Evans, a gospel singer from Chicago, to ask her to go out to L.A. with me. I wanted her to go with me and sing before I delivered the eulogy. There is no voice like Felicia's and I knew whatever was wrong, she would fix it with her angelic voice.

When we got there it was so sad because not only was Marvin dead, but his father was in jail for shooting him. The entire family was just in a state of shock.

That night of the funeral, Bob Johnson from *Jet*, Marvin's bodyguard Andre White, a few other people, and I sat around for hours talking about Marvin.

Andre asked me, "Why didn't you call Marvin back?"

"Why didn't I call Marvin back? What are you talking about?"

"Man, Marvin was calling your house looking for you."

"I told Lil not to tell me when he called."

"Well, that's why he's dead. He told me he was trying to reach you because he knew if he stayed at that house his dad was going to kill him."

I will never forget that. Marvin was trying to get out. When I asked Lil about him calling the house, she told me he had been calling almost daily, but I had asked her not to tell me, and so she didn't. By then I was very much over what had happened with Marvin's accountant. I was just frustrated with Marvin for not getting back on the program for his drug addiction, but I hadn't said so to Lil, so she assumed I still didn't want to talk to him. Marvin's last album was titled *Sexual Healing*, but all of his music was healing. And the world was a better place with Marvin Gaye in it. I miss him.

I don't know if my Formula would have saved Marvin, we will never know. I'm just grateful for the people whose lives it did help and probably saved. In 1980, I got a call from Randy Jackson's father, Joe. Randy, the youngest member of the Jackson family, had had a near-fatal car accident. The doctors were hours away from amputating his right leg when his father called. We immediately started treating him with Formula Four X. I wasn't able to see Jackson personally because I was on my way to Iran, so Lil sent him what he needed by mail. His condition improved dramatically. He went from almost losing his leg to walking within three months. When *Jet* magazine ran a front-page story on Randy several months later, he stated, "I was taking this formula he [Dick Gregory] had given me . . . and the doctors couldn't believe how strong my bones are now."

Now as I've said before, if it ain't in *Jet*, it didn't happen. My phone started ringing off the hook. But as much as I wanted to focus on the needs of my people, there were political situations in the world that I just couldn't turn my back on.

22 Good or Evil

Iranian revolutionaries had taken hostage sixty-six people from the American Embassy in Tehran in November 1979, and they were threatening to kill many of them. I called Lil and told her I was going to Iran to fast and pray for the hostages until they were released. Before I arrived, they had released the Black male hostages and most of the White women. People still don't understand why they released the Black men and most of the White women, but I understood. My belief was that the Southern, Republican reaction back in the United States would have been outrage that they were holding Black men and White women hostage together, and that could have possibly pushed the war button. So I flew to Tehran, checked into a hotel, and started my prayer vigil and fast.

I lost fifty-five pounds on the fast and many of my friends and family were worried about my health. But I continued to fast and pray. I stayed in contact with people back home, mainly Lil. And I did a number of interviews. The one I remember the most was with my good friend Barbara Reynolds, who was writing for the *Chicago Tribune* at the time. They would not print her story about my trip to Tehran, but she wrote it anyway and *Playboy* magazine ran it as their cover story. We still laugh about her jumping under the desk when she heard the bullet and bomb in the background as she interviewed me. There is no better writer than Barbara Reynolds, and she has what many journalists don't have: dignity. She doesn't walk around with a sign that reads "I have a degree from Harvard," because her heart of gold is her greatest asset. But she understands the way this government works and the trickery that comes with it.

In the middle of my stay in Tehran, I received a visit from some of the Ayatollah Khomeini's staff, advising me that the Ayatollah wanted to see me. I said no and told them that I didn't want to get caught up in the politics of what was happening, that I had come there only to fast and pray. The next day, I was standing in the lobby of the hotel talking to Lil on the pay phone because I was unsure whether the telephone in my room was bugged. Suddenly, I heard all this noise. I hung up the phone to go find out what was happening. Before I could ask, I saw all of these men in uniform coming into the lobby. I asked the receptionist what was going on.

"You!" she responded.

"Me?"

"Yes, you. Did you say 'no' to the Ayatollah? They sent the army to escort you to him."

One of the soldiers came over to me and told me that I had to go with them. They politely escorted me out of the hotel. I really don't think I had a choice in the matter. Within thirty minutes, I was standing at the door of the Ayatollah. I didn't know what to expect. I didn't know what to say, nor did I know what he was going to say to me. On the way over, I realized that the soldier assigned to deliver me had never met the Ayatollah before. He was so thrilled by the fact that he himself was about to come in contact with the Ayatollah that he made me nervous.

When I walked into the room, the Ayatollah was sitting at a table at the far end of the room. The soldier escorted me over to where he sat. The moment we reached the Ayatollah, the soldier fell down on his knees and greeted him in Farsi. For the first couple of minutes, they spoke to each other in Farsi. The soldier told me later that he was explaining to the Ayatollah how long I had been on my fast and why I was there.

After they finished talking, the Ayatollah turned his attention to me. He still spoke in Farsi, so the soldier translated for me.

"When will the Black brothers and sisters in America rise up and overthrow their oppressor the way we have over here?"

I responded, "When we get ten million dollars' worth of oil under the ground the way you have, we might try it."

The soldier went crazy. "You can't speak to the Ayatollah that way!" He immediately rushed me out the door and out of the building. As we neared the exit, a White American doctor stopped us.

"Dick Gregory, Dick Gregory, wait," he said. "I need to talk to you. They just tried to assassinate one of Khomeini's aides in Syria today. He was scheduled to speak tonight here in Tehran and that has been canceled. The Ayatollah wants to know if you will speak in his place."

"No," I responded. I said no for the same reason I had said no the day before to meeting with the Ayatollah: I hadn't come to Iran to get involved in their politics. I had come to fast and to pray until the hostages were released.

The soldier said, "You can't say no to the Ayatollah in his house."

"Well, I just did."

The doctor and I talked a few minutes. He had a copy of my book *Dick Gregory's Natural Diet* and he wanted me to know he had read it. He then told me that he was the Ayatollah's doctor and that the Ayatollah appreciated me being there fasting and praying. I told him to tell Khomeini that I would think about his request and would call him later.

The soldier and I left, and I thought we were going back to the hotel. But he took me directly to a pay phone. He called the Ayatollah's office and spoke to his secretary, translating for him what I was saying. I told him to tell them two things: "Tell them that I will speak this evening only if I can talk about their poverty-stricken areas. I can relate to them because I knew poverty as a child. And I will speak on the condition that I can finish my speech by saying, 'If you all ran the Shah out of the country only to replace him with drugs, you might as well have kept the Shah.'"

Those words scared the soldier so bad that he dropped the phone. He said, "You can't say that!"

"I said it, and damn it, I'm sick and tired of you. You are supposed to tell them what I'm saying, so do it."

The soldier got back on the phone and definitely told them what I was saying; I could tell by his response. He turned back to me with a blank look on his face. "Who are you?" he said. He just couldn't believe the Ayatollah had accepted my conditions. From that point on, everything changed with him. He started treating me like I was second-in-command to the Ayatollah.

He took me back to my hotel and came to pick me up later that afternoon for my speech. He also brought me a gift from the Ayatollah. It was something I'd never seen before: a picture of the Ayatollah smiling. So I made my speech that evening with the help of a translator.

A few days after my speech, the Ayatollah's people came back to me and told me we needed to talk. They had a little problem because they had told the people of Tehran that all the American hostages were spies, knowing that only four of them were. They wanted me to hold a press conference to tell the people of Iran that only four hostages were spies and that they should let the others go. Well, I wasn't about to call any Americans spies. But I did want to help.

So I came up with something to say that I hoped would convince them to let most of the hostages go. I said, "All important Americans, wherever they go, have someone to clean up after them and to cook. You know someone has to make the tea. Whoever was sent here to make the tea would never be a spy." Meaning that most of the hostages were innocent people — simple tea makers, not spies.

After that, I thought, they would hold a trial for the four spies and I would stay and fast and pray. They would find them guilty and sentence them to die. Because of my weakening condition, their next step would be to release the four spies to me and we would return home. Of course none of that happened.

I will never forget the morning in Tehran when I woke up and heard then-President Jimmy Carter's voice on a shortwave radio, saying he took full responsibility for what happened in Iran. I was lying there, thinking "Iran? What happened in Iran?" I continued to listen and that is how I learned about the secret U.S. rescue mission to free the hostages, a mission that had gone terribly wrong. The plane had gone down with no survivors. I couldn't believe it. I was thinking that this was the greatest military strategy since Hannibal.

When morning came, the Iranians by the millions were in the streets on their way to Tehran, believing there was going to be an American invasion. American sources said eight soldiers were killed in the plane crash, while the Iranians said it was nine. We later found out it was nine. The Iranians thought it was an act of Allah that the plane went down. I thought it was an act of the CIA because of two things that were found in the crash wreckage. One was six hundred thousand dollars in American money and the other was a notebook with about two thousand names of Iranian military personnel. Iran probably has the third mightiest army on the planet, after the United States and Russia. The Iranian names in that book implied that those people were traitors.

The Iranians went to the crash site and found the book with all the military personnel listed in it and the American cash. They thought the money was a bribe for all those military people to help overthrow the government. Iranian soldiers then went back and killed all of those people, believing they were traitors. They were putting two and three hundred soldiers per day in front of a firing squad.

On the one-hundredth day of my fast, the Ayatollah went on the radio and said, "I want to thank Dick Gregory, who is in the one-hundredth day of his fast and prayer vigil. We pray that the hostage crisis will end peacefully."

To show you the power of the Ayatollah, that very night I just happened to look out my hotel window and it seemed like there were a million people walking towards the hotel. They came with flowers and lighted candles to show their support. That was the first time I realized how much power that one man had.

The next day, I received a visit from the Ayatollah's secretary. He told me that I had to get out of Iran because they were expecting a surprise attack in the morning. I had promised the American people that I would stay in Iran until the hostage crisis was over. So I released a press release saying that I had problems with my tooth and I would have to go back to the United States for treatment. If I had received treatment over there and something had happened to me, no one would ever be able to convince the American people that the Iranians hadn't done something to me. I was coming home to get my tooth fixed and continue my fast and prayer vigil. I would go to the United Nations, hold a prayer vigil, and then walk to Washington, D.C.

So I prepared to go back to the United States. The Iranian soldiers took me to the airport. When I arrived in Paris, I weighed eighty-two pounds. From there I flew to New York, where I held a press conference. I said:

"I'm tired of a handful of men on this planet having the power to decide whether or not we have a nuclear war. I didn't request a meeting with the Ayatollah and the people of Tehran — they asked me. I went to Iran to pray. Prayer, not military action, is needed for our two countries to reach a peaceful accord in this situation. We, the people of the world who believe in God, have something stronger than nuclear bombs. We have something more effective than armies or guns. We have the power of prayer."

Afterwards, I went to the United Nations, as I'd planned, and from there to Washington, D.C., where I sat in front of the White House for thirteen days. Every day Jimmy Carter would send someone outside to ask that I meet with him and every day I would say no. I told them I would meet with a Black staff member if the conversation was recorded. I also told them that the Ayatollah had given me a message for Jimmy Carter that I wouldn't give anyone else. Even when I did meet with the Black staff member, I didn't give him the message.

Actually, when the Ayatollah's secretary had originally told me that he had a message for me to give to President Carter, I had told him that I was not his messenger. He had apologized for asking. But I thought about it for a few minutes and then called him back.

"You know I'm not going to give Jimmy Carter any message, but I would love to know what the message is."

So he told me: "On January 20, 1981, as President Ronald Reagan is being sworn in, the hostages will be released."

On Carter's last day in office, the American hostages in Iran were released, but it was the Reagan administration that largely got the credit.

23 Happy Birthday, Martin

Ronald Reagan was a Republican whom the majority of Black folks felt they couldn't trust. They were right. But, despite his standing with most Black people, Reagan was endorsed by the likes of Sammy Davis Jr., Hosea Williams, Ralph Abernathy, and Medgar Evers's brother, Charles, who was the mayor of Fayette, Mississippi, at the time. On December 9, 1980, one month before his inauguration, Reagan invited Williams, Abernathy, and Evers — the supposed three wise men — to meet with him. They all wanted favors for supporting him. I will never forget what Hosea later told me that Ralph and Charles asked for at that meeting. Ralph, being the Southern preacher that he was, said, "Well, a preacher ain't a preacher unless the president comes to speak at his church. I would like for you to come to Atlanta and speak to my congregation."

Charles Evers said, "Well, I got this dairy farm down in Mississippi, and I sure could use some Jersey heifers."

Hosea, the real wise man, looked at Ed Meese, who was conducting the meeting, and said, "I want President Reagan to make Dr. King's birthday a holiday."

Meese responded, "If King's friend Jimmy Carter didn't make his birthday a holiday, why should we? This meeting is over."

The meeting was over — but the subject of a King holiday was not. Hosea and thousands of other Black folks were not finished with the Reagan administration. They did not stop until they got what they wanted, and what they were determined to accomplish was the establishment of a national holiday in honor of Dr. Martin Luther King Jr.

If I had to go to war and lay my life down for anyone from the Movement, one of those people would be Hosea Williams. I know that he would lay his life down for me, too. Even today, he continues to fight for the poor, and no church in the country has a program like his to feed the hungry on Thanksgiving and Christmas. Hosea is a man of strong convictions, believing deeply in what he feels is right or wrong. That philosophy resulted in him publicly disagreeing with many Black leaders, yet he would gladly die for any of them.

When Nelson Mandela came to Atlanta in 1990, he was scheduled to speak at Georgia Tech because it was the largest available facility in the area. Hosea thought Mandela should have been presented at one of the Black colleges in town, and there was no changing Hosea's mind. He protested from the beginning of Mandela's visit to the end. That night he was arrested and went to jail. Many leaders thought he was wrong and even embarrassing, but I wasn't mad or ashamed of Hosea's actions because I knew he was doing what he felt was right. If any of those people who were embarrassed by his actions were ever under attack, Hosea would be there to defend them — his loyalty is without question.

I will never forget back in 1976 when President Carter allowed Fidel Castro to send mentally deranged criminals to federal prisons in America. Why would America say to its enemy, "Send me your insane criminals," and no one questioned this action? One of the places they sent them was the Atlanta Penitentiary. When I went to Atlanta to protest their imprisonment, Hosea agreed to come with me and picket the federal prison where they were being held. We were out there for about an hour when prison officials escorted Hosea in to see the assistant warden. When he came back out, he had this strange look on his face.

"Nigger, what have you gotten me into?" he asked me. "They said you were crazy. Now there are not ten people in this country that don't believe I'm crazy because of my conviction, and I knew the warden and everyone behind that wall feel the same way. I know something horrible is going on behind those walls for them to call you crazy and talk to me like I'm sane."

"Man," I said, "they have Cubans in there who can't speak English, and they're being used as human guinea pigs for research. That's no different than slavery." We came here from another country and we didn't speak the language. We were brought here against our will, caged like animals, and that's what they are doing to those Cubans.

But Hosea wasn't even listening to me — he already knew something was very wrong, just from the fact that they had tried to convince him that I was crazy and he was not. He knew that they thought we both were crazy. We stood out there for another four hours, refusing to leave. They finally arrested us and took us to jail, but they wouldn't press charges. That was one of the oldest tricks in the book: if they don't charge you with any crime, you don't have the right to ask them any questions. We were eventually released and our protest ended. Months later, the prison allegedly caught fire. How convenient! What really happened to those Cubans is still a mystery to many people. But it was not a mystery to me. Of course they held a press conference and said that some of the Cuban inmates could not be accounted for. They said that many had burned to death and some had escaped. I don't believe that and Hosea, as a true friend, stood by me on that one, just as he had stood up to ask Reagan point-blank to declare King's birthday a national holiday.

Reagan eventually passed a bill that established Martin Luther King Jr.'s birthday as a federal holiday, but it wasn't done out of the goodness of Reagan's heart — it was done because of the brilliance and determination of Coretta Scott King. She put together a coalition of people who respected Dr. King and were committed to bringing about the establishment of a holiday in his name. When Reagan signed the bill, he invited three hundred Black folks to attend the ceremony in the Rose Garden at the White House. I'm glad there were witnesses, because otherwise I would have suspected him of using invisible ink.

Every time I see a "Martin Luther King Jr." highway or street, I think of Coretta, because it never would have happened without her. Today the King Center in Atlanta has an average of 3.5 million visitors per year, including one million tourists from Japan.

Dr. Martin Luther King Jr.'s birthday is the only holiday in the history of America that celebrates the life of a Black man. And it is the only holiday, aside from Christmas, that celebrates the birth of a man who was not president of the United States. Making Dr. King's birthday a holiday said something very important to America. I said a prayer when it was made official. It meant that everything we did during the Civil Rights Movement was official. It meant that all those conspiracies that they had put out there about Dr. King and so many others were lies. Then I thought of all the people who had died — Medgar, the Kennedys, Malcolm, and all the people whose names we don't know. I prayed for all the people who had nervous breakdowns and all the people who were wounded. So many people were framed and just thrown in jail. But that day, they said, we are wrong and you are right. I didn't think this government could do anything better than making Dr. King's birthday a holiday. But in the spring of 2000, they announced that they would build a monument in the nation's capital of Dr. King. What a moment! I can't wait to go and sit at the master's feet, to see a monument of a Black man towering over the nation. When it is finished, we will have monuments to Washington, Jefferson, Lincoln, and Martin, the real king.

I'm glad King's birthday is a holiday, but White folks need to know that we have never needed them to validate who Dr. King was to us. Every year, long before it was an official federal holiday, we went to Atlanta and celebrated in his honor. People were celebrating his birthday all over the country. Parents were even keeping their children out of school. The truth is White folks wanted to make Dr. King's birthday a holiday a long time ago, but they wanted it observed on Sunday. That's when I realized the true strength of Coretta; she said no. She stood strong on her belief that Dr. King's life and work were important enough to interrupt the commerce of America. She joined forces with Stevie Wonder and others in the civil rights community and marched on Washington, demanding that Dr. King's birthday become a federal holiday. Myself, Jesse Jackson, Andrew

Young, Ted Kennedy, and many others showed up. Ted spoke at that march and he said, "There is no way out." He was right. Stevie even wrote a song, "Happy Birthday," that people are still singing twenty years later. The time and effort he put into the King celebration and that march in Washington were incredible. Stevie is more than an entertainer, and he has had a profound effect on this country in more ways than he ever got credit for. I have worked with Stevie on a number of causes, and he can see the way the world should be much better than most people can with their eyesight.

24 Going the Distance

In 1981 I decided to go on a seventy-day fast to prove what happens to the human body when it is deprived of sufficient food and water. This would be different from both times that I ran across country. When I ran from L.A. to New York, it was primarily to dramatize world and domestic hunger — I wanted to establish a Black presence in the world hunger problems. I also wanted to prove that your body does not need food as much as it needs nutrition. This latest fast was to show what goes on inside the human body during starvation. I wanted to know. When the seventy days were up, I was planning to walk and run from New Orleans to Baton Rouge in three days. First, I needed a hospital to make it official.

In July, I checked into Flint Goodridge Hospital in New Orleans. During my fast, the doctors would study the effects of malnutrition and starvation on my body. This fast was mainly for the purpose of research and would be the first study of its kind. Dr. Joseph Allain Jr., an internist, and Dr. James Carter at Tulane University headed the medical research team, along with many other doctors and nurses who monitored me hourly. At forty-nine years old, I dropped from 154 pounds to 104 pounds. At one point during my fast, my condition changed to the "zone of no return," which is a critical condition during fasting when the body defends itself by eating itself, consuming essential body protein. If you don't drink enough water and get the proper amount of rest, it can cause a permanent weakening of the body's immune system, irreversible damage to the brain or body, or a heart attack. At that point my doctors wanted me to end the fast. I would not do it.

The reason for this fast was that I felt it was time that the scientific world stopped making excuses and lend their expertise to helping starving people. During this fast, twenty-eight people were dying from hunger every minute. A total of one hundred thousand people starved to death during the seventy days I was on that fast. The painful part of my fasting was not physical, it was mental — knowing that I could stop anytime I wanted to and millions of others had no choice. The medical community claimed that I had made it because I was in such good condition when I started. I paid them no attention, even though my critics included some of the finest professors of medicine in the country.

Dr. Robert Burch, a professor at Tulane University, said the data was useless because it was only based on one subject and the results would be different for the next hundred people who tried to do what I had done. "Even if you see something," Dr. Burch said, "it doesn't mean very much." He believed that the findings based on my fast were incomparable to those based on children born into a condition of malnutrition. I never responded when they made negative statements. The whole point of my fast was to aid and help those researchers who were looking for information about what happens to the human body and psyche during starvation. That mission was accomplished. My fast was not for doctors who are sitting around eating three meals a day and don't want to open their minds to serious research.

I broke my fast at ten o'clock on September 23, 1981, by ingesting six ounces of Formula Four X, my seaweed-based drink, so I could start a one-hundred-mile walk to the Capitol steps in Baton Rouge. I walked twenty-four miles the first day, but started to experience medical complications and had to return to the hospital. Actually, I collapsed and passed out, but somehow the media missed it and it was not printed until I talked about it later.

The next day, I was back out on my route. I knew I had to finish that marathon. To give up would be the same as saying no to the Civil Rights Movement. You have to finish every race to be effective with the people. The walk I had scheduled for three days actually only took eighteen hours. My oldest daughter, Michelle, was a student at Louisiana State University at the time, and she joined me in Baton Rouge. When we reached the Capitol steps, we knelt down and prayed with Dr. Carter, Dr. Allain, LSU men's basketball coach Dale Brown, and others from the hospital. When we got up from praying, I thought about my main man, Big Mike. *This one's for you, Big Mike,* I said to myself. It was the first time I had completed anything in years without his assistance.

Big Mike died in October 1977 in an alleged car accident in Massachusetts when he was on his way to pick me up at the airport. It was during the time that I was working with Marvin Gaye, and I was supposed to be on my way home to begin my annual birthday fast in October. Instead I stayed in New Orleans with Marvin and his new wife, celebrating all night.

In preparation for my fasts, Big Mike would always put up my tent in the backyard at the farmhouse in Plymouth so I would have total peace and quiet. After he put up the tent that night, he left to pick me up at the airport just as Lil had asked him to do; Big Mike would do anything for Lil. While celebrating with Marvin, I did something I rarely do and forgot to call Lil to tell her not to send Big Mike to pick me up. Thank God I had a late flight so he didn't bring along the children as he usually did. When he got to the airport, of course I was not there. One of the skycaps told me that Big Mike asked several people if anyone had seen me. When they said no he checked the next flight arrival and said he would be back. He then stopped at a tavern and from there we don't know what happened to him, except that my car was later found there. There is no doubt in my mind that he was killed because he was driving my car and mistaken for me. The authorities said he was killed in a hit-and-run accident, but the autopsy report showed that his injuries were consistent with those of someone who had been dropped from a high building.

In the middle of the night, Lil got a call from a Boston police officer who wouldn't give his name. "Mrs. Gregory, I just want you to know your husband didn't die the way they said he did." It was strange, Lil thought, but she knew it was a mistake and didn't panic. But the oddest thing about that night was the tent in the backyard. Lil remembered that shortly after Big Mike left for the airport, the tent just started going crazy. Noises emanated from it, and it started shaking as if a storm were blowing through it. Then it stopped just as suddenly as it had started. We both believe it was around the time Big Mike was being killed. When the wind stopped blowing through the tent, that is when we believe Big Mike took his last breath.

When things like that happen, you don't know what to do other than pray. I just believe that there is a place in heaven with a book that records the names of good folks in it when they leave this earth. I was blessed enough to have two of those people in my life, Big Mike and Jim Sanders. My children were deeply affected by Big Mike's death. He was home more often than I was, and he was the joy of that farm. Before flying his body home to Dallas, we had a memorial service in Plymouth so that all the people who knew and loved him could say good-bye. He wasn't just nice to my family; he was nice to everyone. At Christmastime, he would dress up like Santa Claus and go into town. He'd give all the kids candy, but what they really loved was seeing a Black Santa. Our youngest son, Yohance, who was only four at the time of the memorial, went up to Big Mike's casket and started rubbing his face. I don't know if he understood why Big Mike didn't respond, but he knew something was wrong.

I took my last trip with my man Big Mike when Lil, our older children, and I flew his body home to Dallas for the funeral. My mind raced back to all the war movies that Boo and I had watched: when a soldier goes down on the battlefield, no one stops but the medics. Big Mike was a soldier — he understood that, and so did I. Staying at Marvin Gaye's wedding celebration was like the night I did not go to Medgar's house when Richard Junior died: God had put me here to do His will and He protected me, even from death.

So I ran the distance to Baton Rouge without my friend, and at the end I stood there on the Capitol steps and saluted Big Mike. I will always miss him, and I know my wife and kids still do. He's the guy who was always there. If you said you wanted some watermelon in the middle of a December night, Mike could get it. Really! It was almost as if he weren't real, the way he would make things happen. Even before there were all-night drugstores, if you said you had a headache, Big Mike could leave for twenty minutes and come back with aspirin. He really did seem as magical as I felt walking from New Orleans to the Capitol steps in Baton Rouge — and maybe he was.

25 Let There Be Food

The success of my fast in New Orleans, along with a modified version of my Formula Four X, opened the door for my trip to Ethiopia in 1985. It was a trip I had wanted to take for years. America criticized the Ethiopian government for getting ready to spend millions of dollars to celebrate its ten years in power when it couldn't feed its hungry people. I took a group of Black folks, including Dr. David Allen, Martin Luther King III, and Dr. and Mrs. Joseph Lowery, and we got on a plane with a supply of Formula Four X.

When we got to the capital, Addis Ababa, the U.S. government announced that it was giving five hundred million dollars to Ethiopia's feeding program. But I soon discovered that the main problem Ethiopia had was not its food supply or lack thereof; their biggest problem was with the distribution of food. The people didn't have an infrastructure to feed the poor because the colonial government built the railroads to take natural resources out, not to bring supplies in. The colonial government had been ripping the people off by selling their minerals for years. So naturally, no railroads ran through the cities where the people were.

Now when the Ethiopians had a crisis, they were trying to bring food in with the same transportation system that the colonial government used to take resources away from them. That is when I learned that you will never wipe out world hunger until you understand the politics of hunger. If you are a leader of an African country and other countries send you eight hundred million dollars' worth of food and drop it on your shores, you still have to figure out how to distribute it. If you don't, the poor people are still out there starving in remote areas and the food is not within their reach.

Food companies are paid when the shipments leave their warehouse. There needs to be legislation that says the food companies will receive half the money when the food is shipped and the other half when the food is delivered to the people — not to the shores of their country. In all fairness to these food companies, they are in the business of producing food, not distribution. There is a simple solution: they need to connect with distribution companies to help get the food to the needy. So I decided during our trip to donate one truck to help distribute the food. To this day, I don't know how they found out, but someone from the General Motors corporate office called me and told me they would donate ten trucks for every one truck I purchased from them. I knew it would be great publicity for them, but I didn't care why they were doing it — they were making it possible to feed thousands, maybe millions, of starving people. Unfortunately, the plan didn't work. After a few days, we were told that General Motors trucks were not equipped to travel the roads of Ethiopia, but Toyotas were. So I purchased a Toyota truck instead, and donated it to a program to help distribute the food.

After that, Dr. David Allen and I met with Dr. Demissie Habte, Dean of the Faculty of Medicine at Addis Ababa University. When I showed him the scientific data we had collected in New Orleans, he allowed us to give Formula Four X to children who were close to death. They would not allow the formula in without milk, so we added milk — even though we were sure it cut the effectiveness by 50 percent. But it still worked well enough in the hospital that Dr. Habte wanted the formula distributed in the field (food and distribution centers, resettlement camps, and transit centers). None of the children we put on the formula died, and they all eventually went home. What we did in Ethiopia was barely talked about back in the United States outside of *Jet* magazine. But the lives that were saved were enough for me.

I also left Ethiopia with additional love and respect for Dr. David Allen. I felt very comfortable with the medical staff at all times because he was there. He, like the late Dr. Alvenia Fulton, is one of the finest minds on nutrition on this planet. Soon after our Ethiopia trip, Dr. Allen and I began discussing what to do with my Formula Four X. We also changed the ingredients to suit the needs of obese people. Dr. Allen, my business partner John Bellamy, and I went down to the Bahamas and mapped out a strategy to get the product to the people through the mail order business. John returned to Chicago, where he became president of the mail order company.

In addition to the mail order company, we opened the Dick Gregory International Health Institute in Nassau in 1985. The new facility on Cable Beach would accommodate fifty-six clients, plus a staff of doctors, nutritionists, exercise instructors, and masseuses, and was intended to help obese people lose weight by teaching them a healthy lifestyle. A young man named Reggie Toran, who became a lifelong friend, went down to help get the facility started.

Barbara Cain, a wonderful woman and beautiful spirit, became our program director and immediately moved to Nassau to coordinate everything for our first client — a man named Ron High from Brooklyn, New York. Ron weighed 850 pounds when we first met him. Ron had contacted *Ebony* magazine after reading an article about a young boy whom we had helped to lose weight. *Ebony* contacted us, and we went to visit Ron. He was thirty-two years old and doctors had told him that unless he lost weight, he wouldn't see his thirty-third birthday. When I first saw Ron, I was shocked. He looked like a huge piece of flesh with a head attached, and he was young enough to be my son. I knew I had to help him.

The first thing we had to do was weigh him. It was a task that was traumatic for Ron and for all of us. We had to use two measuring tapes to take his measurements because he was so large. We used a freight scale from Delta Air Lines at La Guardia Airport to get his weight, because a regular scale only goes up to seven hundred pounds. Then we started him on a fitness program. He would get up at 5 A.M. for a walk with staff members and me. After the walk, he would take a swim in the crystal-clear ocean waters that allowed him to exercise muscles that he couldn't otherwise use. The salty water also helped pull toxins out of his body. Next, he would jump rope for a while and then rest. His breakfast consisted of fruit and about ninety vitamins, minerals, and herbs per day. The rest of Ron's day was spent reading, meditating, and attending motivational meetings with the staff and me. We supervised him around the clock, and the doctors monitored his health daily.

Ron was a really nice man, and he was determined to lose weight. Our goal was to get him down to around two hundred pounds, and we figured it would take about two years. He started losing the weight, but the most important thing he had to do was to stay focused. Although Ron lost a considerable amount of weight, things were unfortunately not going as well for the clinic financially. We were forced to close the clinic, and Ron stayed in Nassau with some friends he had met. It would be years before we would hear from Ron High again.

To get things back on track, Larry Depte, an old friend whom I had run into at the airport, and I decided to start a second mail order company. Larry was president of the business affairs department for a recording company — and a certified public accountant. We talked for weeks and decided to start a new company called Correction Connection, Inc., based in Larry's hometown of Philadelphia. It would be an affiliate of Dick Gregory Health Enterprises of Chicago, and I was chairman and CEO and Larry was president.

Correction Connection, Inc., would sell Formula Four X and my new product called Dick Gregory's Nutrition Correction Connection. This new product would combat the nutritional loss caused by abuses of nicotine, caffeine, drugs, and alcohol. With Larry on board, I quickly got back to the business of taking care of obese people, and I continued my college engagements. We ran an ad in *Jet* magazine and the overwhelming response was another testament to the power of the Black press. Our mail order company received two thousand calls the first day the ad ran. Many people wanted to purchase the products, and others wanted to be distributors. We held workshops and seminars to train these new distributors on how to market the diets.

One day I got a call from my good friend Bob Johnson, the late editor of *Jet*, who told me he'd recently run a story about a young man by the name of Walter Hudson. Walter, who weighed fifteen hundred pounds (his waist was 108 inches around, his chest 138, and his right knee 56), had become wedged in his bathroom doorway, and it took paramedics and firemen four hours to free him. Bob promised Walter that he would call me. I agreed to visit Walter, and what I saw made Ron High look like a skinny person. Dr. David Allen went with me, and he, too, was shocked. We agreed that we would try to help Walter lose weight.

Walter Hudson lived in a house in Hempstead, New York. He had been a recluse for seventeen years. His sisters and brothers had tried everything they could to help him, but to no avail. They finally gave up and took care of him as best they could. When Walter got too big to go into the kitchen, they brought the food into his bedroom and would eat in there with him. The whole family revolved around him. He even had his own hot plate and food in the bedroom and would cook for everyone from his bed. It took him fifteen minutes to get out of bed and another fifteen minutes to get to a bathroom that was only ten feet away. He only got up to use the bathroom twice a month.

The first thing we did was set up camp in Walter's house. We had to put an office in the house to deal with the media. Within days of Walter's joining the program, his diet changed from hero sandwiches, Twinkies, and other junk food to fruits, vegetables, and Formula Four X. We were determined that he was going to get out of that bed and live a normal life. He had been so overweight at the time of his mother's death that he was unable to attend her funeral — because he simply couldn't get through the door. Walter didn't want much: he wanted to walk again; he wanted to be able to hang an ornament on the Christmas tree; and he wanted to visit his mother's grave. Within weeks he began to lose weight, and all of us were elated.

Though we had anticipated some media attention, we were in no way prepared for the avalanche of publicity. His story was so incredible that Phil Donahue, who revolutionized daytime talk shows, had Walter, Dr. David Allen, and me on his show. Donahue offered to have a wall taken out of Walter's house so that he could come to the studio. Walter refused, so the show was filmed at his house.

Donahue's producer, Lillian Smith, was very kind to Walter and to all of us. She is a great producer and a nice person. Behind every great talk show host must be a producer like Lillian Smith. The brilliance of Donahue and Lillian, along with *Jet* magazine's coverage, kept Walter Hudson's story in the public's hearts and minds. Walter became an overnight celebrity, the poster boy for many overweight people around the world. He was a man who was determined to lose weight — a lot of weight!

Walter was losing hundreds of pounds and folks were obsessed with him. They would stop me in airports and ask, "How's Walter?" He was a wonderful man and a beautiful human being who just wanted to visit his mother's grave. Sales at Correction Connection were going through the roof.

Meanwhile, I was faced with a moral dilemma: Walter had a phobia about leaving the house. He was seven hundred pounds lighter, and I had a long talk with him about it being time to walk out that door. He refused to leave the house, and I told him that I could not continue his treatment if he did not. I was not equipped to deal with Walter's associated phobia about leaving home, but I didn't want to abandon him. I told him that I could not continue to treat him from his bed; he would have to leave the house to get the specialized care he needed.

We agreed to call a press conference at which time Walter had the choice of either walking out the door or telling the world that he wasn't ready. There were at least a hundred reporters at his door the day of the press conference. I walked to the door with Walter and, God, did the people outside cheer for him! But Walter just could not cross the threshold. I had to explain to the press why we could no longer treat him. It was over. We packed our things and went home.

I was deeply concerned for this man whom I had grown to love and care about. The whole world loved Walter. The next news I received about Walter came three years later from Ron High. They had become friends over the years. Walter was dead at the age of forty-six.

26 Fire with No Flames

Our relationship with Walter Hudson resulted in obese people from around the world calling Correction Connection for help. Walter's story gave them hope. We knew we had to find a new facility to house clients as soon as possible. Most of those people who wanted to come to the facility had no money to pay for it, and some of the people who did have the money didn't want to pay for it, either.

Now, the product itself was another story. It was still selling like mad. And one of the funniest encounters I had while selling it was an incident that I used in my act for years. A three-hundred-pound woman walked up to me one day at the Black Caucus Convention Expo in Washington. My good friend Herb Jubirt and I were sitting at an information booth talking to people about the clinic and the diet when she stopped by. She wanted to purchase the special we were advertising, two cans for twenty-two dollars.

"Dick Gregory," she said, "look at me. I'm a welfare sister, a Black person just like you. I weigh over three hundred pounds. How do you expect me to pay twenty-two dollars to buy that stuff?"

I looked at this big woman. "If you go to the supermarket and pay enough money to get as big as you are, why should I get it off of you for free? You are out of your mind."

She said, "Let me get two cans, my man!" She laughed so hard that they had to pick her up off the floor. People just started lining up behind her to buy the product.

Correction Connection, Inc., was still riding high from the Walter Hudson publicity, and I was invited to Japan to appear on a show called *Super People.* Mike Paltelino, one of the younger guys enrolled in our program, was being presented as the man who had lost the most weight in the least amount of time. I was appearing as the person who had developed the formula that made it all possible. My friend Reggie Toran, who was now a manager with Correction Connection, Inc., and Mike Paltelino went to Japan a day ahead of me. In the meantime, I had a meeting with Larry Depte about some managerial problems we were having. We disagreed about many things in that meeting and decided to dissolve our partnership. I figured that the few days I would be in Japan wouldn't make a big difference and that we could work things out through our respective lawyers when I got back to the States. I was wrong.

When Reggie and I returned from Japan, my relationship with Larry had gone beyond repair. We dissolved our business relationship and ended up in federal court for the next three years. During the entire time royalties I'd earned worth almost three million dollars were tied up. The amazing thing about that year, 1989, was that, due to the publicity from our relationship with Walter Hudson, my weight-loss product was the number-one product sold through General Nutrition Centers (GNC). That was a major accomplishment because GNC was, and still is, the number-one nutrition store in the country — and they still carry my product.

But even the proven worth of our product was not enough to offset the problems that my family and I were about to face. Thank God that Eugene Jackson came into our lives. I don't know what would have happened without his generosity. Eugene had made his fortune in communications and came to my financial rescue. I had known Eugene for many years, but our relationship had grown closer through an organization that we now call "The Family." The Family started in 1985 when two wonderful people, Barbara and Tom Skinner, came up with the idea of having annual retreats called the Skinner Leadership Conference to bring together Black leaders from around the country to come talk about their personal lives, religion, and their children. Tom is now deceased, but fifteen years later Barbara is still the mother of the Family. I'm sure that it was Barbara who made Eugene aware of what was going on with my own family financially.

Eugene has a big heart, and that meant more to us than the money. Lil could just pick up the phone any time we needed anything and Eugene would take care of it. But I don't think Eugene thought our predicament would last for three long years — I certainly didn't. Even with his help, we started to sink into a dark financial hole. At the time, I had six children in college. Things became so bad at one point that two of my children had to withdraw from college for a semester. During this entire time the almost three million dollars that I had was tied up in federal court. God, the pain my entire family had to endure was traumatic for each and every one of us. But I took strength from the fact that our daughter Michelle was the only one of my children who was actually born into poverty. And fortunately, she was not old enough to remember. I kept thinking about that and how we pulled ourselves up from poverty. Surely we would be okay this time.

I didn't want to be bitter. I prayed harder than I had ever prayed in my life. Thank God for the Civil Rights Movement and the whole Dr. King Spirit. Because of the Movement and Dr. King, I never let myself get bitter or angry. I never lost sight of my work for the people and the Movement as the court battle lingered between Larry Depte and me. I still had my college lectures, and there was a new war going on, the war against drugs. Father George Clemens, Reggie Toran, a few other people, and I had been demonstrating in drug-infested neighborhoods across the country for months. But nothing could prepare us for Shreveport, Louisiana. The drug problem was so bad there at that time, I think that if the Colombians had run short of cocaine, they could have borrowed some from Shreveport. Seriously. They had a place that was like an open drive-by market for drugs; it was about eight blocks long, and they were selling so many drugs that they had created a traffic problem so bad that it would take you two hours to drive through.

The Reverends James Green and Joe Gant, both from Shreveport, called me about coming down there to help with the drug problem in their community. I agreed to go and I asked Lil and Father George Clemens to come along with me. Father Clemens had been protesting stores that sold drug paraphernalia for some years, and we decided to confront the problem head-on by holding a press conference in Shreveport about the drug situation. Next we decided to stop at one of the stores that sold drug paraphernalia. We sent Father Clemens in to make the purchase. I just could not understand why, if it was illegal to sell drugs in America, wasn't it illegal to sell drug paraphernalia. So Father Clemens went into the store in his Catholic priest attire. The clerk starts going crazy when she sees him looking at the drug paraphernalia. Father Clemens comes out and tells us what they are selling and how much. We all go back in and Father Clemens asks the clerk to remove it from the store. She calls the police immediately, not because we asked her to take the drug paraphernalia out of the store, but because she had probably never been talked to like that by Black folks. So the police arrive to arrest us and the first thing the Black cop who came said is, "Oh no, I'm not having it on my record in history that I arrested Dick Gregory."

He turns to me. "Mr. Gregory, I don't want to arrest you. Do you mind if I go out and call for someone else?"

Well, the White clerk is looking at us all in total disbelief. So the Black cop calls for a second cop, who was White, to come, and he arrests us all. As they are taking us out of the store, the little hillbilly cashier says, "I ain't never seen nobody that wanted to get arrested before."

So we went to jail and spent the night. We got out the next morning and went back to the same store. The same cashier went nuts when we returned.

"Who do you think you are?!" she shouted at me.

She didn't say it, but she had "Who do you think you are, Nigger?" written all over her face. Now it's become a racial thing.

I responded, "If you think that the good White folks of this town are going to let publicity go out all over the world that this fight is about your right to sell drug paraphernalia, then you really have missed what is going on in this world."

We eventually left the store and went to the real battlefield in Shreveport: we put up a tent in A. P. Palmer Park, which was practically off-limits even to the cops (unless they had backup) because it was so violent. When the police were called in, they had to go in six at a time. The drug dealers were so powerful in this park that they would play basketball for ten thousand dollars each and pile the money up on the ground and no one dared touched it. We held a press conference and announced that this park was now off-limits to all drug dealers. Well, guess what? When we stepped back from the mic, the drug dealers stepped to the mic, raising hell. That's right, one drug dealer got on the mic on local TV and said, "He can't tell us what to do. He must be crazy. How can he tell us what to do? If y'all want to buy drugs, then keep coming."

We stayed all night in that tent in the center of the park. The town went crazy. That was the first time I realized that it's not the drugs that would bring this nation down, it was the fear — the fear that held innocent people prisoner in their own neighborhoods. Although America has only one-twentieth of the world's population, we consume 67 percent of the world's drugs. So now you know the rest of the world doesn't have the drug problem that America has. We must then ask ourselves, is this the price we pay for racism? Is this the price we pay for putting our foot on one group of people to make them stay down? Is this the price we pay to let the foot stay on us, without fighting back? I realized how afraid people really were when I noticed that there were no dogs barking while we marched. That's right, people were so afraid that they wouldn't even let their dogs come outside.

Eventually those same scared people started to come out and march with us. One family came by with their new car and left it there with us for as long as we needed it. They brought food, water, whatever we needed. Old women with aprons on would walk along the sidewalk trying to keep up with us, telling us how grateful they were. They reminded me of that old Black woman in Mississippi who would look at her White boss and say, "I ain't doing this for them, I'm doing it for Jesus." The way I see it, anyone has the right to use drugs and abuse their body if he chooses to. But you don't have the right to abuse an entire neighborhood. Grandmothers are not supposed to have to walk through drug dealers to get to the corner grocery store. So that is what we were fighting for. We noticed that a whole town of people started to smile. They were smiling because they knew that help was on the way. We had people from all over the country come in to show their support: Congressman Charles Rangel, Andy Young, Coretta Scott King, and many others. They came because they know and understand what we are fighting against; they know that there is no such thing as Chicago cocaine or GooseNeck, Tennessee, crack. I tried to tell people fifteen years ago that once this drug war heats up, the drug dealers in the big cities are going to move to the rural, unincorporated areas where there are no narcotics cops. Eventually, that is exactly what happened, and people are still trying to figure out why we have drive-by shootings in towns with populations of one thousand.

The Black brothers who were pushing the dope in Shreveport became so mad at us that they started saying it was a racial thing and they were Black, too. Then they got really crazy and said the White folks had sent us in because the racist White system didn't want to see Black brothers making that kind of money. The main person attacking me, the head drug dealer that we shut down, ended up in jail for robbing a bank. The same White system that he thought had sent me there had allowed him to do what he was doing for so long that he became addicted to the rich lifestyle. When we shut his operation down, he robbed a bank.

Needless to say, I had started to spend so much time in Shreveport that the little money that wasn't tied up in federal court was slowly fading away. You will never believe what happened next, just when I thought we didn't have enough money to stay in Shreveport another day. My stepmother died, and I guess she had an agreement with Big Prez, because each of his children got ten thousand dollars. Can you believe that? Big Prez gave me some money. Lil had gone back to Plymouth and when she called me to tell me the check was there, all I could say was, "Thanks, Pops." So we stayed and marched and prayed until we won.

I eventually left Shreveport and continued my college lecture circuit. My case against Larry Depte continued in court until October 1991, when Judge Joseph L. McGlynn Jr., magistrate of the U.S. District Court for the Eastern District of Pennsylvania, ruled in my favor. After years of struggle, I now had my company back. It was bankrupt, but the war was over.

But in the meantime, we had been evicted from the farmhouse in Plymouth because we couldn't pay the mortgage. Thank God I am a comedian. When you are first and foremost a comic, you can somehow laugh when the family home goes into foreclosure. You can somehow make jokes when you realize that your company, which is now bankrupt, was worth millions just two years earlier. But a sense of humor is the most helpful when your wife is crying her eyes out.

"Give me a break. We haven't paid a house note in two and a half years. What are you crying for?" But I knew why Lil was crying, and it was not funny at all. This was probably my tenth eviction, but it was Lil's first. We just could not work out an arrangement with the bank, and they repossessed the farm. The four-hundred-acre farm had been Lil's safe haven for the past nineteen years; it was a place where she could raise our children in peace. She did not have to be a celebrity wife there, just Lil and Momma. Now she was being forced to leave. When the final moment came, we laughed and she cried. We talked about all of the good times we had in that house and how good God had been to her, to us, and to our children. Then we got on our knees and prayed.

Afterwards, Lil did what she always does: she picked herself up, brushed herself off, and made preparations to move out. I sat there alone for a moment and thought about our children, mainly Yohance and Ayanna, because the farm was the only home they had ever known. And I was sure Christian barely remembered living in Chicago. Now we had to find a new place to call home.

I asked myself the two questions I always ask when in doubt: Have I violated God? *No.* Have I violated the law? *No.* When I can answer no to those two questions, I am always okay.

The good thing about the court order evicting us was that they had to handle the packing and storage of our belongings. They also had to be quick, since we only had forty-eight hours in which to move out. I'm sure Lil was glad we didn't have to pack. It would have taken her forever to pack up the thirty years of our life together that were stored in that house. It had been more than forty years since that landlord on North Taylor Street evicted Momma; now here I was, being evicted again. The difference was that the landlord always let Momma back in. There was no turning around for us. For a split second we were homeless. We watched as the movers labeled the boxes and took them to storage.

Nine of our children had either already moved away or were in college. Lil, our daughter Paula, and Paula's baby, Shayla, went to live in a hotel that night we were evicted, while I had to leave for Washington, D.C., where I had a speaking engagement.

That night after I finished speaking, I went to my hotel room and called Lil. She was no different then than she had been thirty years earlier when she gave birth to Michelle on the floor of Dolores's apartment. Every time I tried to apologize to her about the farm, she would just cut me off with her angel voice and say, "We will be fine, Greg." That was my strength to get off that telephone and keep going. God and Lil are the only things in my life that have stayed the same through all these years. Today when people call me, with good or bad news, if they need help, whatever it is, I tell them to call Lil. Lil has always sorted out the problems. I think if someone called me and told me I had lost Lil like I lost Momma, I would say, "Call Lil." She's just always been there, strong and beautiful. That's the part that hurt so bad after losing the farm. The children had places to live, the money has always come and gone, but hurting Lil was more than I could bear. I was so uptight that I forgot about the money we had, until Lil reminded me.

Eugene Jackson had given her a check for six thousand dollars. I think for a moment Lil had forgotten, too. So within four days, Paula found us an apartment in Plymouth with the money from Eugene. We had to pay month-to-month because, I'll tell you, your credit ain't no good after your house has been repossessed. It's a nice apartment, a good place for Lil. It's the place that we now call "home." I'm on the road a lot and the children are all grown. Therefore, Lil would have been on that big farm all alone if that had not happened. Our family had started out living in an apartment back in Chicago, and we were perfectly content to be in an apartment again. Some days I am actually grateful to God for the eviction.

I'm even more grateful to the higher powers that be when I remember a vision I had one night back in 1973 when I was in jail in Chicago, arrested on a speeding violation. Due to my long history with Daley and the City of Chicago police department, my bond was one hundred thousand dollars. One hundred thousand dollars! I refused to post it. In my cell that night, I dreamed that Chicago was on fire, yet there were no flames. I tried to relate this vision to the Great Chicago Fire of 1871 that raged for twenty-nine hours and covered seventy-three miles of streets. I thought I was dreaming until I saw this guy standing at the door, smiling. I tried to wake up again, then realized that I was not asleep.

Lil was in the hospital giving birth to Yohance when I had that strange vision. And we left Chicago the next week for Plymouth. About three years later, I was reading *The Chicago Tribune* and ran across an article that scared me worse than Mississippi. The article stated that the Hyde Park/Kenwood area of Chicago had one of the highest death rates in the world due to a strange type of bone cancer. It was the same street where we had once lived — Fifty-fifth and Hyde Park — where the pollution was really bad. The article further stated that the authorities and the medical community couldn't explain this phenomenon. I was curious, so I did some research and realized that the first nuclear reaction took place at the University of Chicago at Stagg Field at Fifty-fifth and Cottage Grove, as part of the Manhattan Project. Many years later they had to tear the stadium down, because the radiation was still there. Well, in order to have nuclear reactions, you have to have nuclear waste. The way they got rid of the nuclear waste was to dump it in the concrete every time they got ready to build a new building in the High Park/Kenwood Area. Now someone should go back and ask the University of Chicago, what did you do with the nuclear waste? Then they should do to them what the lawyers did to the cigarette industry. Or better yet, go and check the buildings, to see if they are still radioactive.

I realized that was the vision I had years before, a fire with no flames. Can you imagine what would have happened if I had stayed in Chicago with my wife and ten children? The possibility of one or more of us developing bone cancer was extremely high. So leaving Chicago was a blessing, and I know in some way losing the farm in Plymouth was, too. Whatever the reason, Lil bounced back so beautifully from this latest challenge. She has the strength of Job, and she knows that home is the place where you love and are loved, even if it's an old run-down house on St. Louis's North Taylor Street or an apartment in Plymouth. Paula eventually found an apartment of her own in the same complex and lives right across the way from Lil. When I'm in Plymouth, it's a joy to see Lil's face light up when the grandchildren run across the walkway to see their grandmother.

When I see them together, I know we were not evicted. We just moved on.

27 Nothing from History

I know I used this example earlier in the book, but just as a reference, imagine yourself going up a hill on a battlefield, and your best friend or brother is wounded right beside you. No matter how badly you want to help, no one is allowed to stop except the medics. That's the way life is when you are a real soldier — no one can stop except the medics. I learned that lesson in the Movement. I learned it again when Big Mike was killed. I had to watch soldiers go down and only their names live on. Medgar, Martin, Malcolm, the Kennedy brothers — so many people were killed, and we had to keep going. We would go to a funeral one day and march the next. You simply kept going. This time, *I* was the wounded in a different way, and I knew I had to go on. I'm not comparing my court battle and eviction to losing people I loved to violent deaths, but I felt a similar adjustment to the pain, and this overwhelming feeling that I had to keep going in spite of it all.

Wounded, I continued my college speaking engagements. One day, I got a call from Wyman Smith, a friend in St. Louis. He said that Katherine Dunham, the internationally renowned dancer, was fasting to protest the repatriation of Haitian refugees. He understood her cause but was concerned for her health, and he wanted me to come and check on her. She was calling for a national movement to force then-President George

Bush to change U.S. policy and allow some fifteen thousand Haitians to remain in the States. They had fled Haiti after President Jean Bertrand Aristide was overthrown in 1991. The U.S. Supreme Court had ruled that they were actually fleeing poverty, not the threat of political violence. Poverty, in the eyes of the Court, was not life-threatening. The Court rejected the refugees' argument that they were endangered by the present political climate in Haiti. They were denied political asylum and ordered to return to their native country.

Katherine started her fast on February 1, 1992. I first saw her on the nineteenth day and she did not look well. I was worried, and people around her were concerned. They wanted me to convince her to stop the fast before permanent damage was done. But I understood what she was trying to do and rather than dissuade her, I joined her in the fast. Local activists Cleo Willis and Sylvester Lee joined in as well.

We decided to march to the federal building in East St. Louis. Before the federal workers arrived, we chained the front doors together so no one could get in. After chaining the doors, I noticed a White woman standing on the steps holding a sign in protest of the return of the refugees. She learned about our plans to protest from our press conference and came down to show her support. But she had her own story. Her name was Heddy Epstein, and she told me the story of nine hundred Jewish refugees who escaped Hitler's army in 1939. They arrived in the U.S. thinking they were safe, but instead they were sent back to Germany aboard the U.S.S. *St. Louis.* Upon their return, the refugees, including her parents, were murdered by the Nazis. They only allowed two children to enter the United States, a little boy and, yes, a little girl named Heddy Epstein. I stood there and listened, and I thought about the struggle of people around the world. Before we could finish talking, the federal marshals arrived and used bolt cutters to cut the chains. We refused to leave and they took us to jail. We posted bail and the next morning we were back at the federal building. This time we chained ourselves to the doors. They cut us loose and took us back to jail.

I refused bail, so the government got nasty. Federal prosecutor Stephen Clark informed the judge that I had an outstanding arrest warrant in Washington, D.C., for my participation in a demonstration the year before at the White House. The judge offered to let me pay the fifty-dollar fine for the D.C. arrest, but I refused. So, with taxpayers' money, they transported me back to Washington. They came and got me out of jail at 4 A.M., but no one knew that they had taken me to Washington. First they took me from East St. Louis to St. Louis. If they were trying to scare me they had succeeded, because I know how many Black people, from Emmett Till to the three civil rights leaders in Mississippi, were taken away in the middle of the night and killed by White men. I wasn't foolish enough to think times had changed enough to keep me safe.

While I was being transported cross-country, Heddy held a press conference and told her story again. Then Heddy asked the one-million-dollar question: "Haven't we learned anything from history?" *Hell no,* I thought when I read her story in the paper a few days later. The refugees were returned to Haiti after Aristide negotiated with his government and they promised that he would be put back in power. He made a personal visit to see Ms. Dunham and convinced her to end her fast. I do believe that if Katherine had not ended her fast when she did, she would have died. But I also know that she was willing to die. Like many real human rights activists, Katherine Dunham was making a statement by fasting to the extreme that she did. She was saying that death is better.

The fact that we've learned nothing from history became even more evident a few months after our protest in St. Louis. Thirty years after the Watts riot, all hell broke loose in South Central Los Angeles when three White policemen were acquitted on the charges associated with their brutal beating of Rodney King the year before. If those angry Black folks had crossed Olympic Boulevard into Beverly Hills, it would have been an even worse bloodbath. The National Guard sent in troops who did little to stop the rioting — but they made sure to contain the chaos within the Black community. It was the J. Edgar Hoover days all over again; during the sixties, the government didn't care about Black people rioting as long as they stayed out of White neighborhoods.

Because of the racism that exists in this system, no one is paying attention to the fact that 100 percent of every riot in the Black community since the sixties has had two ingredients: a ghetto dweller and a cop. No riot has ever started over anything else. Not jobs, not poverty, but police brutality. But we didn't need to see the Rodney King incident on film; we already knew that it was happening. White folks needed to see it. Once they saw the film, the White racist system tried to justify it. They had a trial, and the cops were acquitted. The truth about the riots that followed has not yet come out, because there are questions that still have not been answered.

You know something is wrong when parents in a free democratic society have to teach their Black sons and daughters to be very careful and polite when disrespectful, racist White police officers confront them. They are told you don't talk too fast and you can't talk too slow and you must behave yourselves. We never tell our children how to act when a Black cop pulls them over. In many cases when a Black cop stops them, the first thing many of them say with an attitude is, "Why are you pulling me over? Y'all should be out fighting drug dealers." But many of us would never say that to a White cop. The relationship between Black folks and many White cops in this country is so far out of hand, and at some point we Black folks have to start taking some of that blame. We let police brutality run rampant through our community. There are thousands of Black police officers across this country. When have you ever read in the paper that a Black cop handcuffed a White person and shot them in the back of the head? Do you think that the Black cops are not committing police brutality against White folks because they are more spiritual or better trained? No, they don't mess with White folks because they know that the White folks won't tolerate it, plain and simple. When we Black folks decide that we are not going to tolerate police brutality, then it will stop. There's something wrong with a people who have more fear for their enemy than they have love for their children. We have to understand and say to America and the police that enough is enough. We can say it through commerce and shut this country down. Being harassed by a racist cop is worse than being chased by the KKK. At least during the sixties, we could run from the Klan. If you run from a cop today, he thinks he has the right to shoot you, even if you have not broken the law. This new movement that has started against police brutality must and will stop any racist cop from even thinking about harming Black and oppressed people. In the meantime, we have so many scars from what has already been done to us.

One shocking example is the recent case of Amadou Diallo, the young Black man who was gunned down by four White police officers on February 5, 1999, in New York City. Officers Sean Carroll, Edward McMellon, Kenneth Boss, and Richard Murphy claimed that they were looking for a rapist when Mr. Diallo stepped outside and walked into death. The police said they thought his wallet was a gun, and checked it out by shooting at him forty-one times. Nineteen bullets hit their mark. The police said they shot so many times because Mr. Diallo kept bucking — as though he was some guerrilla nigger who wouldn't go down.

The people demonstrated and Reverend Al Sharpton stepped in, and things began to change in the case. Reverend Sharpton is a veteran civil rights leader and president of National Action Network in New York. His organization now has offices across the country. He brought in an independent pathologist, Michael Baden, who discovered that the first bullet that hit Mr. Diallo severed his spine. From that moment, he couldn't even move his eyelids. So how could he "buck" when he was paralyzed? The cops were so vicious that after Diallo fell, they shot him in the heel of his foot. The bullet exited through his kneecap.

The facts of this shooting were so outrageous, even the White press had to report it fairly. They referred to Diallo as a fine young man, a street vendor from Guinea, West Africa. Mr. Diallo had hoped, they reported, that one day his family would move to America, the land of the free. Instead, his parents Saikou Amad and Kadiatou Diallo came to the States to claim his body that had been ripped apart by a racist system that kills hundreds of innocent people for the crime of being Black.

On February 25, 2000, the four officers were acquitted of all charges. Again the justice system had looked the other way as Black America cried out in pain. Of course the attorneys for Mr. Diallo promised an appeal, and I promise you that Al Sharpton will be there fighting until justice is served.

One problem with the cops in racist White America is that they are being overworked, underpaid, and improperly trained. A person in England goes to school longer to become a cab driver than a person in America goes to school to become a police officer. Something is wrong with that. But forget about the bad cop for a minute and think about the good ones. Even they are not adequately trained. Just imagine what happens to them in an emergency. When we are in trouble, we call them. When they are in trouble, whom do they call? If you came home one day and found twenty people dead in your apartment building, you would run outside yelling and screaming and then you would call the cops. When the cops arrived, they would have to make sure that the murderer was not still in the vicinity, check out the bodies, deal with the evidence and the families of the victims. What does that do to their brains? No one has prepared them for that.

When a traffic cop approaches the scene of a horrible accident to find that someone has been decapitated, he or she has to take that image home with them where they are expected to be a spouse and a parent. Where is their therapist the next day? Police officers have the highest divorce rate in this country of any other occupation and many of their second spouses are prostitutes. More police officers die from suicide than are killed in the line of duty, and a large percentage of them die from their own gun. This is a direct result of not being trained to use their guns properly. The same circumstances that make them commit suicide will make them go upside someone's head. And guess whose head is their number-one target? Black folks! Police brutality has gone on in this country for decades.

I will never forget one day in St. Louis in 1992 when I was walking from my hotel to the health food store to purchase some vitamins. I heard a voice say: "Hey boy! Come here." It was a White police officer. I thought he had to be putting me on as he placed his hand on his gun and said it again.

"Boy, I said come here."

I thought I was going to die, because I knew I wasn't going to walk to him. Which meant he was going to come and get me. I threw my hands in the air and said, "First, I'm not your 'boy,' and if you want me, come and get me." My mind was racing and I just kept thinking back to the Movement. *Death is better than being reduced to a boy by this racist White cop*, I told myself.

He came over and handcuffed me. Then he shoved me in the back of the police car and drove me to the health food store across the street. A crowd gathered, and another cop came along and recognized me. They walked away and talked briefly, and then the cop who recognized me walked back to the patrol car. What he said made me madder than the actions of the first cop who had arrested me.

"Mr. Gregory, I'm sorry about this. It was a mistake and you can go now."

"Go?" I responded. "He has arrested me and I am not going anywhere."

By now more cops are on the scene and two of them went inside the store, where they got a White stockboy to say that I was the shoplifter they were looking for. The stock boy came out to the car and identified me.

"Boy," I said, looking him dead in the face, "you know damn well I'm not who they are looking for. I'm Dick Gregory, and I have products in your store. If you want your job, you'd better tell them the truth."

To my surprise, he was not afraid of the cops. "Mr. Gregory," he said, "I'm sorry, they did tell me to lie." He walked away.

After I refused to get out of the car, they had no choice but to take me to jail.

When I got to the jailhouse, a Black female clerk at the desk said to her redneck colleague who had arrested me: "Oh, you have fucked up now!" They all had a good laugh, but it wasn't funny to me. When they were through laughing, they put out a story that I was arrested for shoplifting and the story went all over the world. When I got out of jail, boy, did we go to war! With the support of the Black churches, Black radio and civil rights leaders in St. Louis, we came up with two plans of action. First, *Jet* magazine and the *St. Louis Post Dispatch* printed the true story about what had happened. Second, because of the police's vigorous actions towards me, Black people in St. Louis started protesting, something that mostly White men in St. Louis had enjoyed for the last fifty years: the Stroll, a fifty-two-block area in our Black neighborhood where prostitutes sold their bodies daily.

All over the world, prostitutes can be found in what is known as the "red light districts." It is a place away from children, away from schools, away from family homes, where men come and meet women for the purpose of buying sex. But this is not the case in the United States — the red light district in America is in our neighborhoods (Black neighborhoods), next to our children, our schools and homes. Along the Stroll in St. Louis, we had a situation where mostly White men were driving through, blowing their horns and making indecent proposals to the preacher's wife, the Black woman doctor, mothers, and schoolteachers. The night I was released from jail, we held a rally at one of the churches and something started to happen outside that blew me away. The police came and started doing something they used to do years earlier as a scare tactic: they began writing down all the license plate numbers of everyone who was in the church. They would do that during the Movement and later they would harass the people whose names they had written down. God stepped in and the Black folks in that church came outside and formed human shields around every car that the police got close to. Then they started yelling at the police: "Get out of here! There are no criminals here." The police left. It was beautiful to see Black folks stand up for themselves and righteousness that way.

We held a press conference and told them that the cops had seventy-two hours to close the Stroll. We went to the Stroll and marched and sang songs. This made the prostitutes angry, but we weren't trying to put them out of business; we were just trying to get them to stroll in the neighborhood where their customers worked: downtown! I went on several radio shows and one White interviewer wanted to know where I thought the working girls should go? My answer was simple: "They should go downtown and sit on the bench in front of the First National Bank. That's where most of their buyers are, not in our neighborhood." One of the major forces that kept the Black folks in St. Louis informed of what was going on was radio talk show host Onion Horton of *The Onion Show*. Every day he pumped into Black folks' heads what we should be doing to close the Stroll and why.

As we continued to march, one Black prostitute got so angry that she ran up to us while we were marching and said she was going into her house to get her gun, because we had no right to interfere with the way she chose to make a living. When she came back outside, I was standing on her porch. Beside me stood Cleo Willis, who has been fighting for civil rights and Black folks in St. Louis most of his adult life. We weren't afraid; we didn't move when we saw that gun. I think the person who was shocked and probably afraid at that point was the prostitute. This is where you draw the line, not just with the police, not just with racism, but when wrong is attacking right, you have to look it in the face and say, if this is the way life is, then let it end now. Most of the time right will win over wrong, as it did with that sister that night. I told her that if we had to die, we would die there for what we believed in. At that point, my sister Dolores returned to the Stroll with a police officer and the prostitute dropped her gun and ran.

Our position in the protest was that the police had arrested me for no reason, and we were determined both to punish them for their vigorous false arrest and to reduce the crime rate at the same time. We also wanted to embarrass them for turning their backs on the crimes that took place daily on the Stroll and we wanted to shine some light on it. We did both: the crime rate eventually went down in that neighborhood by 10 percent, and eventually the Stroll faded away. But something else happened while we were demonstrating that bothered me more than anything that has happened during the entire time I have been a part of the Civil Rights Movement.

Though we are good friends now, Clarence Harmon, who was police chief then and is mayor of St. Louis now, fully supported the White police officer who arrested me. That's what the fraternal order of the police department will do — no matter how wrong their officers are, they will stand beside them. But we have to say the same thing to them that we say to the FBI or the KKK: Enough is enough and we are not going to tolerate you anymore.

That incident in St. Louis was very important, because it proved once again that our formula of marching, protesting, and praying works if you have the Black family and the Black church supporting you. Remember, I was not out there marching by myself. Black folks with their children were out there marching every day until we closed the Stroll. Black folks said no, we are not going to stand for this. Not only did we make the White boys pay, we took back that part of our neighborhood. We stood up and said we weren't afraid.

28 Blood off My Shoes

One day there will be some form of healing for Black folks, mainly Black men. I think the first step, and a good one, was Minister Louis Farrakhan's Million Man March in October 1995. I knew four months before the march took place that it was going to be a success. I was in Los Angeles fasting, and one day I walked to the store to pick up three gallons of distilled water. The hotel where I was staying was on a hill. I walked three blocks with those three-gallon jugs of water before I started praying.

"God, please send me someone to help carry this water." Then I saw this Black guy fixing a roof, and he saw me at the same time.

"Hey!" he shouted. "Dick Gregory! You need some help?"

I had never been so happy to be recognized in my entire life. The brother walked me all the way back to the hotel carrying the water. Before he left, he stopped at the door and asked me, "Mr. Gregory, are you going to the Million Man March?"

"Of course. Why?"

"Oh, I'm just asking. I'm going. See?" He reached in his pocket and pulled out his plane ticket. He told me he was so excited that he had been carrying his ticket for two months, and the march was still four months away.

Even White unions with billions of dollars in their coffers hold their marches on the weekend so nobody misses work or during the summer when the children are out of school. But Minister Farrakhan wanted to make a point, so the Million Man March was held on a Monday in October. It was the most beautiful Monday in history for Black folks. Attendees had to take a day off and let the world know that we would make the sacrifice for our people. Point taken! White folks were shocked. I attended with my three sons and Reggie Toran, and a cameraman from ABC's *20/20* followed us around all day. I got up early that morning and took them to see some homeless men. Then we went to the park to witness Black men who had come from all over the country sleeping in the park, just waiting for the march. I wanted my sons to see and know the difference between the homeless men whom we had seen earlier and the brothers who were waiting for the march to begin. The men who were in town waiting for the march slept outside with their dignity, because there were no more rooms; they were waiting for something to happen. The homeless men were just sleeping because they had no place to go and nothing to look forward to.

The White press reported that we Black men didn't accomplish anything at the Million Man March, and that is not true. We went to Washington with our hearts heavy to lay down our hurt, and the world saw that. There were no fights or violence of any kind. Black men said "excuse me" if they stepped on another man's shadow. It was beautiful. There were only two arrests made that day. One was a White man who called in a bomb threat at a phone booth at Fourteenth and U Streets. But he was so dumb that the police kept him on the phone until an officer arrived and arrested him. The second arrest was a Korean guy who was selling hot dogs without a permit.

The White press totally ignored the Million Man March until one week before it actually happened. I was glad the press didn't start covering the march until the last minute so they couldn't take credit for the one-million-plus Black men who did show up. They started writing about the march after they learned that every hotel and rental car agency was sold out within one hundred miles of Washington. You couldn't even get a train into Washington. Hotels ranging from the Ritz Carlton to Motel 6 were booked. That tells you the range of people that was there. No one other than the Pope could bring that many people together. Minister Farrakhan is conveniently not looked upon by the media as a religious leader, though he is the leader of the Nation of Islam. His official title is not a civil rights leader, but a religious leader, just like the Pope is the leader of the Catholic Church. The press attacks Farrakhan at every possible opportunity, but they never discuss his role as a religious leader. When you see members of the Nation selling papers, they are selling religious material as it relates to current events.

Why does this country resent the Nation of Islam? They do everything the old White boys think a "good nigger" should do. They are clean. They are quiet. They work hard and don't bother anyone. So why is it so hard to respect them? Maybe it's because they don't drink, they don't smoke, they don't do drugs. They don't do all the things that a White racist system put out there to cause destruction in our communities. I am so glad that most Black folks don't pay the media any attention when it comes to the Nation. When they see those brothers and sisters in their own neighborhoods doing positive work to improve the quality of life, they are not afraid. They see the Muslims treat their neighbors and themselves with love and respect. The Muslims are not mean or hateful in word nor deed.

But the government resents Farrakhan just like they resented my friend Malcolm X. Their contempt for Malcolm was deeper than most people realized. Was it what he was trying to teach us, or was it his Muslim faith? Or was it because he was a non-Christian? A strange twist in history — no one seemed to notice that the same people who resented Malcolm put him on a stamp in 1999. When I saw the stamp, I could only say, they finally found a way to lick Malcolm.

Even in his grave, the government still tried to attack Malcolm through his daughter. When the government accused Malcolm and Betty's daughter Qubilah of hiring a hit man to kill Farrakhan in 1995, I was very suspicious. It, too, smacked of the FBI's handiwork. The White thug she was supposed to have hired was actually a government agent.

No one wanted to address that fact, and an out-of-court settlement was reached in May 1995. The government decided to settle with Qubilah after it became public information that their so-called hit man was one of them. Qubilah settled for the alleged crime and consented to undergo two years of psychiatric treatment that included treatment for chemical dependency. She further agreed to enroll in school or get a job. But the most telling part of her agreement was that she had to sign an affidavit denying her allegations of an FBI frame-up — or face a possible ninety years in prison and a $2.25 million fine.

Betty and Minister Farrakhan had to find a way to make peace among themselves. Neither of them was going to go along with whatever script the FBI had written. Whatever conflicts they had, they were both smart enough to work it out without the "assistance" of the FBI. When that happened, she was not Dr. Betty Shabazz; she was not Malcolm's wife. She was a mother, doing what good mothers do to protect their children.

I defended Betty's daughter on every radio station that allowed me airtime. We must always protect the children of our leaders whom the system has destroyed; we owe them that. But there was no one present to protect Betty two years later when a fire occurred at her home in New York that severely burned her and led to her death. I went to the hospital almost every day to check on her condition and see her daughters. My son Yohance would sleep there and help the girls. I was glad, because he kept us informed on how they were doing. It was just hard to focus on anything else. It was such a painful day for Lil and me when we heard that Betty had succumbed to her injuries. I thought about how strong she had been when Malcolm died. I figured she would somehow pull through this one, too.

Betty had always been so good to my family and me. When I was really down financially, she would never let me pay for anything when she was around. If we were out to dinner, I'd feel her hand under the table trying to slip me the money to pay the tab. Betty Shabazz never became a "professional widow;" she was Dr. Betty Shabazz, a great educator. When she spoke, she talked about the Movement and the future of Black folks, not about Malcolm. When Coretta and Myrlie arrived at the hospital to see Betty, I wondered what was on their minds as she lay dying. All three of them had shared the trauma of losing their husbands violently. Betty's untimely death created unspeakable pain and was a profound loss to all of us. But many Black folks accepted the authorities' explanation for what happened to our dear Betty, just like we accepted their explanation the year before for the murder of Ron Brown.

Ron Brown's death was one day shy of the thirtieth anniversary of Dr. King's death. Ron was the first Black U.S. Secretary of Commerce. He died in a plane crash that also took the lives of thirty-four others while on a business mission to assess possible post-reconstruction trade projects in Bosnia and Croatia.

A few months after his death, an article appeared in the *Pittsburgh Tribune* alleging that during a post-mortem examination, a hole was found in the top of Ron Brown's skull. A number of military pathologists who performed the autopsy agreed that it appeared to be a bullet hole. One air force doctor, Colonel William Cormley, examined Brown's body and said he concluded that a gunshot wound was an impossibility. He, of course, didn't request an autopsy. But Lt. Colonel Steve Cogwell, who was in the room at the time of the examination, said the head wound could have been caused by a bullet. After that, two senior pathologists with the Armed Forces Institute of Pathology (AFIP) also came forward with their concerns that the hole in Ron Brown's skull could possibly be a bullet wound.

On Christmas Eve, 1997, Joe Madison, the Reverend Walter Fauntroy, radio talk show host Mark Thomason, and I led a protest and prayer vigil outside Walter Reed Army Hospital, headquarters of the Armed Forces Institute of Pathology. I roped off the entranceway with yellow crime-scene tape and was arrested for refusing to leave. I spent Christmas in jail. I hoped that someone would pick up the ball and run with it, but the *Washington Weekly* was the only paper that ran my story right away. Other papers would follow, but the *Washington Weekly* was the only paper to print my statement when I was released from jail. It read:

I got arrested for civil disobedience and I chose to stay in jail from

Christmas Eve till yesterday where I began a fast. I didn't start drinking water till just two days ago [five days after my arrest]. We have a radio show we do here, and I asked the people who have followed me down through the years — I just asked them to fast and pray with me while I'm in jail so that the truth about the Ron Brown fiasco will come out.

This has nothing to do with reports of a bullet hole. We're talking about the way they investigated the crash. Whenever there's a plane crash, the air force investigation is in two steps. First, there's a Safety Board Investigation, which begins by looking for signs of foul play. Once they're convinced that there was no foul play, the next step is an Accident Investigation. In this case, they went right past the Safety Investigation and straight to the Accident Investigation. . . . And so this is why, on that basis alone, we're demanding an independent investigation. . . .

Now, one of the most important things here is the picture of Ron Brown lying on the ground. His body is intact. But there was a report in *The New York Times*, Friday, April 5, 1996 [two days after the crash], with the headline, "14 Bodies Are Airlifted To Makeshift Morgues." The report states that the bodies were so mangled that some of them will probably have to be identified by fingerprints. Now that's not the picture that we saw of Ron Brown. So there appears to be a conflict on that point.

There's another story that ran in *The Akron Beacon*. And this story made the front page because it's about a native of Akron, Ohio. The headline reads: "Aide Calls Commerce Secretary A Father Figure: He Identified Body At Crash Site." Well, I know that can't be true because they wouldn't have let anybody go up the mountain unless they were part of the emergency rescue team. The story says, "Akron native Morris Reed never will forget the weather as he and others struggled to get to the site on the mountain where his boss, Commerce Secretary Ron Brown, and 34 others perished. 'It was like the earth had opened up and was crying,' Reed, 26, Brown's confidential assistant said yesterday. 'There was so much lightning.'" Now, he's not aware that in *Aviation Weekly*, April 8, it said that the weather wasn't that bad.

My reason for reprinting my *Washington Weekly* interview here is to point out just a few of the reasons I kept marching and going to jail regarding the Ron Brown case. Look how many years it took for the public to become aware that the FBI played a part in Dr. Martin Luther King Jr.'s death. There were only a few Black leaders yelling conspiracy back in 1968, and I want the record to show that since 1996, I've said that Ron Brown's death was no accident. When the real truth is finally exposed, people will know that Washington, D.C., talk show host Joe Madison, and long-time editor of the *Amsterdam News* Bill Tatum, and a few others were on target when we challenged the government of the United States regarding Ron's death. The Justice Department ruled Ron Brown's death an accident due to weather conditions, but Bill Tatum fearlessly challenged every inconsistent story printed about Ron's death. "All we want," Tatum said in print, "is the kind of investigation that the president would allow if his dog was run over under mysterious circumstances. Why should we ask less for Ron Brown than we would ask for a dog?" Tatum is the publisher of the country's leading African-American newspaper and makes no apologies. He went on to say, "The American people, and Black people in particular, deserve better than this. I'm really pissed off and you can quote me on that." When I read Tatum's commentary, all I could say was thank God for the real Black press and thank God for Bill Tatum.

Reverend Jesse Jackson, Congresswoman Maxine Waters, and NAACP President Kweisi Mfume requested an investigation, but three years later, nothing has happened. I have protested several times since I first called for an investigation into Ron Brown's "accidental death." I didn't care what the press wrote then, and I don't care now — I will keep marching and praying for Medgar, Malcolm X, Dr. King, Little Emmett Till, and all our other fallen warriors.

I have always said that we have the blood of our ancestors on our shoes. If we don't clean up this mess, including Ron Brown's murder, then the blood will still be there. Each time I'm out there marching, shouting for justice, I think that maybe, just maybe, when I get back home, I'll have gotten some of that blood off my shoes.

29 On Broadway

While I was trying to walk some of the ancestors' blood off my shoes, I made a stop Off-Broadway at the Samuel Beck Theater in New York. For the first time in twenty-four years, I was doing stand-up comedy.

"It was so cold in New York that day, I looked in my closet for my coat and my coat had on a coat."

Opening night was on December 14, 1995. It was a cold, snowy winter night, much like the one thirty-four years before when I had opened for the Playboy Club in Chicago. As I sat backstage at the Samuel Beck Theater, I remembered how I had gotten off the bus at the wrong stop that first night in Chicago and how I'd had to run all the way to the club. And I thought about how Victor Lounge tried to talk me out of going on in front of that audience of White Southerners in town for a food convention. It seemed that racism had dictated my whole life up until that fateful night at the Playboy.

After my first night Off-Broadway, one headline read "Dick Gregory Live, He's Back." When I read the reviews, I have to admit that I was relieved that they were good. One paper called me a "genius." I'm funny, but I'm no genius.

There have only been three geniuses in comedy: Mark Twain, Lenny Bruce, and Richard Pryor. Mark Twain was the only one of the three who came out of the madness unscathed. Of course writing is different from standing flat-footed onstage. But he was so far ahead of his time that he shouldn't even be talked about on the same day as other people. Look what he did with his brilliant satire. For the first time in the history of literature a White man talked about a relationship between a Black man and a White boy. Black men didn't even have names; they were referred to as "nigger." Then he wrote *The Adventures of Huckleberry Finn* in 1884 and talked about "Nigger Jim." Today some people are outraged by that book and they have banned it from many school districts. That's really a shame, because the truth is that Twain was the first writer to refer to us as someone other than a nigger. He attached a name to nigger and made Jim human. Now, we were always human to each other, but Twain's "Nigger Jim" made us human to White folks. They read about Jim and Huck Finn going down the Mississippi River. Nigger Jim was not putting the bait on the hook for Huck — they were fishing together as friends. Twain once wrote an article for *The Buffalo Express* that outraged White folks. It was entitled, "Oh Well, It Was Just Another Nigger." A Black man in Memphis was lynched and then they discovered that it was the wrong man. Mark Twain responded that a bunch of good Christian White folks had lynched a Black man the other day, then found out it was the wrong guy, but so what? It was just another nigger. White folks were outraged. But Mark Twain kept writing and putting a face with the names of Black folks. He was so special that he was born during the appearance of Halley's Comet, which only comes every seventy-five years. When Halley's Comet came again, Mark Twain died that very day.

Almost a century later two other geniuses, Richard Pryor and Lenny Bruce, challenged and strengthened the right to freedom of speech and they both used the stage as their workshop. In order to experience their genius, you had to be there and smell the sawdust. People say that Richard learned from me, and maybe a little of that is true. But Richard Pryor surpassed me in many ways. Richard made it by staying Black. I remember the first time I saw him perform. This White guy came to visit me while I was performing in L.A. He told me there was a new comic in town and that I just had to see him. He also said this new comic would never make it big, because he takes his penis out at the end of each show and shakes it at White folks. This new comic he predicted would never make it big was Richard Pryor. So I went to see Richard for myself and after his show, I went backstage to talk with him.

"Richard," I said, "as a Black father in a racist society, I really have no right to tell you what I am about to tell you. But because this is such a racist country, Black children need to know our Black geniuses. And as long as you end your show like that, they will never know you."

A few years later I was in Atlanta when we passed a theater and I saw all these people standing outside trying to get in. I asked the driver what was going on and he told me that Richard Pryor was in town and had sold out three shows in one night. Over two thousand Black people were still standing outside at the end of the last show. White folks had written him off until he started selling out shows. But after that, they said we'd better bring him downtown. I feel they had written him off because he had stayed Black; he didn't go to the nightclubs to tell anyone's story except that of Black folks and the Black experience.

Until we know more about Richard Pryor, we will never know what made him the comedic genius he is. Perhaps years from now, we will find out what life experiences contributed to making him so brilliant. When Richard started using the word "nigger" in his act, he made it so that every time he said it, it lessened the sting of hearing that word aloud. Richard knew how to play that game — he'd turn every negative thing White folks said about us into a satire and turn the whole thing around. Unfortunately, Richard has been in a wheelchair for years now and he cannot speak very well, because of his M.S.; but his laughter and his ability to make us laugh can never be silenced. If I were a psychiatrist, I would prescribe to Richard the best medicine in the world, laughter. Yep, I would recommend that he get copies of his own tapes and listen to them day and night. He is before his time.

I really took the word "nigger" public in 1963 when I wrote my first autobiography, *Nigger*, with Robert Lipsyte. Dutton Publishing Company thought they were getting a humor book, but they didn't say that in the contract. So I turned in an autobiography. I turned in a book with hard-core facts about Black life in racist White America. Once I had submitted the manuscript and they read what it really was about, they wanted me to name it something humorous to trick White folks into buying it. So Dutton called a big meeting on a Friday and asked me to come back on the following Monday with a humorous title. I went back on Monday and took them the title *Nigger*.

Just imagine a White or Black person walking into a bookstore in New York and saying, "I want a copy of *Nigger*." People were afraid to ask for my book, and bookstore owners were afraid to put it in their stores. Some Black folks would go into a bookstore and say, "I want one of Dick Gregory's what-you-call-it." They just couldn't say the word. And White folks would say, "You named that book a title I just can't say." Or they would complain, saying, "I just can't stand the name of your new book." I didn't hear White folks complaining about the word *nigger* when I was growing up. I only heard them using it. If they had complained about the word *nigger* in the past, there would not have been a need to name my book *Nigger*. Titling my book *Nigger* meant I was taking it back from White folks. Mark Twain threw it up in the air and I grabbed it.

Lenny Bruce was another genius who had the same attitude about the word *nigger* that I did: If people felt free to use it in private, then we could use it in public. That was the edge Lenny had: he would use the word *nigger* and make many White folks ashamed, because they knew they were using it, too. God, what they did to Lenny. He was one of the few White Americans that the government treated as badly as they treat Black folks. The White folks hated him; they considered him a nigger-lover.

Lenny and I were friends, and I will always remember that he understood what the word "nigger" really meant. Lenny knew that word was a symbol of White folks' hatred of us. He knew what it meant to the point that he was afraid to go down South when I asked him to, and he was not afraid to admit it. In one of his books, Lenny mentioned that time I'd asked him to come down and march with us. Not only did he admit he said no, he did not lie about the reason, like a lot of entertainers would have. He admitted he was afraid of White folks' anger towards Black folks. That's how honest Lenny was. It was that honesty that made the racist White system hate and destroy him. They reported that Lenny overdosed in his home in Los Angeles. I do not believe that for one minute. The same government that tried to silence him had finally killed him.

I was so hurt to see the way the police officers treated Lenny's death. They left him lying in an open doorway while people just walked in off the street to look at his nude body with needles in his arms. But his work was far more brilliant than the system that destroyed him, so I guess Lenny had the last laugh.

If you really want to know who Lenny Bruce was, go get copies of his albums. They are still out there, just like Richard Pryor's. The great thing about both Lenny and Richard was that they were unique. You couldn't duplicate their comedic brilliance if you spent the rest of your life trying. There just was no one else like them.

Bill Cosby is another great comic. He can tell a story and no matter how long it takes for him to finish, people will wait to hear the punch line. That's one hell of a talent. I, personally, could never do that. I never did long jokes or stories; I do one-liners and then I am out of there. But Bill gives it to you in parts and you can just wait for that punch line to come and the roar of the audience. That's what comics call "cooking": when you have reached that special high. The audience's reaction and the chemistry in the room let you know when you have reached that point. If comics knew how to recreate that chemistry every night, they would do it. But if you did it every night, I think you would go crazy. I do know that sometimes I would sound so good, I'd wish I were in the audience listening to myself.

Many comedians have come and gone since my first gig at the Playboy when I made people laugh at the racist system that had destroyed Momma. I like some of today's comedians, but some of them use too much profanity. Don't get me wrong, I speak two languages: English and Profanity.

The real problem is not the profanity; it's the fact that they use it on TV If you want to hear something really filthy, go to the Friars Club in New York City and listen to their profanity. But that's never aired on national television like *Def Comedy Jam.* And the sister who comes on *Def Jam* talking about "she wouldn't suck her man's penis until he pays the rent" is out of her mind. You will never see a White woman talking like that about herself on national TV Never! The comedians who want to get on *Def Comedy Jam* know that they have to be filthy to even be considered. There is no room on that show for clean comedy. I honestly believe that if *Def Jam* allowed Black comedians to insult Italians, Irish Catholics and White women the way they insult Black women, that show would no longer be on the air. It's about respect.

While I don't appreciate some of the comedy routines on television, they are not nearly as devastating as gangster rap — and certainly not as disrespectful. The other thing is that comedy doesn't require the same effort as music does. People learn the lyrics to music, but how many people learn a comic's act? They laugh and then they go home. A little child will learn a record from front to back or sing along with the record the entire time. I don't know why, it's just something about music. I'm not talking about the kind of rap we hear from Queen Latifah or LL Cool J. I'm talking about gangster rap. Gangster rap is an insult to the Black family. Take a minute to look up the definition of "gangster" and "rap." Gangster means a member of a group of people banded together for some purpose, usually bad or negative. Rap means to deliver short, light blows. For our children, gangster rap means a succession of criminal messages.

Two of the strongest forces in the history of America are and will remain the Black woman and the Black church. Gangster rap was not created by Black folks; it was created by White folks, created to destroy the Black woman and the Black family. Imagine that you are a Swedish woman on vacation in the United States. You get in a taxi and the Black driver is listening to a gangster rapper calling Black women bitches and whores. This is your first time in this country, and you don't know anything about Black women. Stay with me now. The next week, you go home to Sweden and two Black American women executives from Xerox with Ph.D.'s are there on vacation. Well, you don't see them as two Black women from corporate America — you see them as bitches and whores because that is the image that has been planted in your mind the week before by a Black gangster rapper.

I believe gangster rap has also had a negative effect on the relationship between Black women and White cops. Consider the case of Tyisha Miller of Los Angeles, an innocent young woman who had an epileptic seizure while sitting in her car in 1998. She waved down a White man and asked him to take her young nephew to her family because she felt the seizure coming on. He did, and her family came back to help. They arrived at the car to find Tyisha suffering from a seizure with the doors locked. When they could not wake her up, her mother made the fatal mistake of calling the police.

When the White police officers arrived, they didn't see a frightened young woman, according to them. Instead, they saw what the gangster rappers call our sisters, a "bitch" who allegedly had a gun. When they hit on the window, she jumped, and they started shooting within seconds. I believe if they'd seen a White woman in the car, they would have relied upon a completely different set of assumptions.

While I blame the cops foremost, I believe the brothers and sisters out there singing gangster rap have to share some of the responsibility. They created this new and negative image of our Black women that has set the stage for violence. The cops said Tyisha fired the first shot. But guess what? There was no pin in the gun, and the gun was not registered in her name. We don't know if Tyisha ever even had a gun or if it was planted on her. Thank God for Johnnie Cochran, who is representing her family, and for Al Sharpton, who started demonstrating against the police department immediately. Hundreds of people protested with us, including Kim Fields, Reverend Randel Osburn, Reverend Walter Fauntroy, Joe Madison, Danny Bekewell, and Martin Luther King III. But we cannot expect them to do it by themselves.

To add insult to injury, when we went out to demonstrate the murder of Tyisha, we were met by other demonstrators. In the beginning the officers who shot her were only suspended with pay and we were protesting for them to be terminated and prosecuted. In support of those officers, over one hundred police officers shaved their heads. Like skinheads, they didn't say "I'm Klan" with a sheet — they just silently shaved their heads and went to work. It took months, but eventually all the officers were fired and are awaiting trial. But we simply have to stop letting them insult our Black women. We have to stop accepting their explanation for what happened in incidents like this.

Sometimes they insult our Black women in ways we don't even realize; it's almost in code. What I mean by in code is, for example, when a White man dresses like a woman, he is called a transvestite or a cross dresser. But when RuPaul dresses like a woman, the same media refers to him as a beautiful Black woman. What they are really doing, in my opinion, is making a statement to Black women: We are getting ready to kill you: kill your image of beauty, kill your image as a mother, as a sister and an aunt, and eventually kill your spirit.

You know there was a time, even as they were hanging Black men, when our Black women were the White man's darlings. Not that that's a positive. It is not. But at least when they were the "darlings," White men were not putting bullets in their Black heads. People will never believe this, but more Black men were lynched in America over Black women than over looking at White women. That's right, one day when the truth comes out, people are going to be shocked to find out that Black men were lynched more often for just looking at the White man's Black mistress than for looking at a White woman.

Many Black women no longer tolerate that kind of behavior and they are no longer the White man's darling, which makes them the enemy. Many of these Black women are nurses, teachers, mothers, and many of the White men who resent them have to listen to them give orders all day because those White boys are working for the sisters now. These women are not their secretaries; they are members of Congress, like Maxine Waters. And believe me, they are running the show and sending that White boy to get them files from the basement. What do you think that does to many of those White boys' heads?

Now on top of that, you create gangster rap to give many White men a negative image of our sisters. At some point, we as Black men have to accept responsibility for our sisters.

If we go back to slavery days, when White men came to Africa to enslave Black men and women, we know that they had no love for our people — they were merely stealing a commodity. They stole us away from our homes to sell us to American landowners; they would go to the Black male slave and demand that he have sex with a Black female slave he didn't even know in order to produce a child, so that the White man could sell the child, too. Those slaves were not having sex for enjoyment; they were having sex to stay alive.

Now think about the Black man who looked that White man in his eye and told him, "I'm not going to screw her, you do it. Because there ain't nothing that you can put in her that will produce a product that you can sell. Nothing." If he could have, the White man would have done it himself or gotten some little White boy to do it. But no one was buying Yellow slaves. So think about the dignity of all those Black men who said no. Yes, there were Black men during slavery who refused to have sex with their enslaved sisters — they chose death instead. They were chopped to death with an axe in front of all the other slaves to teach them a lesson. But God, it is their light that shines; it is the light of the man and woman who said no that gives us vision today. In the darkness of night, that is the light, and one day we will honor the ones who said "I choose death over doing what you want me to do. Death is better," many of them said. Can you imagine how many Black sisters had to fight off the Black brothers who wouldn't say no to the White man, the ones who wouldn't choose death? I can hear them cry out in the night, "How can you do this to me?" How many brothers held those women down so other brothers could do this? How many of those pregnant sisters jumped off a cliff and said, "I will kill myself before I produce something of mine for you to sell and use." But it didn't end with slavery.

That's right, another horrifying moment in history for Black women happened sixty-eight years ago in Tuskegee, Alabama. We have talked about the Tuskegee Experiment for all these years, but never mentioned the Black woman. President Clinton even brought the survivors to the White House recently and apologized. I was glad to see that happen, but I kept waiting for someone to say I'm sorry to the women who were also affected by that experiment. Everyone seems to forget that those four hundred Black men, who were injected with syphilis under the false pretense of a scientific study on colds, had families. They had girlfriends and, yes, babies were produced. What happened to them?

This experiment started in 1932, the year I was born, but what most people don't realize is that the public health service in Alabama didn't end the experiment until the seventies, when the media uncovered the story. Now let's discuss why they chose Tuskegee. Well, the White colleges that would accept Blacks — and there were not many — accepted only their quota. The other best and brightest Black minds went to all-Black universities. And Tuskegee was the Citadel for the Black intellectuals. Many wealthy Blacks from all over the world sent their children there. So you had the best and the brightest under one roof. Well, if we Blacks knew that was the case, White folks knew it too, and that is when they said, "Look at all these niggers under one roof, let's poison this well." I believe those who poisoned the well had it all figured out. All you need is for one of the men who has been infected to sleep with one woman in town. A month later, that same woman sleeps with a male student from Tuskegee. One month later, that male student sleeps with a girl back on campus. And there you have it: you are knocking out thousands of brilliant Black minds.

The most devastating part was that after the U.S. Bureau of Health got caught, we let their system dictate the protocol for their apology — and they never apologized to that Black woman whose lover unknowingly gave her syphilis. What about the Black baby she passed syphilis on to? The government can't undo what they did to all those Black folks, but someone someday will show how broad the entire racist act really was. Then the Black people have to stand up and say, yes, you infected me, but what about the Black woman? An apology is owed to our sisters. I wish that one of those gangster rappers would write a song called "Hey, What About the Sisters?" Young people, a serious price has been paid.

I have faith, however, and I believe that our sisters will survive. I relate their survival back to an incident that happened many years ago. When we lived on the farm in Plymouth, Lil had a part of the driveway paved so that the children could play basketball. One day I came home and there were holes all over the Blacktop. I couldn't believe it. It was less than a month old and I thought the children had caused the destruction. I didn't ask Lil what happened because she had this strange look on her face. You know the look, the "Don't mess with my children" look. Finally she said, "Do you know how the Blacktop got all those holes in it?" "No, I don't." "Mushrooms," she replied. That's right, mushrooms. You can cover me up, but I will rise again, even through the toughest times, right through the Blacktop like one of God's mushrooms.

Our women will rise above gangster rap and even some of the lyrics in blues songs that I also see as negative. Think about it. Hillbilly blues songs go like this: "I'm sorry baby that I hurt you." Some Black blues songs say: "I caught my baby with my best friend." Now, I have never heard any White man singing a negative hillbilly song about their woman; they sing about something they have done wrong to their woman. So why would the person from Sweden or Europe who has heard a gangster rap song or a negative Black blues song see an American Black woman with a Ph.D. and think anything positive? My question for gangster rappers is, why don't you sing about Black women who are scientists or great mothers? Many adults defend gangster rap, because they believe that these children are singing about their real-life experiences. My answer to that is a question: Why are we the only people singing about the negative side of our lives? Where is the rap about the Catholic priest who has been ripping off little boys? When will the Mafia do their rap? When will the White folks who have been dumping nuclear waste in oppressed people's neighborhoods do their rap? And as long as we're singing about negative things, will there ever come a day when they rap about bigger issues, like the Black men and women who were lynched in America? Or about how White business bankers are laundering drug money? Will they ever rap about that same banker denying Black folks loans every day? Or rap about the poor quality of schools and houses that they put our children in?

Bob Marley expressed himself and the conditions of oppressed people without cursing and calling Black women bitches and whores. I didn't understand the power of Bob Marley's music until we actually performed together in the early eighties. I got a call from his manager, saying that Bob had been asked to perform a concert in Harvard Yard at Harvard University and the only way he would do it was if I joined him. I didn't know what his request was about at first, but my children went crazy. We all went up there and when I listened to his music, I was blown away by his lyrics — he sang about this oppressed world and got his point across. That much is evident, because his music is still played all over the world; they still have Bob Marley tribute concerts every year and he has been dead for many years. Everyone from Lauryn Hill to Johnny Cash performs at these concerts and I understand it is beautiful. Maybe listening to Marley's music would provide some insight for gangster rappers into how to write songs that matter without cursing and disrespect.

There are just so many ways to express yourself as an artist, through song and words. There are so many positive issues and Black role models we should be celebrating. Take, for example, the brilliant Xernona Clayton, who every year gives us our Oscars. She has been with Turner Broadcasting for twenty-five years. Seven years ago she started the Trumpet Awards to honor African Americans ranging from golf great Tiger Woods to Jesse Jackson. She had the insight to honor Tiger before he rocked the world of golf. Even if she held the Trumpet Awards every month, there would still be Black folks left to honor, and why can't gangster rappers sing about them? Maybe some of the rappers could write a news article or a book to express their views. Then my three-year-old grandchild wouldn't hear their music just walking in the mall. We have to say to the negative blues singers and gangster rappers that they have done a disservice to the Black women of the world. Second, we must shut their income off by not buying the product. That's what C. Delores Tucker was trying to say. So instead of some young performer being mad at C. Delores Tucker, I would advise you to listen to her — she was fighting for the rights of the children who attack her today before they were born. Back in 1995, Ms. Tucker called me to say she was holding a demonstration at "Sam Goody's" against gangster rap. She wanted me to go with her. I didn't know what Sam Goody's was, but I did know that anything C. Delores Tucker did was righteous for our people.

When Ms. Tucker, Joe Madison, Reggie Toran, Mark Thomason, and I got to the music and video store, we started to demonstrate and I saw the store manager dropping a dime in the cops' ear. Let me tell you, I have been in jail for marching more than I've been out. I know when and from where the cops get their instructions. The store manager was telling the cops not to arrest us. Again, if you don't get arrested, you don't get any press. When I saw that exchange go down, I knew this was about more than just some nasty records being sold; it was bigger than that. We kept marching and refused to leave. Strangely enough, while we were marching, a bomb threat occurred in the same block and the cops tried again to make us leave. We refused, and because of the bomb threat, they had no choice but to arrest us. They really didn't want to take us in because, again, if you don't get arrested, you don't get the press.

That demonstration at Sam Goody's was the beginning of a long-running battle between C. Delores Tucker and the record industry. When you take on an entire industry the way Ms. Tucker did, you don't know what's going to happen next. She even bought stock in Warner Brothers so she could attend their stockholders' meetings. Lawsuits were filed and eventually they were all thrown out of court. I always knew that show business was a ruthless business — more so today than back in the sixties when I started. But I must admit, the music business is far more ruthless. However, C. Delores Tucker just stayed out there on the battlefield fighting for young Black folks and they don't even know it. Trying to protect them from themselves, trying to protect them from a racist system that they fall prey to.

Most of our youth don't even know they are a target of a racist system. That does not exclude my own. I learned that on July 11, 1996, during the Riddick Bowe vs. Andrew Golota boxing match at Madison Square Garden. I was in a hotel room watching the fight on HBO and talking to Lil on the phone. People were rioting for about thirty minutes, and we just couldn't believe how long the police were letting it go on. I was still talking to Lil when I saw the cops beating this young Black guy with dreads. I said to Lil, "That looks like our Yohance." I took a second look and said out loud, "That's Yohance!" At the same time, the phone rang on Lil's end and it was one of Yohance's friends from Tokyo, who was also watching the fight. Lil didn't have HBO, thank God.

My son Gregory was also there and he had tried to help Yohance. The police beat them both, threw them in a police car, and drove them downtown. I decided not to go to New York immediately, because Lil and I cannot go around telling Black folks that death is better, then when one of our children is beaten by a cop, we run to the scene of the crime. We tell other people to stand up to a mean racist system even if it means death, and we have to say the same to our own children. I told Lil they were all right and to let them stay in jail a minute. But when I got the news that false charges were being filed against both my sons, I went to New York.

When I arrived, I found that Gregory was not seriously injured, but Yohance had suffered a concussion, a blood clot in the brain, bruises, and lacerations to his neck and upper body. I was devastated to see Yohance like that and even more sickened to learn that the police had continued to verbally abuse and taunt them both with foul, racist slurs and epithets as they took them away. One of the cops looked at Yohance's dreads and, thinking he was Jamaican, said, "If you were in the Bronx, nigger, you would have a bullet in your head."

It's too bad that the cops didn't check Yohance's I.D. They would have been shocked to know that they had beaten one of the men who decided their pay rate. At the time, Yohance was one of the financial analysts for the New York City Council. What Black folks have to understand is that when some White folks see you, they don't see a schoolteacher or Ph.D.; they don't see you as president of a Fortune 500 company, or as a son or father; they don't see kindness; they don't see love — they see nigger. Yohance was employed by the City of New York, just as the officers who beat him were. He is also a graduate of Phillips Academy in Massachusetts, a high school that at one time 85 percent of the leaders of Fortune 500 companies had attended. Also, thirteen of the past presidents of this country went to Philips Academy. Yohance went on to

Howard University and graduated with one of the highest averages in the history of the School of Finance. But to the White cops, it was, "Oh well, just another nigger."

The cops saw none of that — they saw niggers when they beat my boys. Not only did they beat them for being Black, they tried to railroad them. Before my plane had landed in New York, they had charged Gregory and Yohance with assault, disorderly conduct, and resisting arrest. I immediately sent a letter to Attorney General Janet Reno, asking that she "investigate the criminal and unjustifiable attack" on my sons and prosecute those responsible to the fullest extent of the law.

I think about how close my sons came to death in New York, just as I had in St. Louis that day. Then I thought about the fact that they were Dick Gregory's sons and how it made national news. But what about Tom Smith's boys? They are just dead or imprisoned niggers. All the charges were dropped, and neither Janet Reno nor the Justice Department ever responded to my letter. I don't know if they investigated the matter, but I do know I never received a response. I have known Janet Reno for years, but she has yet to respond to my letter. So I wonder how many other people Janet Reno and her department ignore daily?

What chance do Black folks with no visibility have to seek justice? Their chances are as good as those Blacks and Latinos in Los Angeles who have been robbed, wrongly imprisoned, and even murdered by the LAPD. When that story started to unravel in 1999, the nation appeared shocked, but how can you be shocked when just eight years before, you saw them beating Rodney King with billy clubs on national television?

The LAPD scandal came to light when an officer named Rafael Perez was accused of stealing six pounds of cocaine from headquarters to sell on the street. When it was time for his trial he made a deal with the DA officers. A big deal! He has provided the DA with two thousand pages of testimony naming former colleagues in incidents that would land them in jail. He also admitted that he and his partner shot an unarmed nineteen-year-old man named Javier Francisco Ovando. After they shot him in the head, heart, and hip, they placed a rifle in his hand and said he attacked them. Well, surprise, surprise, he did not die, but he is paralyzed and will probably never walk again. When Ovando appeared at his sentencing hearing on a gurney, the judge lambasted him for endangering two police officers before sentencing him to twenty-three years in prison. The judge also lambasted him for not showing any remorse. Ovando had no reason to show any remorse; he was as innocent as my two boys were in New York that night. He just didn't have anyone to defend him and he couldn't defend himself. When I think about that incident with my boys, I just know that if my sons had beaten the cops, the Justice Department would have responded. I know if you want justice in America you can't call the Justice Department. That is the reason men like Reverend Al Sharpton will always be a vital part of New York City and the world. I was proud of my sons who fought for their civil rights.

While I thought my sons had been treated horribly, it didn't compare to the recent case of Abner Louima. He was at a nightclub in New York when a fight broke out and he was arrested along with everyone else. But for Louima, that was just the beginning of the horror. At the police station, several officers beat him and Officer Justin Volpe pushed a plunger handle into Louima's rectum, then pushed it in his mouth, breaking out his front teeth. I wondered what could possibly have been going through this young man's mind as he faced the possibility of such a brutal death.

Thanks to Brother Al Sharpton, Louima's case did not go away. I knew it wouldn't because I know Al Sharpton. On December 13, 1999, Justin Volpe was sentenced to thirty years in federal prison while his partner, Charles Schwarz, who was accused of holding Louima down, was given a separate trial and eventually found guilty. Volpe was ordered to pay Louima restitution of $277,495 and to pay $3,555 to another man who'd been victimized, Patrick Antione. Patrick's name and near-death experience have been overshadowed by the more horrendous abuse Louima suffered. Patrick Antione was beaten over the head with a flashlight that same night, for no reason, as the police searched for a Haitian. I guess they just finally said any Haitian will do. It never occurred to them that both men were innocent. Even if they knew, like Twain wrote, "Oh, well, it's just another nigger." When the verdict was read in the Louima case, brother Al stepped to the mic and said, "A deposit was paid on justice, but we were not paid in full. But twenty years ago, we couldn't get that." The thirty years Volpe did receive was largely because Al Sharpton and the people of New York consciously said no to the racism that allows some of the NYPD to beat Blacks and other minorities for a hobby.

I personally would rather live in a New York with Al Sharpton than to live in one without him. Al is always on point, marching to his own beat. When there are killings and other injustices, he's been there. They tried to write Al off, but when he ran for governor, he drew a sizeable share of the vote. When he ran for mayor, he pushed his opponent into a runoff. That's when funny things started to happen to Brother Al. The IRS suddenly discovered that Al owed them one hundred thousand dollars just when they thought he might become mayor. But none of that stopped him. Scarred, beat-up Brother Al just kept on going — sometimes all by himself. This guy is regularly ridiculed in the New York press and he doesn't care. White folks in New York know that if you do wrong, Brother Al will be there.

If you are in the glamorous city that never sleeps, forget about Broadway, Saks Fifth Avenue, or the Waldorf Astoria Hotel. If you want some real entertainment in New York, go find brother Al. He will take you to a show on injustice. He will show you the spot where they held Abner down and raped him with a plunger handle. Brother Al can take you to the location where they shot Diallo nineteen times. Then he will take you over to the Bronx and show you all the Black folks who fear that they may be next. If that doesn't entertain you enough, let Brother Al gather fine folks like former mayor David Dinkins and Ossie Davis. Ruby Dee will come along and march with Al to the street corner where they beat Patrick Antione and many other oppressed Black people for being "just another nigger." In the town that never sleeps, yes, that's Broadway.

30 Sitting on the Couch

When the producers of *The Jack Paar Show* called me thirty-eight years ago to appear on the show, I initially said no. I declined because Billy Eckstine had told me that Black entertainers were not allowed to sit on the studio couch when they were guests. Although I watched the show every night, I had never noticed that when Black folks performed on the show, they left the stage immediately after their performance. But many White people didn't; they were invited to sit and talk with Jack afterwards. Maybe no one would have noticed that I didn't sit on the couch, but *I* would know — and I knew how I would have felt when I got back to Chicago.

I cried because I knew it was a huge opportunity, and I knew I'd missed my big break. Minutes after I hung up with the producer, Jack Paar himself called.

"Dick Gregory? This is Mr. Paar."

"Hello, Mr. Paar," I responded.

"Why don't you want to come on the show?"

"I can't because Negroes are not allowed to sit on your couch."

"Sammy Davis Jr. sits down."

"Yes, he does, but he's a guest host."

But even then, Sammy wasn't sitting on the couch; he was sitting at the host table. Paar talked to me for a few more minutes.

"Come on in, Dick, you can sit on the couch."

My life is different because I demanded to sit on the couch. When I arrived at the studio, Jack Paar had no problem with it. I can honestly say there was no harassment. I kept wondering why it had never happened before. It was almost like an oversight on Black folks' part. We had just automatically accepted that treatment.

You have to understand the power of Jack Paar in the sixties to understand the importance of my appearance on his show. Not until Oprah has there been a TV talk show host in recent years with the power of Jack Paar. Going on his show was like having your book chosen as Oprah's book of the month. And we all know that every book that has been chosen since Oprah started her Book Club in 1997 has become a bestseller. But Oprah's true power was shown on April 16, 1996, when she ran a show about dangerous foods and Mad Cow disease. A former cattleman, Howard Lyman, explained on the show that anyone who eats beef could easily contract E-coli and Mad Cow disease because some cattlemen feed their cattle animal parts. Oprah said that information stopped her cold from eating beef. That one statement, cattlemen claimed, caused beef prices to fall and they didn't rise again for two weeks. Soon afterward a group of Texas cattlemen sued Oprah. She won the case on February 26, 1998, but she showed the world something else — she showed them the power of one little Black girl from Mississippi. That lawsuit proved that her audience didn't watch her show to hear the topics; they turned on the show to see Oprah.

Oprah comes with pure talent and you talk about reparations for Black folks, Oprah is it. She proved to Black folks, to all oppressed people, that once you realize you have earned something, you don't have to stand on the back porch and wait for master to tell you to come on in. Even when you haven't accomplished everything you think you should, you just wait it out — your day will come. We have been standing at old master's backdoor for so long, we don't understand that we have a right to be inside.

Consider some of the inhuman acts White folks have put upon us just in the past thirty years that we as Black folks should have demanded an explanation for. Look how long Nelson Mandela languished in a jail cell before Black people began to protest his incarceration and to boycott South Africa. What Mandela did for us and for South Africa is something we can never adequately repay. In 1987 Lil and I decided to protest in front of the South African Embassy. We held a press conference and went to Washington. When we first got there, we knocked on the door and asked to see the ambassador. They said, yes, and told us to wait. We waited until someone came back and told us that the ambassador was in Johannesburg. We told them that we were not leaving until we discussed the release of Nelson Mandela. When they realized that we were not leaving, the police came in and arrested us. I had been arrested hundreds of times and it didn't bother me or Lil. What was horrifying was that the cop who arrested us told us that no one had ever protested in front of the South African Embassy before. That was shocking to me. With all the Black folks living in Washington, D.C., I couldn't believe it. Fortunately, that would be just one of the many marches, protests, and sanctions against South Africa that would eventually help to bring Mandela home. People were going to jail daily. Black folks said we are not taking it anymore; we want to discuss the release of Nelson Mandela — or else.

After Mandela's release, the world started looking at South Africa in a totally different light. The continent of Africa is the key to the salvation of Black folks in the United States. Thanks to great men such as Randall Robinson, president of Trans Africa Network, we know more about Africa than we ever did in the past. Black folks in this country do what our Jewish brothers and sisters did for Israel, we will be free for the first time in four hundred years. Some of the top Jewish minds in this country, Europe, and countries all over the world went to Israel, taking with them the power of their collective intellect and finances. When many Black Americans decide to take their collective skill and intellect back home to Africa, the world will realize their importance. More importantly, Black folks will realize their own power and strength. The world treats Africa worse than any other place on earth. When two African countries are fighting, the whole continent is referred to as savages. In contrast, a war in Belfast, Ireland, is referred to as a "religious hassle." And no one has ever accused the whole continent of Europe of being savages.

Reverend Dr. Leon Sullivan of the OIC takes thousands of Black people to Africa every two years. I, too, have taken the journey with him because I know that Rev. Dr. Sullivan does not have a hidden agenda. What you see in him is what you get: a man trying to tell us that it is okay to go home. Rev. Dr. Sullivan knows that we are getting a false picture of our ancestral home from the press, and he is trying to show us the real beauty of Africa. And then there are brothers like Eugene Jackson, president of Jackson Communications. He got tired of the insulting treatment he received in this country and decided to go "back home." He moved to South Africa and put his considerable talents to work there.

One day I hope Black people will get tired of training many White folks to do a job only to watch those same White folks get promoted over them. When we are totally fed up, I hope we will go back home rather than live in America with no dignity. We can take our knowledge, our love, and our beauty home to Africa. I just hope it's not too late.

When I look around this place called America, I see a handful of Black folks who have succeeded financially and have also managed never to compromise their dignity as human beings. Eunice and John Johnson are two of those people. Through *Jet* and *Ebony* magazines, the Johnsons have documented the whole of Black struggle and Black progress in this country. They have not only documented the Movement, they have also recorded our day-to-day lives; they have been our voice when no one else cared about our perspective. If there was a hurricane in Money, Mississippi, and Black folks were affected, *Jet* and *Ebony* reported it. Those two magazines were and still are our "friendly ink." They reported the progress of artists before they were stars. During the Movement, some of the White press would report that those of us in the Movement were "harassing the police." We wondered how we could harass the police when we were nonviolent and they had guns, clubs, and water hoses. But *Jet* was always there to pry out the truth. Black folks should pray that we always have *Jet* and *Ebony* to tell us what the White press wouldn't.

And of course there are a few Black TV talk shows that are our verbal friendly ink, like *Tony Brown's Journal.* Tony is brilliant and he is a good researcher who is always on point. Tony's show taught me that White folks watch us more than we realize. I was on his show one night, probably ten years ago, talking about nutrition and home remedies. I told the audience that burned toast could settle an upset stomach, because of the charcoal. A few days later I was walking through the airport when this White guy yelled, "Hey, Mr. Gregory, that burned toast really works." Then it just kept happening, people kept coming up to me about the toast, but the people were mostly White. I thought this was strange until I called Tony and told him about it. That is when he told me that 71 percent of his audience is White.

Then there is Tom Joyner, who, as Oprah said when she won her case against the Texas cattlemen, shows that "freedom of speech rocks." This guy, along with his great sidekicks, J. Anthony Brown, Sybil, and Ms. Depree, wakes Black folks up every morning with his "in your face, White boy"attitude. His show is providing Black folks with information that we are not going to receive on a White radio station. What's so hip about Tom Joyner is that he feeds you this information in seconds, in between songs; it's not like he has a four-hour talk show. He is playing music and telling you like it is at the same time. In addition, Tom has Tavis Smiley on the show with political and social commentary on issues that Black folks should know about. Now, Tavis is a walking *Jet, Ebony, Black Enterprise, Wallstreet, New York Times,* all in one. Together Tom and Tavis wake up seven million people every day and say "Good morning, Black folks, let me tell you this." Another influential radio host is Les Brown, who appears with his sidekicks, George Wallace and C. T. Bandit, on the *Les Brown in the Morning* show. In addition to being a brilliant radio personality, Les is one of the best motivational speakers of our time. So not only is he feeding you information, he is inspiring Black folks on their way to work. Both of these shows are needed.

God, was I glad to see Bryant Gumbel back on the air. Forget who has the highest rating. When you turn on your TV at 7 A.M. and see Bryant it just confirms what Black folks already know about themselves: "Yes, we are brilliant and we can do what White folks do." This was always the seed that John and Eunice Johnson wanted to plant. They made their publications into something out of nothing, and they did it with dignity and courage. No one wanted to take a stand back then, and sorrowfully, few people do today. No one wanted to talk about racism, but the Johnsons did. Even today, people don't want to talk about it. But racism is a form of insanity in this country that we can no longer afford to ignore. Where do the Black church, the White church, the synagogue stand on racism? Many of the Black churches and most of the White churches never mention the word. The Christian church is supposed to represent a reflection of God, Jesus, and love, yet they never talk about racism. We have to talk about it every day until it goes away. Racism is like a brain tumor; ignoring it will not make it go away. You have to acknowledge the presence of the tumor, then cut it out. It may be painful, but it will save your life. America wants the tumor of racism to just go away without the pain of talking about it. But not Eunice and John Johnson.

Ebony and *Jet* not only provided opportunities for Black journalists, but also set an example for young people to go into business for themselves. By going into business for themselves, young Black people can start shaping their own destiny. In the meantime, Black folks need to confront businesses in their neighborhoods that are owned by people from outside those neighborhoods. Go to the dry cleaners that's paying its Black employees minimum wage and demand that they be accountable to the community in which they're doing business. Why is there an Italian- or Irish-owned business in my neighborhood, but no Black-owned business in their neighborhood? Demand that they start adequately training our people and offering them partnerships. Tell them you want answers and that their behavior is no longer acceptable. If they don't respond appropriately, take your business someplace else.

Another thing we need to do as a people is stop accepting the insults to the Black family. Black women should not take that "single-parent-household" stereotype. Telling our Black women that the problem in the Black community is the absence of a man in the home is a terrible thing to say. Jackie Kennedy raised her children in a single-parent household, and they became the darlings of America. Queen Elizabeth, the richest woman in the world, raised her children in a two-parent household, and you can't find a more dysfunctional family. Hey, Jack the Ripper had a daddy at home. We simply have to stop taking the insults.

Talk about insulting Black folks, do you remember the day Bill Cosby gave $20 million to Spelman College — with no strings attached — and the White system retaliated by announcing the same week that Walter Annenberg, the White CEO of *TV Guide,* was giving $50 million to the United Negro College Fund? Once you checked it out, you realized that Annenberg pledged the money to UNCF, meaning they had to match that amount in order to receive his "gift." The catch is "match." Bill Cosby gave Spelman $20 million; Annenberg pledged $50 million. UNCF rose to the occasion by matching the money eventually, but who got the press? If Black folks had our act together, we wouldn't tolerate that kind of treatment of a man like Bill Cosby.

Cosby never had a problem with the media until he donated that money to Spelman College and started talking about buying NBC. White folks had to put him in his place. Bill not only had the money to buy NBC, he had the intelligence to run it. So they tried to shut him down. Bill and Camille have done so much for the education of young people. Most of it is probably never even reported because they have never asked for the press to cover anything they do.

Unless you are a part of the Movement, you would not be aware of most of the work Camille does. She works very hard with women like Dr. Dorothy Height to further educate all oppressed people. One thing people missed when the Cosbys' son Ennis was killed was how the real murderers wiped out the Cosby name. They told us when Ennis's murder was first reported that it wasn't a robbery and Ennis still had his cell phone, money in his pocket, and credit cards. But when they finally arrested the Russian immigrant charged with the crime, they decided it was a robbery attempt. When I researched the case, I learned that the suspect was in Mexico at the time of the killing. The next morning, a little twenty-year-old girl named Autumn Jackson came out of nowhere, claiming that Cosby is her father. I don't believe any of this was a coincidence. I just pray that one day the truth will come out. The press fed us what they wanted to, just like they did in the sixties, when they were wiping out Black men in the Movement.

The government was so slick during the Movement that I can't imagine what they are doing to men like Bill now. It's fair to say, I think, that the American government should just come clean, like other countries. At least Nazi Germany did not pretend to like the Jews. This country pretends they are the melting pot and we have freedom of speech and equal rights for all. But in my experience, it's just a lie.

Until Bill tried to buy NBC he was called "America's Favorite Dad." Because of Bill, television shows opened their doors to a lot of Black actors, and he has done so many fine humanitarian things for people. As a father, I just want to say thanks to him and Camille for all they have done. I want them to know that they are still a shining light that the system cannot put out.

We as Black people have to recognize and appreciate our own achievements. A century ago, we were in terrible shape. Never before in the history of this planet has a group of people made the progress that we Black folks have in the past thirty years, in spite of what the racist system has tried to do to us. The only reason we have not gotten it all is because America is not honest and Black folks are still playing games instead of calling it like it is. We all need to join organizations like the NAACP, the Urban League, and the SCLC and use our collective economic power to bring this country to its knees.

A day when Black people should have come out in force was May 13, 1996, when the "Dark Alliance" article was published in the *San Jose Mercury*. It was a day when we should have demanded to talk to the directors of the CIA and the DEA; we should have demanded an explanation of why thousands of kilos of cocaine were dumped in South Central Los Angeles in the eighties. Carl Nelson, a producer and talk show host from

Stevie Wonder's radio station in Los Angeles, called me and told me about the article entitled "Dark Alliance: The Story Behind the Crack Cocaine Explosion," written by reporter Gary Webb. Within minutes, I received a call from radio talk show host Joe Madison, who faxed me further information on the story. Maxine Waters was on the case immediately and held many rallies in Los Angeles that were barely covered by the White press. Over five thousand people showed up at some of those rallies and the *Los Angeles Times* never printed one story. Black radio hosts like Madison and Nelson kept that story alive. *60 Minutes* reported a story on how the CIA brought over one billion dollars' worth of cocaine into the inner cities, and not one newspaper did a follow-up story. If the NAACP or the Urban League were accused on *60 Minutes* of bringing a million dollars' worth of cocaine and dumping it in a White neighborhood, there would have been indictments and investigations.

The article stated that agents of the CIA placed crack cocaine in the hands of Los Angeles gang members during the eighties. Profits from the sale of the cocaine were to be used to finance the U.S.-backed contras, who were trying to overthrow the revolutionary socialist government of Nicaragua. Danilo Blandon, a former Nicaraguan government official, had come forth and told Webb the details of his role in the matter. According to Blandon, he had provided the thousands of kilos of cocaine that flowed into the hands of L.A. gang members between 1982 and 1986. In 1992, he pleaded guilty to cocaine trafficking and admitted having gone to work as an undercover agent for the U.S. Drug Enforcement Administration. His job had been to sell cocaine to inner-city gangs to raise money for the guerrilla army in Nicaragua. He testified that his biggest customer had been a drug kingpin named Rick "Freeway" Ross. Ross in turn had used the drugs to make crack to sell on the street. In 1994, Ross received a life sentence for his involvement.

Another source who served to confirm the *San Jose Mercury* exposé was Celerino Castillo III, a former narcotics agent for the DEA. Castillo came forward with documentation that his agency knew of the shipments of cocaine from Central America to the United States. According to Castillo, he began recording the narcotics trafficking while investigating narcotics activity at Ilo Pango, a U.S. air base in El Salvador. Castillo's story is so ugly and such an insult to Black people. He logged the shipment of huge amounts of cocaine, phone numbers of informants, the names of pilots, and airplane identification numbers, dating as far back as 1986. Castillo claimed that he sent the information he had accumulated to Washington, but never got a response.

When this information began to surface, many of our leaders came forth. Maxine Waters, Kweisi Mfume, and the Reverend Joseph Lowery picked up the ball and started a small movement. Joe Madison, who was at a White radio station at the time, and I went to DEA headquarters with the information we had obtained. Joe Madison is now at Cathy Hughes's radio station, WOL, in Washington, D.C. But even before he went to WOL, he was out there on the front line fighting for justice with his voice. He not only understands the media, he understands the Civil Rights Movement. He sat on the board of the NAACP for many years and never stopped working for oppressed people. Because of Joe Madison and Cathy's radio station, WOL, five thousand people showed up to support us while we were in jail.

That's the beauty of Cathy Hughes. She started her radio station with no money and had to sleep in the building where the station was located for eighteen months. She simply had a vision, and she started that vision every morning with a prayer on her station at 6 A.M. She touched the hearts of Washington with her prayers and sensibility. Meeting Cathy and doing a radio show with her was definitely one of the powerful turning points in my life. I didn't understand the power of radio because my audience has always been visible. When I'm on stage, I can look out there and see, hear, and feel the audience laugh. But even with all the technology, radio is still the most difficult media because you have to create an environment and a relationship without seeing who you are talking to. You can go to GooseNeck, Tennessee, and do a radio station program for thirty years and no one knows what you look like; you just become a voice they believe in. That's what Cathy Hughes became and still is to Black radio: a voice you can trust. I will never forget once, when Washington, D.C., had one of the highest murder rates in the country, Cathy and I got on the radio and said, "Let's have prayer that this weekend there are no murders in Washington, D.C." Well, we checked that Monday and there was not one murder in the district that entire weekend. That was the power of Cathy Hughes, then and now. She never backed down or out when we needed her during the protest.

As for our protest at DEA headquarters over the whole cocaine and CIA involvement, Joe and I were arrested immediately, but we continued to take matters into our own hands. We held a press conference at the JW Marriott in Washington, D.C. That afternoon, I went with Joe Madison, Reverend Joseph Lowery, Celerino Castillo, and others to DEA headquarters and requested a meeting with the chief administrator. Of course, the chief administrator refused to see us, so Castillo requested a copy of the DEA's file on him, a request that was also denied. After the DEA refused to give us a copy of Castillo's file, we knelt down and Reverend Lowery led us in prayer:

"In the name of all the people destroyed by drugs, we don't want to believe that our government would engage in activities that are detrimental to the American people."

On December 2, 1996, the *Washington Post* ran an article confirming the CIA's knowledge of all the activities of which they'd been accused. It wasn't printed anywhere else, and no formal statement was ever made by the CIA. I thought about Dr. King and all the years that he had knelt down in prayer in front of men like Bull Connor. Dr. King never knew whether or not he'd be knocked in the head before he could get up. I find it difficult to believe that we still have to pray for justice. We've already paid a high price for something that should have always been free.

31 Callus on My Soul

Well, here we are folks. It's the year 2000. Just think where we were at the turn of the twentieth century. We have gone from "nigger" to "colored," from "colored" to "Negro," from "Negro" to "Black," and from "Black" to "African American." Our Black children have gone from youngsters to boys and girls, our Black men from "hey boy" to men, and our Black women have gone from "gal" to beautiful women. Long before those days, we were proud African people — kings, queens, princes, and princesses. Then White folks brought us over here, shackled like cattle to the bottom of ships. On the way over, they dropped Black folks' grandmas off in the Caribbean and our grandpas off in Mississippi. Our aunts were taken to Charleston, South Carolina, and our uncles to Virginia.

Many of the Black women were pregnant when they arrived, having served as bed warmers for the overseers night after night on the slave ship. Some of the babies were sold as future house niggers, while their darker cousins were sold as field workers. Then the majestical slave ship slowed down and a few great men and women jumped off. They were tired and started to fight back. They fought long and hard until White folks told us that we were free. But free to do what? Free to go where? So we became sharecroppers, though we never got our share. The only thing we got to share was the pain while they got all the crop.

But it was not over, for men such as Paul Robeson came along demanding justice for all. White folks could not silence him, so they destroyed him. They destroyed them all, one by one. From the days of Nat Turner to the present, they destroyed everyone who tried to help us. They murdered Malcolm, Medgar, Martin, Chaney, Goodman, and Schwerner. They killed King and the Kennedy brothers and people whose names we will never know. Name one other movement in the history of this planet in which *every single leader* has been murdered. If we could go back in time and undo all of the assassinations, character assassinations, and frame-ups, and put all of those heroes back on this earth, where would we be now?

We were in a race for our lives, but we were never allowed to reach the finish line. If I am running a marathon, you cannot fault me for running slowly if you keep putting fifty-pound weights on my back every five miles. And that's what they did every time they killed one of our leaders. You cannot judge the Movement without taking into consideration the assassination of half our warriors. You must evaluate the Movement from a look-what-you've-done-to-us angle. Where would we be if they had not beaten our Freedom Riders almost to death?

Ask yourself before you close the pages of this book, where would this country be today if Dr. King had not been murdered? What would the outcome of the Poor People's Campaign have been? How many more people would Medgar Evers have registered to vote, if he had not been gunned down in 1963? What would Harlem be like if Malcolm X had not been killed and Adam Clayton Powell had been allowed to stay in office? And we also have to consider the loss of all the unsung, unknown heroes. Who did those body parts belong to that we discovered as we searched Mississippi for Chaney, Goodman, and Schwerner? As people were killed to stop the Movement, wives were losing husbands, husbands were losing their wives, and parents were losing their children. Think of all the children who never knew their fathers because they were still in their mothers' wombs when their fathers became casualties of the Movement. We must never forget those fatherless children or the little children who were murdered. Remember Emmett Till, Jimmy Lee Jackson, and the four little Birmingham girls? Those girls were friends with Angela Davis; maybe they, too, would have become social activists and respected professors at the University of California, Santa Cruz, like Davis. Who knows what impact they would have made if they'd lived? But we will never know the answers to any of those questions.

So how does a White racist system stand before me now and teach family values? I think a Black person would have to be insane to let a White person discuss family values with him. Just imagine if Hitler were still alive; would Jews let him come to America and discuss ethics with them? He would have no right, and the White racist system has no right to teach morals to me. We are the Black family. You cannot talk to me about family values when you are the ones who created the law that said my great-great-grandmother could not marry my great-great-grandfather. Keeping their African tradition, they jumped over the broom you probably made them sweep your house with to consummate their union. You passed a law barring my ancestors from learning to read or write. I have been married for forty-two years and have ten brilliant children. Thank God there is not a book in the library at Yale or Howard University that my children cannot read from front to back. So what you tried to do to us did not work.

At the age of sixty-eight, I look back on all those years in the Movement and all those people who are now dead, and I know that their legacy lives on. We don't know why or how men like Medgar Evers became a part of the Movement. Maybe they just got tired of the pain, the way Lil and I did. We did not march and go to jail because we wanted to; we marched and went to jail because we had to. We refused to adjust to the pain that Momma had gone through. Poor Momma would walk miles in the snow in order to feed her children. She simply would not give up, and her cheap, tight shoes made calluses on her once-beautiful feet. It's like Black folks: we have rubbed against America the way those cheap, tight shoes rubbed against Momma's beautiful feet, until we have become a callus on the soul of this country.

Perhaps racism made me this way; maybe it was the White man who knocked my teeth out when I was a child. But it was really the way they treated Momma that made me want justice. I remember the way they expected her to serve them to the last minute, even on Christmas Eve. Momma would have to rush home to make it Christmas for us, then put on those White folks' clothes before Big Prez was supposed to show up. (Of course he rarely did.) Maybe my momma just wanted justice for being obscenely underpaid for the work she did, and for all those times the man of the house patted her on the butt in the kitchen while Miss Ann slept late.

Back then, many White men sent their wives and children away for the summer and the maids like Momma were no longer needed. So Black women had to look for summer jobs. White men would run ads in the papers advertising fake jobs in empty apartments just to get the Black women to come over. When they arrived, they would rape them. I mean, who were the women going to tell? Men like Big Prez, who weren't home? Momma and her friends got smart and started going on interviews in twos. But what a way to have to live to feed your children.

When people like Lillian Gregory came along, White folks still thought they were going to treat Lil and women like her the way they'd treated Momma, but they were very wrong. Though my Lil is too much of a lady and too kind to curse, her soul said *hell, no!* She fought back and even went to jail, leaving her babies at home. She left them because she knew going to jail meant freedom for all Black little children. I think she, too, was trying to get reparation for all the inhumane treatment that Black women had suffered at the hands of the system. I don't know when it will happen, but I will continue to work towards complete reparations for all the hurt that Black folks have suffered. God will not let White America off the hook until it cashes that check Dr. King tried to cash at the March on Washington in 1963.

Until that check is cashed, there will be reminders: Our ancestors will continue to cry from their watery graves along the Middle Passage, starting in West Africa where the slaves came from, and where all the hurricanes begin. Their spirit will travel across the Atlantic Ocean to the Caribbean, where the slavedrivers dropped off our great-great-grandmas. Not one slave was taken off those ships until they arrived in the Caribbean, and I think it's no coincidence that no hurricane jumps above water until it arrives at the Caribbean. Once it hits land there, it will go up the East Coast all the way to Maine. Canada is right across the street from Maine, but the hurricane has never crossed into Canada, because Canada has never treated the Black women the way America has. This hurricane is the spirit of the Black woman, Black women like our great-great-great-grandmothers who traveled the Middle Passage and watched the White man drop off their sons in the Caribbean. Then the ships stopped in Florida, where their daughters were dropped off. When those slave ships stopped in Charleston, South Carolina, they said good-bye to their brothers, too. All the way to Maine, our great-great-great-grandmothers traveled, and when they got there, they were all alone.

God, I know that you are watching over us, and I know that my ancestors are crying from the sea, demanding justice for their great-great-grandchildren. Until then, we will remain a callus on the soul of this country, strong like the eye of the hurricane.

As for me, finally, yes, finally, I understand the calluses Momma got from her old, worn-out tight shoes. The shoes were made by man, but they could not wear out her feet, made by God. Those precious feet wore those shoes down, like Black folks will wear down this place called America if things don't change. It was that change that Momma was trying to make for her children.

I didn't understand then, Momma, but I do now. I didn't understand why your shoes were worn-out and your dress wasn't. They were a symbol of a weary soul. You were walking for all the Black mommas, for all the Lils, for all the Black daddies, for oppressed people all over the world. I understand now, Momma, I understand the calluses on your soul, because I now have my own.

The following excerpts are reprinted from Dick Gregory's Natural Diet for Folks Who Eat: Cookin' with Mother Nature! by Dick Gregory (Harper & Row, Inc., 1973).

FASTING

THE WHAT OF FASTING

What is fasting? It is simply the voluntary withdrawal of food for a period of time. Or, in other words, it is to choose to stop eating. People go on a mild fast, a very brief fast, every day of their lives and don't even realize it. When you go to bed at night, you don't eat until the next morning. Unless, of course, you get up in the middle of the night and have a midnight snack. But then you don't eat again until you wake up. So there is always a period of, say, six to eight hours when you don't eat.

When you get up and eat your first meal, what do you call it? Break-Fast! When you have your breakfast, you are "breaking the fast" of the night before. Your whole body has been resting, including the parts of the body machine that have to work out during the digestive period. Those glands and organs need a period of rest, which means a period when food is not being taken in for them to digest.

The fasting that occurs while you are asleep is only indirectly a voluntary abstaining from food. You don't say, "It's time to stop eating now," but rather, "It's time to go to be bed." But it is the result of your body saying to you, "For heaven's sake, go to bed. I need rest from the further ingestion of food so I can do something with what you've already thrown in here." So your body is making the choice for you.

It is interesting to note that when you go on an extended fast, the body requires less and less sleep. The body is not involved in the constant process of exerting energy to digest food, and as more and more waste matter and poisons are eliminated from the system, the body is in need of less rest. The opposite side of that observation is what happens after you eat a big meal, as at Thanksgiving or Christmas. First of all, the meal has probably contained the most impossible combinations of food for your body to handle. You've probably eaten a huge amount of turkey, maybe ham too, untold startches, etc., all of it cooked. Your body is so busy trying to handle all that holiday mess you don't even have energy left to walk around.

There is a difference between fasting, starvation, and malnutrition. Malnutrition is closer to starvation than to fasting. Malnutrition means "bad nutrition," from the Latin word *malus* meaning bad, ill. Malnutrition is bad nutrition or malassimilation, the failure of the body to be able to assimilate and use the food that has been taken in. Malnutrition can be the result of very few scraps of food being eaten, or it can come from large amounts of food being eaten, none of it useful to the body. Well fed but undernourished, in other words. The Ellen H. Richards Institute at Pennsylvania State College concluded in a report that "only one person in a thousand escapes malnutrition."

The marks of malnutrition are the same whether the malnourished person is underfed or overfed. If you look around you, you can see the signs passing by on the street every day. Or perhaps you can use a full-length mirror for the same observation! Two obvious signs of malnutrition are a bloated belly (a bay window) and a bald head or patches of thin, poor quality hair. The bloated belly is usually the sign of a diseased colon and the bald or mangy head usually indicates a lack of vitamin B, calcium and protein. Of course, if meat is used as the source of protein the chances of producing an impacted and diseased colon are greatly increased. In terms of some of the items that the Dick Gregory Natural Diet menu suggests, protein is supplied by soybeans, pumpkin, squash and sunflower seeds, vitamin B by wheat germ, sunflower seeds, soybeans and sesame seeds, and calcium by kelp, almonds, sesame seeds, soybeans and filberts. As I look over charts of nutritional value of food, I'd say the soybean is the most likely "hair restorer" around.

Starvation occurs when food is denied to the body at a time when the body is in need of substenance. There is a big difference between the voluntary withdrawal from food and the denial of food, just as there is a big difference between true hunger and plain old hunger, or appetite. When mealtime rolls around we feel "hungry" for all kinds of reasons, not the least of which is that it is part of the eating ritual — mealtime, three times a day. Although we feel "hungry" and have an appetite for food, the body machine is in no way going through the throes of true hunger.

When you get up in the morning, before you break your fast of the night before, if you look in the mirror and stick out your tongue you will notice it is coated. A chalkish coating, sometimes yellowish in color and sometimes white, is on the surface of the tongue. This is an indication that the body is not yet in a state of true hunger; although the chances are you feel hungry from the force of habit.

If you go on a long fast, the tongue will remain coated during the entire period the body is cleaning itself of impurities. After the third week of the fast, the body will begin a complete overhaul by cleaning out poisons. When that overhaul is completed, the coating on the tongue will disappear, starvation will set in, and true hunger will return. Then nourishment must be supplied and denial of food beyond this point would result in death.

After the third or fourth day of a fast, hunger leaves. I don't mean to say you do not get hungry, or experience the nagging pangs of appetite. But hunger disappears. It is the mental or ritualistic aspects of eating that are most bothersome. If a person is on a short fast, and one day dinnertime rolls around and that persons gives in to the pangs of appetite because he or she has passed a restaurant, or friends are eating, or whatever, invariably the fasting person will say later on in the evening, "Now why did I do that?" If the person could only have avoided the temptation of the dinner hour and its accompanying hunger pangs, the fast could have continued.

I frequently tell my audiences that sometimes during a fast I have dreams of the "hot dog parade" marching on me! Again, it is appetite playing games with me long before true hunger has set in. It is strange that, as certain poisons and stored up wastes begin to be flushed out of the system, old tastes return. The "hot dog parade" plagues me though I have long since given up eating hot dogs. Even if I were eating I would parade on past the hot dog stand!

The mental aspect is very important, I believe, in understanding the difference between fasting and starvation. Some people starve to death in much shorter periods of time than I, for example, have fasted. I think there are two reasons for this.

First, it is important to drink a lot of water to assist the process of elimination of waste matter. The person who has been denied food through factors out of his or her control does not look upon the denial of food as a fast. Such a person does not carefully consume the proper amount of water necessary to flush out impurities. And of course such a person does not aid the process of elimination with enemas.

Secondly, the mental attitude is an important factor. When a person chooses to go on a fast, the mind is at ease because the person knows exactly why he or she is refraining from eating. The mental attitude is calm, relaxed, and therapeutic. But if a person wants to eat and cannot get any food, the mental attitude is entirely different. Rather than being calm and relaxed, the person is panicked and desperate. The person is worried about starving to death, and I personally believe this mental attitude is a contributing factor when death results. If proper concern is given to the process of elimination and water intake and the mental attitude is calm and relaxed, it is physiologically impossible for a person to die from fasting until Mother Nature gives her clear sign on the tongue.

I would hasten to add one important qualification. If there is an organic disease in the body to such an extent that the organs involved are damaged beyond the point of their ability to repair themselves during fasting, death may occur during a fast. But fasting is not responsible for the death. Death would have occurred anyway and it just happened to come during the fast. And, as Linda B. Hazzard points out in her book *About Scientific Fasting*, "It is conclusively demonstrated that in a scientifically directed fast, although death in the conditions cited (organs degenerated beyond the stage of repair) cannot be averted, yet because of organic labor lessened, life is prolonged for days or weeks, and distress and pain, if present, are much alleviated."

The Why of Fasting

There are at least three reasons why people may go on a fast: religious, political or scientific (rational). I do not mean to suggest that the religious and political reasons are irrational, but rather to emphasize that people come to the rational decision that fasting is good and necessary for the body without any political or religious overtones.

Religious fasting is sometimes an act of deprivation of the body as a means of penance for past sins. But when I speak of religious fasting, I mean fasting for the purpose of heightened spiritual awareness. It is an act of piety, of freeing oneself from the demands of bodily appetites to be in closer communion with Mother Nature, the Ground of Being, God, the Supreme Being, or whatever name one chooses to call the Universal Force and Intelligence

Religious fasting is best done in secret; that is, without telling people you are fasting. Jesus called attention to this aspect in the Sermon on the Mount: "Beware of practicing your piety before men in order to be seen by them, for then you will have no reward from your Father who is in heaven". When fasting is done for this purpose, it is best to be in the closest possible contact with Mother Nature. Time should be devoted to being in the open air and sunlight. If possible, one should seek to be near a fresh water stream, lake, or at the seashore to soak and bathe in the tingling freshness of Mother Nature's water. It is also desirable to go into the woods and share communion with Mother Nature's trees and vegetation. The religious fast is an attempt to blend and unite with the creative order.

The political fast is public. In my own view, the political fast is more appropriately termed a hunger strike. The political fast is undertaken to call attention to some form of injustice, or to protest a failure to redress just grievances. My own public fasts have been in this hunger strike category. My political fast is a witness, an example, and a symbol that is shared by all who also protest the particular injustice.

As a witness, it has a public and private effect. When I went on my fast of eating no solid food for two and a half years until the war in Vietnam was over, I became conscious of the war and its effects more frequently than ever before. For example, any time one of my kids walked through the house eating an apple, my mind immediately focused upon the war in Vietnam. In the same way, people all over the country who knew about my fast, whether they shared my views on the war or not, became conscious of the war when they sat down to a meal.

I personally believe you do not conduct a political fast to make "bad" people "good" or to change the hearts of the tyrants and oppressors. Rather, you go on a political fast to provide a rallying point for all the moral forces and the ethical forces needed to displace the negative forces responsible for the perpetration of a particular injustice.

Scientific or rational fasting is undertaken for the purpose of cleaning out the system, eliminating all toxic poisons collected in the body. It is a detoxification of the body. Scientific fasting is based upon the conviction that toxemia is the basic cause of disease. The symptoms of disease that we recognize and seek to treat are really the effects of the body trying to restore itself to a state of health. When we continue to push food into the body as it seeks to heal itself, or shoot chemicals into it, we are forcing the body to use vital energies for purposes other than the restoration of health. Thus, the best way to help the body when the symptoms of disease appear is through fasting, relieving the body of digestive function, or taking only juices, which provides help in the process of healing.

When we are sick, the desire for food is usually absent. Parents and friends — those most concerned about us — think they are doing us a favor when they urge, "You got to eat something." And they are fond of reciting the old cliché "Feed a cold and starve a fever." It is interesting to note how far that particular cliché has strayed from its original wording, "Feed a cold and you'll have to starve a fever."

The Who of Fasting

To trace the history of fasting would take an entire volume, more likely a series. But I suppose the history of fasting begins with the instinctive tendency of animals to fast when sick. In both the Old and New Testaments of the Bible, fasting is a frequently mentioned activity. Moses fasted forty days, as did Jesus. The Hebrew prophets and the apostles engaged in prayer and fasting. The Pharisees, a Hebrew sect at the time of Jesus, practiced semiweekly fasts.

The Roman theologian Tertullian wrote a treatise on fasting in A.D. 210. Earlier, in A.D. 110, Polycarp urged fasting as a means of warding off temptation and lust. The Druid priests among the Celts were required to undergo a probationary period of prolonged fasting before initiation into the mysteries of their cult. In the Mithraic or sun-worshipping religion of Persia, a fifty-day fast was required.

It is reported that Egyptian hospitals at the time of the French occupation by Napoleon were using fasting as a treatment of venereal disease. Avicennaa, the Arabian physician of the tenth and eleventh centuries, prescribed three-week fasts for this patients, especially as a cure for smallpox and syphilis.

In the mid-nineteenth century, therapeutic fasting began to come to the attention of many through the treatment of Dr. Issac Jennings of Oberlin, Ohio. Others continued to spread the word of benefits of fasting, including Sylvester Graham, Dr. Edward Hooker, Dr. Henry Tanner and Bernard Macfadden. Dr. Tanner, for example, undertook an experimental fast in Chicago at the age of fifty. He fasted for forty-three days. Ten years later, he fasted for fifty days. The thin gray hair he had when he began the first fast had been replaced by a thick crop of black hair by the time of his second fast. He died at the ripe old age of ninety-three.

Gandhi was probably the most famous practitioner of the political fast. But in recent decades, many others have fasted for varying lengths of time for political purposes, including the former H. Rap Brown, Cesar Chavez, David Dellinger, Paul Mayer and Sean MacStiofain.

The When of Fasting

In discussing the "when" of fasting, we must make a distinction between the long fast and the short term fast — what we might call an "extended breakfast." It is very good for cleaning out the body to go on a twenty-four-hour or a thirty-six-hour fast once every week. During this period of time, only fresh, pure water is taken, in very plentiful supply. This means no fruit or vegetable juices. You may add a teaspoon of freshly squeezed lemon juice to each glass of water and sweeten with maple syrup. Persons suffering from diabetes should use tupelo honey, which is available at the health food store. The first meal after breaking the twenty-four-hour or thirty-six-hour fast should be a raw vegetable salad, like grated carrots and cabbage, which will act as a broom, sweeping out the intestines and colon.

Dr. Otto H. F. Buchinger in his book *About Fasting* offers an extended list of ailments which make it advisable for a sufferer to go on a longer fast, two weeks or more. Some of them are as follows:

1. Metabolism disorders such as being overweight or underweight, rheumatism, the initial stages of diabetes.

2. Diseases of the heart, circulation and blood vessels such as high and low blood pressure, coronary thrombosis, early cases of arteriosclerosis.

3. Skin diseases such as psoriasis, eczema, acne, boils.

4. Diseases of the digestive organs such as loss of appetite, liver and gallbladder difficulties diarrhea, stubborn constipation.

5. Diseases of the respiratory organs, chills, asthma, aftereffects of pneumonia attacks.

6. Kidney and bladder disorders.

7. Female complaints such as menopausal symptoms, disturbances in the menstrual flow, chronic inflammations of the womb.

8. Allergies and nervous complaints such as nervous exhaustion, migraine, recurring headache, neuritis, neuralgia, insomnia, depression, sexual weakness or overstimulation.

The above list is by no means complete, but it is an indication of the great variety of illnesses that might be relieved by a prolonged fast.

Thus, the when of fasting depends upon the individual. When your mind and body are convinced that you have been disobeying Mother Nature, an extended fast may be in order.

The How of Fasting

Once the decision to put the body on an extended fast has been made, certain preparatory steps should be taken. The most important is to start the cleaning process in the body which will be intensified during the fast. It is advisable to go on a diet of only fruit ice for at least a week before starting the complete fast. If the decision is made well enough in advance, you could begin by eating only fruit for a week, then going to fruit ice and finally into the fast. During this preparatory period for the fast, it would be a good idea to start taking enemas, every other day or every third day.

When the fast has begun, only pure water will be taken. The best water is rain water that has been warmed by the direct light and rays of the sun. Distilled water may also be used, but never use fluoridated tap water.

The water consumed should not be too hot or too cold. Room temperature is all right, though some fasting authorities insist upon body temperature (98.6 degrees Fahrenheit). Water should be taken when thirsty or hungry. Every attempt should be made to take as much water as possible; a gallon a day is good. Do not give up water consumption even if you are "turned off" by water at some point during the fast.

Remember you may add the strained juice of two or three lemons, a little honey, and/or black strap molasses if available. Once the fast has begun, daily enemas should be taken to assist the process of flushing out impurities in the body.

Daily bathing is also important during the fast. Take tub baths in preference to showers if at all possible. The body is flushing impurities out through the pores of the skin, so bathing is very important. A bath in the morning and a bath in the evening before retiring are sufficient. I would not take more than three baths daily. Never use a harsh soap when bathing. The morning bath might be with Epsom salts rather than soap (use two pounds of Epsom salts for a tub of water) and the evening bath with a natural soap from the health food store (coconut, cucumber, etc.) or Ivory soap. Massage the body gently when bathing.

It is also very important to keep the body warm during the long fast. If you go to work, remember to dress warmly, especially in the summer if you work around air-conditioning. At home you should avoid air conditioning and never sleep in an air-conditioned room.

Light exercise, such as moderate walking, is all right during the fasting period. Do not lift anything during a long fast, and avoid sudden movements, such as getting up suddenly or changing positions suddenly. Sometimes people make such sudden movements, experience a feeling of dizziness, and take it as a sign to break the fast. Remember the cleaning process the body is going through, especially the cleansing of the bloodstream, and you will realize the sudden movement was merely a shock to the system in the process of renewing itself.

I hate to mention it, but it is important to practice celibacy (no sex) during a water fast, a week before and two weeks after. But don't be too depressed. You'll be a lot better at it once the body is purified. Nothing can beat pure sex.

When breaking the fast, only fruit juice should be consumed, one day of it for every five days you were fasting. Thus, in breaking a forty-day fast, fruit juice should be taken for eight days. The fruit juice should be heated like soup. Grape juice from the bottle may be used. It sounds like a contradiction, I know, since the pasteurizing process will have destroyed the enzymes. But during the fasting period, those little villi will have actually fallen asleep. The fresh enzymes in the pure fruit juices would be too much of a shock for the sleeping villi — like throwing ice-cold water in a sleeping person's face!

It is very, very important to break your fast correctly. While it is not possible to die on the fast (except under the special conditions mentioned earlier), it is possible to do extreme or even mortal damage by breaking the fast incorrectly.

Of course, it should go without saying that the kind of diet you adopt permanently after the long fast will determine the real benefits of fasting. After the long fast and the cleansing it brings, you should go on a natural diet of raw foods and increasingly more fruit. It's the only way to stay clean, look young, feel even younger, and be around well into the twenty-first century!

The Result of Fasting

The long fast puts the entire body through a cleansing. That also includes toxic accumulations in the brain. And as the brain is cleansed, the mind is released. During a long fast you will notice a heightening of ethical and spiritual awareness.

One of the things that happens during a long, cleansing fast is that you lose the six basic fears that plague humankind:

Fear of poverty
Fear of death
Fear of sickness
Fear of getting old
Fear of being criticized
Fear of losing your love

All six, or some combination of these fears, haunt everyone who is captive to the usual nervous imbalances accompanying toxic diet. But when those fears disappear, you are really at home with Mother Nature and happily at peace with life in Mother Nature's world. You can shout the words of the familiar freedom phrase and they will have a meaning only you will truly realize: "Free at last!"

Dick Gregory's Weight Loss System

Herbs

Burdock	3 capsules in the morning, 3 in the evening
Buchu	3 capsules in the morning, 3 in the evening
Dandelion	3 capsules in the morning, 3 in the evening
Uva Ursi	3 capsules in the morning, 3 in the evening
Juniper Berries	3 capsules in the morning, 3 in the evening
Golden Seal	1 cup in the morning, 2 cups in the evening
Comfry (Tea) (sweeten with maple syrup)	2 cups in the morning, 2 cups in the evening
Herbal Laxative	2 capsules in the morning, 2 in the evening

Vitamins and Supplements

Zinc	1 capsule in the morning, 1 in the evening
Evening Primrose Oil	1 capsule in the morning, 6 in the evening
Vitamin B6 (500 mg)	1 capsule in the morning, 1 in the evening
Vitamin B2	1 capsule in the morning, 1 in the evening
Vitamin B12	1 capsule in the morning, 1 in the evening
Vitamin C (2000 mg time-released)	3 capsules in the morning, 3 in the evening
Vitamin E (400 I.U.)	1 capsule in the morning, 1 in the evening
Enzyme CoQ10	2 capsules in the morning, 2 in the evening

Menu

Breakfast: Nothing but fruit before 12 noon.

Lunch: Eat all raw vegetable salad or just fruit.

Dinner: Cook ½ cup of rice (brown or white). While rice is cooking, mix the following in a blender: ½ onion, 4 pieces of garlic, 9 Tbsp. olive oil, 6 Tbsp. Braggs Liquid Amino Acids. After blending, pour mixture in a sauce pan, heat, and pour over the rice once it is cooked.

Water: Always drink a minimum of eight (8) glasses of spring water each day.

Beverage: Squeeze the juice from 8 lemons, 4 oranges, and 2 grapefruits, and mix with 1 ½ cups of pure maple syrup in a one-gallon container. Fill up with spring water.